Palgrave Politics of Identity and Citizenship Series

Series Editors
Varun Uberoi
Brunel University London
London, UK

Nasar Meer
University of Edinburgh
Edinburgh, UK

Tariq Modood
University of Bristol
Bristol, UK

The politics of identity and citizenship has assumed increasing importance as our polities have become significantly more culturally, ethnically and religiously diverse. Different types of scholars, including philosophers, sociologists, political scientists and historians make contributions to this field and this series showcases a variety of innovative contributions to it. Focusing on a range of different countries, and utilizing the insights of different disciplines, the series helps to illuminate an increasingly controversial area of research and titles in it will be of interest to a number of audiences including scholars, students and other interested individuals.

More information about this series at
http://www.palgrave.com/gp/series/14670

Abdi Hersi

Conceptualisation of Integration

An Australian Muslim Counter-Narrative

Abdi Hersi
Griffith Centre for Social and Cultural
  Research
Griffith University
Nathan, QLD, Australia

Palgrave Politics of Identity and Citizenship Series
ISBN 978-3-319-91234-9   ISBN 978-3-319-91235-6   (eBook)
https://doi.org/10.1007/978-3-319-91235-6

Library of Congress Control Number: 2018940762

Cover image: Christopher Biggs/Getty Images

Printed on acid-free paper

This Palgrave Macmillan imprint is published by the registered company Springer International Publishing AG part of Springer Nature
The registered company address is: Gewerbestrasse 11, 6330 Cham, Switzerland

I dedicate this book to my beloved parents:
My father Col Mohamud Hersi Muhumed and my mother Miss Mihiya Aw
Muhumed Mubarak Ti'bile.
"My Lord! bestow on them Thy Mercy even as they cherished me in
childhood" (Quran 17:24)

Foreword

It is a pleasure and a privilege for me to write these lines of recommendation for what is in the first place an interesting and very original book on the conceptualisation of integration. As an academic who has been working in the field of migrant integration for several decades I must say that I have hardly come across a book that is as comprehensive and as insightful as Dr. Abdi Hersi's study. He clearly shows in how many different ways the notion of integration can be and has been conceptualised and interpreted, not only in the literature, but also in practice.

This does not always make things easier for newly arriving immigrants who are expected to integrate into their new society, but who receive vague and often contradictory signals on how to achieve this. Nearly always it is the receiving society and its members who define the conditions for integration, and these conditions sometimes even change as the integration process advances. It happens much more rarely that the integration process is being looked at from the perspective of those who are expected to integrate, that is the newcomers themselves.

This is precisely what Dr. Hersi has done in this book. He has carefully studied views on integration as held by the Muslim community in Australia, which mostly consists of relatively recent immigrants and which he knows from the inside. He has discovered and analysed a variety of interesting and often unexpected perspectives. Contrary to what is sometimes believed by the dominant population, Muslims have a strong desire to integrate, but they understand integration primarily as participation, and certainly not as assimilation.

A form of integration that also accepts and accommodates differences in culture, religion and—at least in the private sphere—language can work quite well as long as everyone respects the fundamental rights of the other and as long as there is a sufficient degree of mutual respect. Integration certainly is a two-sided process: the receiving society has to make adjustments as well. Such two-sidedness, however, can never imply abandoning the basic values of society.

The Australian Muslims interviewed in Dr. Hersi's study are well aware of this, and they are fully prepared to integrate into Australian society under the conditions just described. The politicisation of immigration and integration as well as worldwide shifts in the appreciation of Islam outside the Islamic world have not made that integration process easier. More than in the past do Muslims encounter prejudice and discrimination, as has also become apparent from this study.

The empirical parts of this book focus on Australia. This is good, because relatively little is known about this country in other Western countries. Australia has a long—and turbulent—tradition of dealing with immigration and multiculturalism. Most Muslims, however, have arrived in Australia relatively recently, and they have added to the country's religious pluriformity. When comparing Australian Muslims to those in most European countries, however, one must keep in mind that the former often have higher schooling levels than the latter. This may have a positive impact on their successful participation in Australian society.

I do hope that the readers of this well-written book will enjoy reading it as much as I have done.

Rotterdam, Netherlands   Han Entzinger
                                        Professor Emeritus of Migration
                                              and Integration Studies
                                          Erasmus University Rotterdam

Preface

This book deals with the highly topical subject of Muslim immigrant integration in Australia. In its recent history, Australia has been a model multicultural nation that welcomed immigrants and refugees from different countries and continents. The country is now a proud vibrant multicultural nation with citizens that hail from multiple regions, nationalities, religions, and ethnicities. But despite this, Muslims in Australia faced significant challenges, as their loyalty and allegiance to their own nation is being constantly questioned. Anti-Islam and Muslim sentiments are high in Australia, and discrimination and prejudices experienced by Muslims are frequently reported in the media. There is abundant research that discusses conceptions of integration but none is concerned with the immigrant's conceptualisation of integration. In writing this book I intended to bring to light the possible counter-narrative of the meanings of integration held by Australian Muslims.

The primary purpose of this book is to broaden public and policy discussions about Muslim integration by shifting the debate away from simply demands of Muslim integration but rather making Muslims part of the integration conversation. The book is based on empirical research that investigated Australian Muslims' conceptualisation of integration.

It is the first book of its kind that provides a comprehensive overview of Muslim conceptualisation of integration with full acknowledgment of other competing interpretations of the concept of immigrant integration. The idea of writing this book stemmed from my long-held belief in equality, social justice, and community cohesion. The book is intended to plea to academics and students engaged in the fields of migration, mobility, integration and social cohesion as well as, policy-makers and ordinary citizens to consider integration conceptualisation more broadly and to appreciate the perspectives of immigrants themselves. Though the journey of writing this book was extensive, the experience was inconspicuously unmatched, fulfilling and highly rewarding.

I thank Allah for giving me the strengths and His blessing in completing this book.

I would like to express my gratitude to Associate Professor Halim Rane from Griffith University in Australia and Professor Ian Woodward from the University of Southern Denmark, for their guidance, fervent encouragement and useful critiques of this research work.

My deepest thanks go to my caring, loving and supportive wife, Meimuna Aden Affey and to my children, Mohamed, Hafsa, Hamza, and Adam, for their understanding, continuous patience and immense support during the long hours I dedicated to writing this book.

I also extend my thanks to colleagues in the Griffith Centre for Social and Cultural Research, the School of Humanities, Languages and Social Science and friends from the National Centre of Excellence for Islamic Studies for their help in offering me resources and a collegial environment to undertake this research.

Finally, I offer my sincere thanks to all participants from the Australian Muslim communities who have granted me permission to interview them in this study. Without their support, this project would not have been completed.

Brisbane, Australia   Dr. Abdi Hersi

Contents

1 Introduction   1
Polarised Debates About Migration and Integration   5
Evolution of Australian Discourse on Integration   10

2 Muslims in Australia: Context and Background   19
Diversity of Australian Muslims   23
The Social and Economic Position of Australian Muslims   25
Higher Educational Attainment   26
Labour Market Participation   29
Occupational Group and Industry   32
Average Weekly Income   33
Home Ownership   34

3 Problematic Conceptions of Integration   43
Proliferated Meanings of Integration   45
Absence of Agreed Indicators of Integration   49
Perceptions and Suspicions   52

4   Determinants of Integration   65
     Participation   73
     Belonging and Acceptance   77

5   Detractors of Integration   83
     Institutional Detractors   84
     Individual Detractors   94

6   Muslim Frames and Schemas of Integration   105
     Functional Versus Cultural Schemas of Integration   107
     Citizenship Schemas   111
     Good Citizen Schema   111
     Flexible Citizen   114
     Productive Citizen   118
     Respectful Citizen   120
     Loyal Citizen   123

7   Clash of Integration Frames   131

8   Conclusion   149
     Implications   155
     Recommendations   156
     Research Limitations   159

Bibliography   163

Index   185

About the Author

Dr. Abdi Hersi is Adjunct Research Fellow at the Griffith Centre for Social and Cultural Research, Griffith University. He was the manager of the award-winning Reporting Islam national research project, that developed suite of research-based training and education resources for Australian media practitioners to encourage more mindful reporting of Islam and Muslims. He has worked on other research projects undertaken by several major Australian universities including The University of Queensland and Curtin University. He has published a number of refereed journal articles in reputable international journals on issues and matters that affect immigration in general and in particular the Muslim communities in Australia. His journal articles have been featured in the *International Journal of Legal Pluralism, International Journal of Humanities and Social Sciences, Media International Australia, Journal of Studies on Alcohol and Drugs* and the *European Scientific Journal.* In addition to his academic work, Dr. Hersi had a long and distinguished career in the Australian Public Service and over a period of more than ten years worked across the spectrum of Australia's Federal Department of Immigration and Border Protection in different capacities including managerial roles.

Abbreviations

AAR	American Academy of Religion
ABS	Australian Bureau of Statistics
AHURI	Australian Housing and Urban Research Institute
AMEP	Adult Migrant English Language Program
ANES	American National Election Survey
CC	Cognitive Complexity
CMEB	Commission on Multi Ethnic Britain
DHA	Department of Home Affairs
DIAC	Department of Immigration and Citizenship
DIBP	Department of Immigration and Border Protection
DIMA	Department of Immigration and Multicultural Affairs
GC	Good Citizen
GSS	General Social Survey
IOM	International Organisation for Migration
IS	Islamic State
MIPEX	Migrant Integration Policy Indicator Index
MP	Member of Parliament
SACC	Standard Classification of Countries

List of Tables

Table 2.1   Count of persons (excluding overseas visitors) by religious
            affiliation by highest educational attainment   28
Table 2.2   Age profile of Australian Muslims and non-Muslims
            seeking employment   29
Table 2.3   Comparison of employment and unemployment between
            Australian Muslims and non-Muslims, by age   31
Table 2.4   Count of persons (excluding overseas visitors) by religious
            affiliation, by occupation, by industry   33
Table 2.5   Average weekly income of the Muslim and non-Muslim
            population in Australia   34
Table 2.6   Home ownership* by the Muslim and non-Muslim
            population in Australia   35
Table 3.1   Focus groups and participants   52
Table 3.2   Participant country of origin   54
Table 4.1   Determinants of integration   72
Table 5.1   Barriers to integration   84
Table 6.1   Functional and cultural schemes of integration   107
Table 6.2   Volunteerism among Muslim and non-Muslim Australian
            citizens   113

1

Introduction

The integration of immigrants into their host societies continues to be a hotly debated topic around the world today. As people migrate from one place to another, they inevitably come into contact with strangers, and they are expected to, or sometimes ordered to, assimilate and become part of the wider society. However, the adopted processes and programmes to incorporate immigrants into their new societies vary. A clear definition of integration eludes researchers, governments and host communities. Immigrant incorporation is thus explained as being the "most pressing policy and social challenge that liberal nation-states face" (Goodman, 2010, p. 769). The purpose of this book is, therefore, to examine the concept of integration and its meaning through the eyes of Muslims in Australia. This study departs from the focus on policy and institutional frameworks which reduces integration to a concept, and a model of incorporation adopted by a state. Instead, it attempts to initiate an approach that acknowledges that there may be variations in how different ethnic, cultural and religious groups interpret integration, and recognises that integration is a lived social experience involving complex subjective and objective levels. Research into the ways in which Muslims conceive integration, and whether or not proposed

© The Author(s) 2018
A. Hersi, *Conceptualisation of Integration*, Palgrave Politics of Identity
and Citizenship Series, https://doi.org/10.1007/978-3-319-91235-6_1

government policies of integration are cognisant with Muslims' under-standings, has been largely unexplored to date.

This book sets out to make a meaningful contribution to the broader scholarly debates about migrant integration, specifically within the sphere of Muslim migrant integration. The importance of addressing this gap in the literature cannot be underestimated, as this is a study of everyday social actors' perceptions of core national values such as belonging and social inclusion into the nation-state. It is essential to gain an understanding of how simple everyday things are shaping feelings of social inclusion and belonging to the nation-state. The entire symbolic universe that exists in our suburbs, markets, schools and places where we come into contact with people on a routine basis orients us towards, or away from, others (Schaeffer, 2013; Zagefka & Brown, 2002).

Immigrant integration is an issue of concern to policymakers and the broader society because of its potential impact on the social har-mony and cohesion of the nation (Hugo, 2005). This is the case because Muslim immigrants play a vital role in our society and Australia prides itself as a country of immigration. Muslims are one of the larg-est groups of immigrants to settle in Australia and Islam is the fastest growing religion in Australia (Hassan, 2015). Policies surrounding the integration of Muslim immigrants are high on the agendas of a num-ber of migrant-receiving nations. A strong rationale in undertaking this book is the importance of understanding what integration means and the processes by which immigrants become integrated or not integrated into the wider society, and how that changes the host society and the individuals involved. It is important to integrate immigrants in order to create and maintain a harmonious and cohesive society.

At the core of the contemporary debates about migrant integra-tion in Australia is the issue of Muslim integration. A number of researchers have found that Muslims in Australia face challenges relat-ing to the wider society's perception that their integration is problem-atic (Celermajer, 2007; Poynting, 2006; Saeed, 2003; Samani, 2007). However, since the tragic events of 11 September 2001, Muslims in Australia have experienced and encountered increased difficulties in being completely integrated into the wider Australian community. The fact is that there is an implicit assumption on the part of some, including the media, that Muslims in Australia are not integrating or are unable to be integrated (Aly, 2007; Dunn, Klocker, & Salabay, 2007; Ho, 2007; Kabir, 2004; Poynting & Mason, 2007).

This book is designed to fill a significant research gap concerning Muslim conceptualisations of integration. It uncovers an issue that remains unexplored in the literature thus far, which is how Muslims in Australia interpret the concept of integration. It specifically contests academic literature and current government policies, which advance a top-down belief about how to integrate immigrants into the wider society, with no regard for how these policies are received by the immigrants themselves, or by members of the wider society. However, in addition to its specific focus on Muslim conceptualisation of integration, this line of inquiry may set the scene for future research to shed light on the extent to which different layers of society, social institutions and groups subscribe to perhaps different and contradictory definitions of integration. The author acknowledges that a critical issue that needs to be examined is the extent to which meanings of integration are similar or different between different constituent actors in the process of integration. However, this book is limited in its scope, and it explicitly addresses Muslim conceptualisations of integration. Previous research has overlooked the extent to which communal opinions of the concept of integration, be it those of immigrants or the wider society, match with those of the state and vice versa. The author recognises this fact and understands that integration is a complex process that has multiple actors and players:

1. the individual immigrant who decides to migrate;
2. the host society that is made up of individuals and social institutions with collective values who receive these immigrants;
3. the state or government that makes the policy determinations and laws concerning who should migrate to that country and how they should be integrated; and
4. the media who arguably influences the public and political discussions of integration.

The complexity of the interactions between these various actors and their understandings of what integration means is not what this author intends to evaluate. However, this is not to say an examination is not warranted into whether or not the textual interpretations of the term *integration*, which bureaucrats are bound to uphold by legal writ and conduct, differ from how immigrants, including Muslims, perceive integration.

The author develops an innovative approach to examine what integration means to Muslims in Australia, employing dual methods to reach an understanding of what meanings of integration are advanced by Muslims in Australia. For example, the first study relies on a series of focus group discussions conducted with Muslims in the South East Queensland region, whereas the second study utilises in-depth interviews with members of the Muslim community in the South East Queensland region, Australia. While the first study alone provides sufficient information about what meanings Muslims assign to the term *integration*, the intent of this study is to go further than the definitional terms of integration and therefore employs the cognitive psychology theory of schema (Cerulo, 2002; DiMaggio, 1997) to understand the research participants' cognitive interpretations of the concept. The application of this cognitive psychology theory of schema lends increased credibility to the research findings and complements the findings of the thematic analysis in the focus group discussions.

Chapter Outline

Chapter 2 explains the polarised nature of the debates about international migration, and in particular, the subject of migrant integration. As a background to the core research question of integration, it highlights international levels of migrant movement and briefly explains reasons why migrants move from one place to another.

Chapter 3 presents an overview of the Muslim community and deals mainly with the context and background of Muslims in Australia. This chapter addresses issues of the early migration of Muslims to Australia, recent trends in Muslim migration to Australia regarding population size and the composition of the Muslim migrant cohort. The chapter analyses Australian Bureau of Statistics (2011) data on the Australian Census of Population to provide a context to the topic currently under study.

Chapter 4 discusses the proliferated meanings of integration in literature and the absence of any consistently agreed indicators of successful and/or unsuccessful integration. It also highlights findings of this empirical study, revealing how Muslim respondents in this study held suspicions about the concept of integration.

Chapter 5 presents findings based on data from four focus groups conducted in Brisbane and in South East Queensland and discusses the meanings Muslim respondents assigned to the term *integration*. It specifically explains research findings about Muslim belief systems and practical elements of integration.

Chapter 6 pushes this empirical examination further by going beyond the pattern of responses that informants provided at the focus group discussions and looks into the cognitive schematic constructs that individual participants employ to define integration.

Chapter 7 engages in an integrated analysis and discussion of the findings of the two empirical studies in Chapters 5 and 6. It carries out in-depth discussions of the findings from both the thematically varied definitions of integration offered by study participants in the initial focus group discussions and the richer cognitive schemata of integration in the second empirical study.

Chapter 8 provides a summary of the research, discusses implications and limitations and makes recommendations about ways in which this research can be continued in the future.

Polarised Debates About Migration and Integration

In the broader field of international migration, the integration of migrant individuals and groups receives significant attention. Throughout Europe, North America and Australia, the integration of migrants is a topic of enormous controversy and one that generates fierce debate. The manner in which this important debate about immigration and integration is conducted is contentious among researchers, politicians and the public alike (Andersson, 2012). Polarities of the debates arise in different forms: racial labelling (Samers, 2002), increasing anti-immigrant sentiment across many parts of Western Europe (Segovia & Defever, 2010), and politicisation of the immigration and integration debate (Van Heerden, de Lange, van der Brug, & Fennema, 2014). These polarities may have created a somewhat antagonistic space in which debates and discussions about immigration and integration lack objectivity and balance.

Increased anti-immigration sentiment across many countries in the West has led to the emergence of invigorated right-wing political parties. Examples include the analysed trend data and public opinion about immigration in the United States collected by the American National Election Survey (ANES), General Social Survey (GSS), the Gallup Poll, the Pew Research Centre and media surveys from 1992 to 2012 (Segovia & Defever, 2010). The above surveys found that there has been a steady increase in anti-immigrant sentiment in the United States, especially following the period from 11 September 2001. Similar negative polling results were found elsewhere, including in Australia, where the Lowy Institute found that 73% of Australians endorsed tightened immigration policies in dealings with asylum seekers (Lowy Institute Poll, 2014). Some scholars cast doubt on the accuracy of these polls (Muste, 2013) but despite their cautious remarks, it remains the case that immigration is a polarised and divisive topic in the national discourses of many countries in the West.

Immigration and integration are also characterised by controversies and excessive politicking and suffer from what Poppelaars and Scholten (2008) describe as responsiveness to a serious of focus events and mood swings. The polarities of the debates about immigration and integration are evident in how some prominent leaders in Europe, such as Germany's Chancellor, Angela Merkel, former UK Prime Minister, David Cameron and former French President, Nicolas Sarkozy all openly attacked the concept of multiculturalism (Novotný, 2011). Angela Merkel addressed members of the Christian Democratic Union party stating: "Germany's attempt to create a multicultural society has utterly failed" (Weaver, October, 2010, n.p.). In Australia, the former conservative Prime Minister, John Howard, is alleged to have polarised the debate about asylum seekers coming to Australia (Van Onselen & Errington, 2007).

The diversity of integration models, policies and programmes in the available academic literature further polarises the debate about immigrant integration and arguably produces differences in how the concept is perceived. Immigrant integration programmes vary and sometimes overlap, and it is critical to explain from the outset that a range of terms is used to describe the processes of incorporating newcomers (immigrants) into the receiving societies. For example, these integration processes are explained to mean "integrate, absorb, and assimilate" (Weiner, 1996, p. 46). Other terms used include "acculturation, assimilation, adaptation, incorporation, inclusion, insertion, settlement and citizenship" (Lacroix, 2010, p. 11). Nevertheless, it is noted that *integration* appears to be the term that is widely used in the public debate about immigrant incorporation.

Lacroix (2010) explains how the 2008 national elections in Austria and the United States, the 2007 French presidential elections, and the 2006 and 2003 Dutch general elections were all dominated by national discourses linked to immigration. Wyss, Beste and Bächtiger (2015) assert that immigration and integration debates have become not only polarised in recent times but seem to have declined in quality. The authors researched parliamentary debates on immigration in Switzerland from 1986 to 2014 by using a psychological construct known as cognitive complexity (CC). They found that in the Swiss parliament, the CC of debates on immigration has decreased over the period. This decline in the quality of the debate is also true in other Western liberal democracies. Some extreme specific examples of the nature of polarised debates about immigration and integration include the language used and the way in which public and political discussions are framed. For example, Ercan (2015) argues that framing "honour killings" in Germany as being specifically Muslim cultural acts, rather than a form of violence against women that occurs in many different cultures, polarises the debate and is unsustainable.

In Australia, debate about illegal immigration and those arriving by boat put immigration at the forefront of public discussions (Crock &

Ghezelbash, 2010; Koser, 2010). For instance, Lacroix (2010) states that the subject of integrating migrants raises the alarm on all fronts, and receiving societies have a fear of new immigrants diluting national culture, changing the established way of life and becoming a burden on social systems. Receiving nations also perceive that there will be an incompatibility between the host community's values and culture and that of the immigrants, conceivably leading to clashes between Islamic and Western societies (p. 1). These tensions are mainly due to "out-groups" coming into contact with "locals". The tragic events of 11 September 2001 in the United States of America (USA) caused further concern about immigrant integration, and government and public opinion linked the terrorist attacks to national security and safety of the wider society (Zimmermann, Gataullina, Constant, & Zimmermann, 2008). The polarities in the debates about integration are evidenced by the way in which the Australian federal government struggles to find consistent ways to accommodate the increasing number of immigrants residing in Australia.

The immigration debate is topical and featured prominently in each of the last three of Australia's federal parliamentary elections. For instance, immigration and the asylum seeker issues which arose during the 2001 Tampa standoff are claimed to have cost the Australian Labor Party the opportunity to win office in the elections of that year (McAllister, 2003). Similarly, other Australian federal election results could be partly attributed to the polarised debates about immigration and asylum seekers. In the 2007 election, Federal Minister Kevin Andrews singled out African immigrants and refugees and alleged that they were not integrating to his satisfaction (Farouque, Petrie, & Miletic, 2007). As a minister and senior member of the Liberal and National Coalition government, Minister Andrews made this statement "Some groups don't seem to be settling and adjusting into the Australian way of life … as quickly as we would hope … slow down the rate of intake from countries such as Sudan" (Farouque et al., 2007, n.p.).

In the 2013 Australian federal election, the "Stopping the Boats" campaign could arguably be credited with helping the then opposition conservative coalition of Liberals and Nationals ultimately to win the election and form government. Similarly, traditional migrant-receiving countries such as Australia have recently adopted policies that make it harder for some international migrants to reach their borders. These restricted movements are manifested in campaigns to stop boat people arriving in Australia.

For example, in 2014, the Abbott government launched an operation code-named "Operation Sovereign Borders" by using the Department of Immigration and Border Protection (DIBP, 2014). A survey conducted by an Australian think tank found that 73% of Australians endorse the government's policy to turn back boats carrying asylum seekers when it is safe to do so (Lowy Institute Poll, 2014).

In more recent times, the arrival of often unseaworthy boats carrying hundreds of asylum seekers attempting to reach Australian shores has completely overshadowed the immigration debates which had been going on since the turn of the century (Collins, 2013; Klocker & Dunn, 2003; O'Doherty & Le Couter, 2007; Pickering, 2001). The heated debates about asylum seekers attempting to come to Australia by boat reached new heights, as these arrivals and the government's policies seem to have affected Australia's relations with its important neighbouring Muslim majority countries, such as Indonesia and Malaysia. Koser (2010, p. 3) states that "Boat arrivals are near the top of the political agenda in Australia and have been the focus of a flurry of policy making in 2010". The polarisation of the debate is not limited to the management of boat people attempting to arrive in Australia but extends to the management of asylum seekers once they are in Australia, or to apprehending them in Australian or international waters.

In some cases, the so-called "boat people" aren't even allowed to land in Australia but are shipped off to offshore detention camps such as Manus Island in Papua New Guinea and the Pacific island of Nauru. Public and political discussions in this area include those that criticise Australia's mandatory detention regime, claiming the adverse impact of prolonged detention on the mental health of asylum seekers (Newman, 2013). Such claims of inhumane treatment of asylum seekers in detention centres failed to persuade the high court judges in Australia to make detention laws illegal, and instead, the court ruled that detention of asylum seekers was legal (Brennan, 2015). While these debates are outside the realm of immigrant incorporation, it is understood that they have a direct influence on the perceptions of how Australia receives and manages its new arrivals, including those seeking protection under the refugee and humanitarian grounds governed by the 1951 United Nations' Refugee Convention that relates to the status of refugees.

Despite the politicking about immigrant integration described above, it is worth noting that Australia as a country is unique in its history as a nation, its self-conception and its geographical location. The country prides itself as one that has a long history of migration and successful settlement of people of diverse cultural and linguistic backgrounds. Australia's current demographic profile speaks for itself. In fact, about 23.5% of Australians are born overseas (Biddle, Khoo, & Taylor, 2015, p. 28). In contemporary Australia, immigration is seen as being a way to build the nation, and in 2010 the Department of Immigration and Border Protection celebrated 65 years of nation building (DIBP, 2014). For the most of this period, the department's core functions included the successful incorporation of culturally, linguistically and religiously diverse groups of immigrants into the host society.

Evolution of Australian Discourse on Integration

Australia is a major resettlement country and has a long history of migration. Millions of people from across the world with diverse ethnic, cultural and religious beliefs have resettled in Australia since the Second World War. Policies and programmes to integrate immigrants into the wider society have evolved over the years. Australia has gone through phases such as the introduction of the White Australia Policy (1850), the adoption of an *Immigration Restriction Act* (1901), an assimilationist phase (1947–1966), an integration phase (1966–1972), a multiculturalism phase (1972–1996) and a post-multiculturalism phase (1996–2007) (see Jupp, 2011). In its early history, Australia enforced segregating and discriminatory migration policies and programmes. A document prepared by the National Multicultural Advisory Council (1999) states that prior to 1949, the legal status of people living in Australia who were not "aliens", was that of British subject. With the passing of the *Nationality and Citizenship Act 1948*, which came into effect on 26 January 1949, most of these people became Australian citizens automatically.

The evolution of Australia's immigrant integration policies has been explained as having taken place due to several reasons, including the changing demographics of the community (Jayasuria, 1990, pp. 50–63) and the apparent failure of unrealistic policies of assimilation (Poynting & Mason, 2008, p. 231). Whatever the reasons, migrant integration has remained an important function of governments of all persuasions in this country. However, some political parties and leaders are credited with having left significant immigrant integration policies as their legacies. Political leaders who are attributed with enacting better and more humanitarian immigrant integration policies include Gough Whitlam, Don Dunston and Harold Holt (Jupp, 2011, p. 46). Similarly, former Prime Minister Malcolm Fraser has been commended for pioneering multiculturalism, and under his leadership multiculturalism became official state policy in Australia (Poynting & Mason, 2008).

Former Prime Minister Malcolm Fraser not only encouraged cultural diversity in the nation but also practically implemented this by establishing the Special Broadcasting Services (Mayne, 2009; Poynting & Mason, 2008). Former Prime Minister Bob Hawke is also recognised as having defended multiculturalism from a fierce political opposition which rejected multiculturalism outright, thus discarding a bipartisan approach to the policy between the major political parties (Jupp, 2011). Succeeding Bob Hawke, former Prime Minister Paul Keating continued to support multiculturalism and held the view that in a globalised world, a multicultural society with all its diverse language and cultural capital is more competitive economically than a monocultural one (Johnson, 2000).

A contentious issue in the integration debate is what form of multiculturalism is adopted and what the concept means to ordinary Australians. When John Howard was elected as the new Prime Minister of a Liberal–National coalition government in 1996, it was apparent that the Coalition government had a determined policy of moving away from multiculturalism, back to integration (Tate, 2009). This move was described as being, "A radical restructuring of many of the practices and institutions created under 13 years of Labor" (Jupp, 1997, p. 29). The change of government in Australia in 1996 highlights how Australia's immigrant incorporation models shift with time, depending on the ruling party at a particular period. For example, under the federal Coalition led by John Howard, an alternative to multiculturalism was a "constitutive" model, premised on an ideal of assimilation (Tate, 2009). Researchers such as Poynting and Mason (2008) point out that integrationism replaced multiculturalism during John Howard's leadership. The Howard government's introduction of the citizenship test is explained as proof of the government of the time's final departure from multiculturalism.

In Australia, the debate about multiculturalism has continued for decades. There appears to have been a partisan policy shift between the conservative Liberal and National parties and the Australian Labor party, moving between multiculturalism and integration. Bloemraad (2006, p. 233) points out that Australia, a country which previously embraced multiculturalism, is now retreating from this method of integration, and is adopting a laissez-faire immigrant integration system similar to that of the USA. Bloemraad's comments appear to be in reference to the hard-line approach to refugees arriving by boat taken by the Liberal and National coalition parties. This apparent retreat from multiculturalism is revealed in the shift of policy and approach in matters relating to migration and integration between the two major political parties in Australia. It is quite apparent that removing the reference to multiculturalism from the department's name is an attempt to focus on citizenship and values, in line with discontent with the concept reported in many parts of Europe and elsewhere. It can be argued that the emphasis placed on citizenship, together with the requirements of citizenship tests imposed on immigrants, may be creating a vetting process to deny citizenship for some, or to ensure that their conformity to the mainstream is enforced.

However, Portes, Rumbaut, Fernandez-Kelly and Haller (2006) report that there is a widespread view among the members of many host societies, in particular the USA, that having a distinct cultural and ethnic identity undermines unity and social integration. Others such as Jongkid (1992, p. 365) assert that, "Keeping one's own culture further increases feelings of alienation". Overall, Tate (2009) claims that under the Liberal Government led by former Prime Minister John Howard (1996–2007), government support for multiculturalism waned as support for cultural unity, assimilation and integration increased. However, Howard's policies did not last forever. Once in office, in 2011 the Australian Labor Party re-embraced the concept of multiculturalism. In a speech at the Sydney Institute, the then Minister for Immigration and Citizenship, the Honourable Chris Bowen MP referred to Australia's multiculturalism as being "unique" and different from that of Europe and refers to it as "genius multiculturalism" (DIAC, 2013). The fact is that in a period in which multiculturalism was condemned in most of Europe, in Australia it has been pronounced as being resilient and effective and is claimed to have served Australia well for over 40 years— much longer than a policy of assimilation (Tavan, 2012).

The immigration portfolio is turned into a political football, and departmental name changes often occurred after changes of governments in office, suggesting that immigration has become the most highly politicised federal public service department in Australia. In 2007 as a signal of their departure from multiculturalism former Howard government changed the name of the federal Department of Immigration and Multicultural Affairs (DIMA) to the Department of Immigration and Citizenship (DIAC). During the time of writing this book, the Liberal and National coalition government formerly led by Tony Abbott and now by Malcolm Turnbull, departed further from multiculturalism and again changed DIAC's name, this time calling it the Department of Immigration and Border Protection (DIBP, 2014). Depending on the politics of the day, the emphasis on integration moves between citizenship, border protection and multiculturalism. The latest of these name changes is the creation of the new Department of Home Affairs (DHA) consisting of an amalgamation of national security, law enforcement, emergency management, border control, immigration, refugees, citizenship and multicultural affairs (DHA, 2018). This gives conservative Minister Peter Dutton an extensive oversight and responsibility of all the listed agencies. Despite these politicking, there is little doubt that immigration continues to be an important agency in the development of a robust economy in Australia. Australian

Muslims were part of this successful migration history, and the next chapter provides context and background about who Australian Muslims are and what their presence in Australia signifies.

References

Aly, A. (2007). Australian Muslim responses to the discourse on terrorism in the Australian popular media. *Australian Journal of Social Issues, 42*(1), 27–40.

Andersson, M. (2012). The debate about multicultural Norway before and after 22 July 2011. *Identities, 19*(4), 418–427.

Australian Bureau of Statistics. (2011). *Australian Standard Classification of Countries* (SACC). Retrieved from http://www.abs.gov.au/ausstats/abs@.nsf/Lookup/1269.

Biddle, N., Khoo, S. E., & Taylor, J. (2015). Indigenous Australia, White Australia, multicultural Australia: The demography of race and ethnicity in Australia. In R. Sáenz, N. Rodriguez, & D. Embrick (Eds.), *The international handbook of the demography of race and ethnicity* (Vol. 4, pp. 599–622). Rotterdam, The Netherlands: Springer.

Bloemraad, I. (2006). *Becoming a citizen: Incorporating immigrants and refugees in the United States and Canada*. Berkeley: University of California.

Brennan, F. (2015). High court fails high seas detainees. *Eureka Street, 25*(2), 46.

Celermajer, D. (2007). If Islam is our other, who are 'we'? *Australian Journal of Social Issues, 42*(1), 103–122.

Cerulo, K. A. (2002). *Culture in mind: Toward sociology of culture and cognition*. New York, NY: Routledge.

Collins, J. (2013). Multiculturalism and immigrant integration in Australia. *Canadian Ethnic Studies, 45*(3), 133–149.

Crock, M., & Ghezelbash, D. (2010). Do loose lips bring ships—The role of policy, politics and human rights in managing unauthorised boat arrivals. *Griffith Law Review, 19*, 238.

Department of Home Affairs (DHA). (2018). *Welcome to the department of home affairs*. Retrieved from https://www.homeaffairs.gov.au/.

Department of Immigration and Border Protection. (2014). *Operation sovereign borders*. Retrieved from https://www.border.gov.au/about/operation-sovereign-borders.

Department of Immigration and Citizenship (DIAC). (2013). *Key facts about immigration.* Retrieved from http://www.immi.gov.au/media/factsheets/02key.htm.

DiMaggio, P. (1997). Culture and cognition. *Annual Review of Sociology, 23*(1), 263–287.

Dunn, K. M., Klocker, N., & Salabay, T. (2007). Contemporary racism and Islamophobia in Australia racializing religion. *Ethnicities, 7*(4), 564–589.

Ercan, S. A. (2015). Creating and sustaining evidence for "failed multiculturalism" the case of "honor killing" in Germany. *American Behavioral Scientist, 59*(6), 658–678.

Farouque, F., Petrie, A., & Miletic, D. (2007). Minister cuts African refugee intake. *The Age.* Retrieved from http://www.theage.com.au/articles/2007/10/01/1191091031242.html.

Goodman, S. W. (2010). Integration requirements for integration's sake? Identifying, categorising and comparing civic integration. *Journal of Ethnic and Migration Studies, 36*(5), 753–772.

Hassan, R. (2015). *Australian Muslims—A demographic, social and economic profile of Muslims in Australia 2015.* International centre for Muslim and Non-Muslim understanding, University of South Australia. Retrieved from http://www.unisa.edu.au/Global/EASS/MnM/Publications/Australian_Muslims_Report_2015.pdf.

Ho, C. (2007). Muslim women's new defenders: Women's rights, nationalism and Islamophobia in contemporary Australia. *Women's Studies International Forum, 30*(4), 290–298.

Hugo, G. (2005). *Migrants in society: Diversity and cohesion.* Geneva: Global Commission on International Migration.

Jayasuria, L. (1990). Rethinking Australian multiculturalism: Towards a new paradigm. *The Australian Quarterly, 62*(1), 50–63.

Johnson, C. (2000). *Governing change: Keating to Howard.* Brisbane: University of Queensland Press.

Jongkid, F. (1992). Ethnic identity, societal integration and migrant's alienation: State policy and academic research in the Netherlands. *Ethnic and Racial Studies, 15*(3), 365–380.

Jupp, J. (1997). Tacking into the wind: Immigration and multicultural policy in the 1990s. *Journal of Australian Studies, 21*(53), 29–39.

Jupp, J. (2011). Politics, public policy and multiculturalism. In M. Clyne & J. Jupp (Eds.), *Multiculturalism & integration: A harmonious relationship* (pp. 41–52). Canberra, ACT: ANU Press.

Kabir, N. A. (2004). *Muslims in Australia: Immigration, race relations and cultural history*. London, UK: Routledge.

Klocker, N., & Dunn, K. M. (2003). Who's driving the asylum debate: Newspaper and government representations of asylum seekers. *Media International Australia Incorporating Culture and Policy, 109*, 71–92.

Koser, K. (2010). *Responding to boat arrivals in Australia: Time for a reality check—Analysis*. http://m.lowyinstitute.org/files/pubfiles/Koser,_Responding_web.pdf.accessed17/03/2014.

Lacroix, C. (2010). *Immigrants, literature and national integration*. Retrieved from http://www.palgraveconnect.com/pc/doifinder/10.1057/9780230281219.

Lowy Institute. (2014). *Poll*. Retrieved April 16, 2014, from http://www.lowy-institute.org/publications/lowy-institute-poll-2014.

Mayne, A. J. C. (2009). *Delineating multicultural Australia*. Doctoral dissertation, Wakefield Press.

McAllister, I. (2003). Border protection, the 2001 Australian election and the coalition victory. *Australian Journal of Political Science, 38*(3), 445–463.

Muste, C. P. (2013). The dynamics of immigration opinion in the United States, 1992–2012. *Public Opinion Quarterly, 77*(1), 398–416.

National Multicultural Advisory Council. (1999). *Australian multiculturalism for a new century: Towards inclusiveness*. Retrieved September 19, 2013, from http://www.immi.gov.au/media/publications/multicultural/nmac/chapt_2a.htm.

Newman, L. (2013). Seeking asylum, trauma, mental health, and human rights: An Australian perspective. *Journal of Trauma & Dissociation, 14*(2), 213–223.

Novotný, V. (2011). Opening the door: Immigration and integration in the European union. *European View, 10*(2), 269–271.

O'Doherty, K., & Le Couter, A. (2007). "Asylum seekers", "boat people" and "illegal immigrants": Social categorisation in the media. *Australian Journal of Psychology, 59*(1), 1–12.

Pickering, S. (2001). Common sense and original deviancy: News discourses and asylum seekers in Australia. *Journal of Refugee Studies, 14*(2), 169–186.

Poppelaars, C., & Scholten, P. (2008). Two worlds apart: The divergence of national and local immigrant integration policies in the Netherlands. *Administration & Society, 40*(4), 335–357.

Portes, A., Rumbaut, R. G., Fernandez-Kelly, P., & Haller, W. (2006). *Religion: The enduring presence*. Unpublished manuscript.

Poynting, S. (2006). What caused the cronulla riots? *Race and Class, 48*, 85–91.

Poynting, S., & Mason, V. (2007). The resistible rise of Islamophobia anti-Muslim racism in the UK and Australia before 11 September 2001. *Journal of Sociology, 43*(1), 61–86.

Poynting, S., & Mason, V. (2008). The new integrationism, the state and Islamophobia: Retreat from multiculturalism in Australia. *International Journal of Law, Crime and Justice, 36,* 230–246.

Saeed, A. (2003). *Islam in Australia*. Crows Nest, NSW: Allen & Unwin.

Samani, S. (2007). Rhetoric and realities of multiculturalism: The perpetuation of negative constructions of Muslims in Australia. *International Journal of Diversity, 7*(2), 113–119.

Samers, M. (2002). Immigration and the global city hypothesis: Towards an alternative research agenda. *International Journal of Urban and Regional Research, 26*(2), 389–3402.

Schaeffer, M. (2013). Inter-ethnic neighbourhood acquaintances of migrants and natives in Germany: On the brokering roles of inter-ethnic partners and children. *Journal of Ethnic and Migration Studies, 39*(8), 1219–1240.

Segovia, F., & Defever, R. (2010). The polls—Trends American public opinion on immigrants and immigration policy. *Public Opinion Quarterly, 74*(2), 375–394.

Tate, J. W. (2009). John Howard's "Nation": Multiculturalism, citizenship, and identity. *Australian Journal of Politics & History, 55*(1), 97–120.

Tavan, G. (2012). No going back? Australian multiculturalism as a path-dependent process. *Australian Journal of Political Science, 47*(4), 547–561.

Van Heerden, S., de Lange, S. L., van der Brug, W., & Fennema, M. (2014). The immigration and integration debate in the Netherlands: Discursive and programmatic reactions to the rise of anti-immigration parties. *Journal of Ethnic and Migration Studies, 40*(1), 119–136.

Van Onselen, P., & Errington, W. (2007). From vitriolic criticism to ungainly praise: Locating John Howard's political success. *Australian Quarterly, 79*(2), 4–39.

Weiner, M. (1999). Determinants of immigrant integration: An international comparative analysis. In S. Vertovec (Ed.), *Migration and social cohesion*. Northampton, MA: Edward Elgar Publishing.

Weaver, M. (2010, October 17). Angela Merkel: German multiculturalism has utterly failed. *The Guardian Newspaper*. Retrieved April 22, 2016, from http://www.theguardian.com/world/2010/oct/17/angela-merkel-german-multiculturalism-failed.

Wyss, D., Beste, S., & Bächtiger, A. (2015). A decline in the quality of debate? The evolution of cognitive complexity in Swiss parliamentary debates on immigration (1968–2014). *Swiss Political Science Review, 21*(4), 636–653.

Zagefka, H., & Brown, R. (2002). The relationship between acculturation strategies, relative fit and intergroup relations: Immigrant-majority relations in Germany. *European Journal of Social Psychology, 32*(2), 171–188.

Zimmermann, L., Gataullina, L., Constant, A., & Zimmermann, K. F. (2008). Human capital and ethnic self-identification of immigrants. *Economics Letters, 98*(3), 235–239.

2

Muslims in Australia: Context and Background

An investigation into Muslim conceptualisation of integration in Australia is difficult to achieve without some context, background and understanding of the history of Muslim migration and settlement in Australia. Indeed, providing this context enables the reader to contextualise the findings and discussions in the book's later empirical chapters. Public discussions about Muslim integration and migration naively suggest that this migration is a recent occurrence. However, these discussions usually ignore the fact that Muslims have been a part of the population of this country for a very long time (Cleland, 2002; Jones, 1993; Jones & Kenny, 2007). The extant literature on early Muslim contact in Australia is scarce and generally refers to the Afghan cameleers and the Indonesian Muslim Macassan fishermen (Jones & Kenny, 2007). The contact between Muslims and the first Australians, which occurred long before European settlement, is documented in the cave drawings of the distinctive Macassan boats and in artefacts found in northern Aboriginal communities (Jones, 1993; Saeed, 2004). Although small in number and maybe not as diverse as today's communities, Muslims have been present in Australia for centuries. However, it is disputable whether either group, the Macassan fisherman who came in the

© The Author(s) 2018
A. Hersi, *Conceptualisation of Integration*, Palgrave Politics of Identity and Citizenship Series, https://doi.org/10.1007/978-3-319-91235-6_2

1600s or the Afghan cameleers who came in the 1800s, established permanent communities. According to Jones and Kenny (2007), Australia gained a small permanent Muslim population only about 150 years ago.

The first regular settlement of Muslims began in 1886 with the arrival of three camel drivers from British India (Yasmeen, 2008, p. 5). Other researchers, such as Saeed (2003), claim that Muslim contact with this country predates European settlement. Saeed (2003) presents the example of the Macassan fishermen from Sulawesi, Indonesia, who are reported to have arrived in Australia around 1750. It is the arrival in 1840 of the Afghan camel travellers, known as the Afghan cameleers, who are credited with the opening up of the vast interior of Australia to European settlement (Cleland, 2002). Historians such as Ganter (2012) reveal the deep and meaningful engagements that early Muslim settlers had with the indigenous populations of Australia. Other researchers such as Deen (2011) state that it was not uncommon for indigenous people to encounter camel caravans passing through their land and to establish relationships with camel drivers.

Some of the contributions that early Muslim migrants have made are well-documented, and the period between the late nineteenth century and early twentieth century is known as the period of the "Afghan Camel Invasion" (Cleland, 2002, p. 41). Camels were needed to access remote parts of Australia to trade and transport goods, and the Afghan cameleers had the specialised knowledge and skills needed to drive the camels. The Maccassans and the Afghan cameleers were not the only Muslim groups who travelled to Australia as early migrants (Jones, 1993). In fact, it is estimated that in 1875, 1800 Malays were working in Western Australia in the pearling industry as deep-sea divers (Jones, 1993). Evidence of a Muslim presence in this early period included the 1861 building of a mosque in Marree, South Australia (Peucker & Akbarzadeh, 2014).

Muslim migration to Australia continued after Federation in 1901. However, the experiences of early Muslim settlers have not been well-documented. After Federation, Muslims, like other non-Europe groups, were subjected to social and legal restrictions (Kabir, 2004; Samani, 2007). During this early period of Muslim migration, Australia's immigration laws were by their nature discriminatory.

The *Immigration Restriction Act* of 1901, which later became the *Naturalisation Act* of 1903, officially put a seal of exclusion on "coloured" people, and they were barred from becoming Australian citizens (Samani, 2007). The policy of sourcing migrants strictly from English-speaking countries was directed against groups which were considered to be unable to be integrated (Jupp, 2002, p. 14).

It is quite clear from the literature that those deemed or suspected to be unable to be integrated into society were not singled out because of their faith alone. In fact, in the case of the early Afghan Muslim settlers, it is argued that the discrimination encountered by this group was also aimed at members of non-Muslim faith groups, for example, Irish Catholics, "Simply because these groups were distinguished from the wider society in terms of a range of criteria including colour, religion and language or accent" (Kabir, 2004, p. 43). Other minority groups such as "Chinese and Melanesians were equally discriminated against by the majority white society" (Kabir, 2004, p. 42). Researchers such as Northcote and Casimiro (2010, p. 146) advance that "Australia's early migration program was both Euro-centric and Christian-centric". The discrimination that Muslims faced during this early migration period around the early 1900s is directed at particular groups of migrants coming to Australia. Northcote and Casimiro (2010, p. 146) explain that a "Muslim who looked European (Turkish) was acceptable as an immigrant and a non-European who was a Christian (Lebanese) was also acceptable". However, the people of both of these groups may well have been the same, as Lebanon was then a province under the rule of the Ottoman Empire and, "The people from Lebanon were sometimes referred to as Ottomans or Syrians" (Convy & Monsour, 2008, p. 2).

Arguably, the small number of Muslims who came to this country during the late nineteenth century and early twentieth century lived simply and did not enjoy the same privileges that contemporary larger Muslim communities commonly take for granted. These privileges include a diverse Australian population which did not exist in those early days and a great many Muslim community organisations and peak bodies which today serve contemporary Muslim communities all over the country. However, early Muslim settlers observed their religious duties such as following Islamic burial rites and keeping to a strict *halal* diet. These early immigrants also had *imams* (religious leaders) who conducted marriages, and they were able to pray in Islamic mosques (Jones, 1993). A major difference between the early Muslim settlers in Australia and contemporary Muslim communities in Australia is the ferocity of debate over Muslim women's dress codes. The *hijab* (or headscarf) is a phenomenon that appeared among Muslims in Australia in the late 1990s as part of a global emphasis on outward expressions of Muslim identity.

The period between 1920 and 1930 saw an increase in Muslim people's migration to North Queensland to work on sugar cane farms and to Victoria to work on fruit farms (Department of Immigration and Citizenship, 2009). However, it was not until the end of World War II that large-scale Muslim migration to Australia began. Poynting and Mason (2007) state that at the end of the World War II, Australia undertook the second largest migration intake per capita in world history, after Israel (p. 66). Turkish Cypriots began to arrive in Australia in the mid-1950s and 1960s, and Turkish immigrants followed between 1968 and 1972 (Humphrey, 2001). In the post-World War II era, migration to Australia was in full swing, and the immigration of thousands of Muslims from many different countries began (Akbarzadeh & Saeed, 2001). By the late 1960s, the migration agreements the Australian government had with traditional Western Europe countries had peaked and it became necessary to source migrants from non-traditional Western European countries.

Just as many of today's new Muslims immigrants are fleeing from wars in parts of the Middle Eastern countries such as Iraq and Syria, post-war Muslim immigrants, including those from Yugoslavia and Cyprus, were displaced by wars (Jones, 1993). Similarly, demand for labour was at its highest, and the migration agreement was extended to Turkey in 1968 and the former Yugoslavia in the 1970s (Jupp, 2002, p. 23). Migration from countries with a majority of Muslims in their populations, and from countries with significant Muslim minorities, was the beginning of a large influx of Muslims, and the Muslim population in Australia grew after the World War II (ABS, 2011). Since the World War II, many other Muslim groups have made Australia home, and predominantly, their reason for migration is that they are fleeing from war-torn countries.

Diversity of Australian Muslims

The Australia of today is different from the one in which Bouma (1994) described a normal Australian as being a "…member of the Church of England and of British background" (p. 285). In fact, Bouma (1994) argues that one of the unintended consequences of this massive migration program comprising people of Middle Eastern and Asian origin is the emergence of a very religiously plural society. According to the Australian Bureau of Statistics (2011), as a proportion of the general Australian population by religious group, Muslims have the fourth highest number of people (61.5%) born overseas, after Hindus at 84.3%, Buddhists at 69.4% and non-Christians at 67%. This shows that a large proportion of Muslims were born overseas and came to Australia from all over the world. Muslims in Australia are part of the significant demographic changes that are potentially altering how Australians view themselves. They are from mono-cultural societies such as Afghanistan and Pakistan and from countries where there is cultural and religious diversity, such as Albania, Lebanon and Nigeria (Jones, 1993).

Australian Muslims are a diverse group of people coming from a vast range of ethnic, national, language and cultural backgrounds. The diversity in the Australian Muslim population is also a direct reflection of the transnational migration nature of the world's Muslim population. More than 300 million Muslims—a fifth of the world's total Muslim population—live in countries in which Muslims are not a majority (Pew Forum, 2009). Ethnic diversity appears to be the most prominent and visible difference between all people of Muslim faith in Australia. The Australian Muslim community is also diverse in nationality, coming from all continents, and as a result, the people of this community are disparate in their cultures and their languages. English is generally the preferred language of communication and is justified by certain realities such as the diversity of ethnicity and nationality of congregants of mosques in Australia (Saeed, 2004). Even where members of one ethnic group manage a particular mosque, the fact that the congregation may come from different ethnicities and nationalities often dictates that English be substituted for local group languages such as Urdu (Ali, 2012).

Muslim community diversity extends to the legal and theological spheres, and members of the two major sects in Islam, the *Sunnis* and the *Shiites* migrated to Australia (Saeed, 2004). Muslims are categorised into several religious groupings, just as their Christian counterparts have been traditionally classified as churches, sects and cults (Saeed, 2007). Within theological and legal spheres, *Sunni* Muslims follow one of four major schools of thought; these are *Hanafi, Maliki, Shafi'i* and *Hanbali* (Blanchard, 2005). Throughout the Muslim world, these schools of thought influence the practices of Muslims in different parts of the world. While these ancient classifications are important, in the recent past, Muslim communities have been categorised and classified in other ways. In fact, Saeed (2007) states that one of the challenges in classifying religious groups is difficulties with changes in classification criteria over time.

Contemporary Muslim societies include adherents of the following six schools of thought: scholastic traditionalism, *Salafi* literalism, *Salafi* reformism, political literalist *Salafism*, liberal or rationalist reformism and *Sufism* (Ramadan, 2003, pp. 27–28). Other scholars such as Saeed (2007) discuss the diversity of Muslims in the legal and ideological domains and make these general classifications of Muslims: legalist traditionalists, theological puritans, militant extremists, political Islamists, secular liberals, cultural nominalists, classical modernists and progressive *Ijtihads*. However, a slightly different classification of the legal and theological domains of Muslims is proposed by Ramli (2013) as follows: fundamentalists, traditionalists, reformists, post-traditionalists, modernists, literal *Salifis*, reformist *Salifis*, political *Salifis*, liberal/rational reformists and *Sufis*. In reality, the above-mentioned classifications hold no meaning for the average non-Muslim Australian. However, assumptions that are often made about the legal and theological affiliation of an individual Muslim suggest that these categorisations may have some influence on their levels of integration.

In many Western societies, Muslims have been categorised as "moderate" and "extremist" (Kundnani, 2012). These labels suggest that moderates are easily integrated, whereas extremists are difficult to integrate into society. However, Kundnani (2012) states that the moderates are held responsible for failing to stop the extremists, thus labelling all

Muslims as being unable to fit into modern society. The classifications above also fail to acknowledge how the religion and the identity of many Muslims in the Western world intersect. For instance, Jacobson (2006) poses that the religious identities of young Muslim Britons range from devout adherence to nominal affiliation, or the state of being a cultural "non-practising" Muslim. Based on the above facts, Brasted and Khan (2012) explain that it is not quite right to class Muslims as essentially monolithic, to class them as coming from one culture, and to associate all Muslims with the tragedies taking place in the Middle East.

To date, little research has been carried out into the extent to which Muslims' legal and theological traditions influence their levels of integration. However, the literature does contend that ideological and theological identification are significant factors in integration and immigration (Campese, 2012; Cruz, 2008; Minkenberg, 2008; Peschke, 2009). In a later empirical study (Chapters 5 and 6), this research finds that Muslims use their religion as an important factor which influences their levels of integration into aspects of local culture in Australia. This does not mean that all Muslims agree on the influence of their faith on matters regarding their integration. This will differ between one individual and another and in different contexts and environments. While discussions regarding the early migration of Muslims to Australia and their rich diversity are necessary and historically relevant, an appreciation of their social and economic conditions in Australia is more important.

The Social and Economic Position of Australian Muslims

The Australian government takes a Census of the population every five years. Amongst many other factors, the Census reports the number of persons reporting an affiliation to a religion. The number of Muslims in Australia recorded in the recent Australian Bureau of Statistics (2011) Census data is 476,300, constituting about 2.2% of the Australian population. This is higher than the number of Muslims recorded in the previous Census data of 2006, in which Muslims in Australia constituted 1.7% of the total Australian population. It is worth noting that the 2011 ABS Census data shows a higher proportion of recent Muslim arrivals reporting an affiliation to Islam than was reported by longer-standing migrants, a figure of 8.4% in the 2011 Census and 4.7% in the 2006 Census. With the exception of the "no religion" category, Hindus and Buddhists, Muslims scored higher rates of new arrivals reporting religious affiliation than some of the other religious groups (ABS, 2011).

The increasing population of Muslims in Australia is not of itself an indicator of how well Muslims are faring within the wider Australian society. Instead, the relative social and economic position of Muslims in this country is a better indicator of their integration (Hassan, 2010). Therefore, in order to research this area, some evidence-based key indicators of integration must be used, and these are Muslims' educational attainment, average weekly household income, labour market participation and data on home ownership (Ager & Strang, 2004; Phillimore & Goodson, 2008; Spoonley, Peace, Butcher, & O'Neill, 2005). Nevertheless, it is not claimed that Muslims' socio-economic position is the best indicator of immigrant integration. In fact, it is quite possible that non-migrant societal groups might have low levels of education, higher unemployment and lower income, and yet it would be problematic to describe them as unintegrated. While integration cannot be solely measured on these functional indicators, the importance of this aspect of integration for immigrants is stressed, as it is vital in enabling them to play their part in the social and economic fabric of the nation.

Higher Educational Attainment

From the 2011 ABS Census data, the total number of the Census population who reported attaining a postgraduate level of education is 631,122. This includes the 22,711 people who did not state their religion in the population Census. The fact that there is a chance that some Muslims might be included in this group dictated that this amount be deducted from the total of the Australian population who attained a postgraduate level of education. This makes the total actual number of Australians who attained a postgraduate level of education

608,411 persons. Out of this group, Muslims who attained a postgraduate level of education constitute 25,386, which is about 5% of the total number of people who attained a postgraduate level of education. Correspondingly, the total number of non-Muslims in the same Census period comprising people who stated that they either have a religion other than Islam or have no religion at all (termed as non-Muslim) was 583,025, which is about 3% of the population. It is clear that in percentage terms, significantly more Muslim Australians, more than twice their overall population count, have completed a postgraduate level of education. Other categories in which Muslims had higher levels of education than the non-Muslim population in the 2011 Census include completing year 12 at school scoring 17%, compared to 14% in the non-Muslim population. However, this simply means that a higher proportion of Muslims in Australia have high school as their highest qualification. Those who attained year 8 and lower levels of education were about 5%, as compared to 4% in the non-Muslim group. An important point to note is that, despite their higher educational attainment in the postgraduate-level education category, Muslims report a slightly lower percentage in the count of all higher education than the non-Muslim cohort.

In the graduate diploma and graduate certificate levels of educational attainment, both Muslims and non-Muslims report a low figure of 1%. However, Muslims report lower levels of educational attainment at the bachelor degree level at 11%, and 5% in the advanced diploma and diploma levels, as compared to the non-Muslim figure of 2 and 7%, respectively. The data concerning Muslim educational attainment in school years 10 and 12 is of particular interest. As the table 2.1 shows, Muslims do poorly in completing year 10 of high school and report about 6% completion in comparison with the figure of 11% reported by the non-Muslim group. A reasonable explanation for this phenomenon could be the higher levels of Muslims' completion of schooling in the year reported above. This could be an explanation as to why the numbers of Muslims completing year 10 is so low (Table 2.1).

Overall, while data on religious affiliation by highest educational attainment is generally sound, Muslims report a significantly higher level in the *no educational attainment* category at 3%, as compared to

Table 2.1 Count of persons (excluding overseas visitors) by religious affiliation by highest educational attainment

Level of highest educational attainment	Muslim	%	Non-Muslim	%	Total
Postgraduate degree level	25,386	5	583,025	3	608,411
Graduate diploma and graduate certificate level	3052	1	283,944	1	286,966
Bachelor degree level	51,073	11	2,209,119	12	2,260,192
Advanced diploma and diploma level	24,726	5	1,321,648	7	1,346,374
Certificate level	26,694	6	2,533,949	13	2,560,643
Year 12	83,207	17	2,686,562	14	2,769,769
Year 11	16,637	3	955,607	5	972,244
Year 10	29,024	6	2,150,943	11	2,179,967
Year 9	11,653	2	775,463	4	787,116
Year 8 or below	23,355	5	802,992	4	826,347
Inadequately described	5131	1	231,209	1	236,340
No educational attainment	14,671	3	109,194	1	123,865
Not stated	22,761	5	908,344	5	931,105
Not applicable	138,919	29	3,639,781	19	3,778,700
Total	476,289	100	19,191,780	100	19,668,069

1% of the total population. It can therefore be stated that Muslim data on educational attainment is at worst mixed, or perhaps reasonably good, based on the figures reported above. So, if education is a good predictor of the high levels of integration of migrants, then Muslims in Australia are reasonably integrated and potentially have the necessary human capital to contribute to the development of Australia as a nation.

These statistics correspond with the earlier findings by Hassan (2009) who found that the 2006 ABS Census data shows that in all categories except one, Muslim citizens have reached similar or better educational attainment than their non-Muslim counterparts. Bouma (1994) found similar results and concludes that in the attainment of higher education, Australian Muslims match up well with the wider Australian society. Bouma further claims that the high value which Muslims place on learning and education, plus the labour market's preference for migrants with qualifications, are reasons for their high educational attainment. It is also the case that the Australian migration program favours skilled migrants and this could be a factor in the higher educational levels of Muslim immigrants.

Nevertheless, caution is advised in interpreting the data on Muslims' higher educational attainment. For example, it is difficult to determine how many of these postgraduate qualifications are obtained overseas before migration and whether or not they are recognised in Australia. On the other hand, there may be uncertainty about how these qualifications enable Muslims to be adequately employed in the labour market.

Labour Market Participation

Labour market participation is understood to be an indicator of successful immigrant integration, as indicated by numerous studies by Ager and Strang (2004), Entzinger and Biezeveld (2003), Phillimore and Goodson (2008) and Spoonley et al. (2005). The question is then how are Muslims faring in Australia's job market? But before this comparison takes place, it is important to note that there is a disparity between the age profiles of the Muslim community and the non-Muslim community. In particular, the 2011 ABS Census of Population data shows that the Muslim community is largest within the age group brackets of 20–24, 25–29, 30–34 and 35–39 (see Table 2.2).

Table 2.2 Age profile of Australian Muslims and non-Muslims seeking employment

Age range (years)	Muslim employable	%	Non-Muslim employable	%
0–14	0	0	0	0
15–19	9780	6	635,774	6
20–24	23,743	14	1,011,753	10
25–29	30,242	18	1,109,284	11
30–34	29,286	17	1,059,397	11
35–39	23,053	13	1,122,164	11
40–44	19,040	11	1,166,975	12
45–49	15,395	9	1,149,703	11
50–54	10,509	6	1,075,853	11
55–59	6253	4	854,421	8
60–64	3142	2	573,621	6
+65	1428	1	318,388	3
	171,871	101*	10,077,333	100

* More than 100% due to small rounding error

The employment and unemployment rates for each age category for Muslims and non-Muslims have been calculated and compared (see Table 2.3). In comparison with their non-Muslims counterparts, Muslims report lower levels in the total employed category comprised of all age groups (87%) as opposed to the recorded 95% of the non-Muslim group. Certainly, this percentage difference is not very high, but still it shows that Muslims record lower levels in the employed category than their non-Muslim counterparts. This data corresponds with the comparative unemployment data figures of all age groups between Muslims and non-Muslim depicted in the same table, which shows 13% unemployment for Muslims and 5% unemployment of the non-Muslim group. However, the data on this table also illustrates that Muslims show poor participation, in particular in the age group 15–24 (below 90%), in which they record unemployment levels of 12–28%, and then gradually improve in employment participation of older age groups, recording 93% for 65 years and over. In fact, unemployment rates for 65 years and over drop to 7%.

In a period of uncertain economic climate and high levels of national debt and deficit, Muslims in Australia are disproportionately affected by unemployment and face the challenges of underemployment in a competitive Australian labour market. The 2011 ABS Census data concerning Muslim labour force participation is consistent and shows that in all age groups, Muslims report high unemployment percentages as compared to non-Muslims. Figures in different age groups evidently vary, but the Census data reliably reports that youth unemployment is specifically a major problem faced by Muslims in Australia. For example, Muslims between the ages of 15 and 24, who are of course in their most optimal working years, are not active in the labour force. It is indeed important that governments pay attention to this high rate of youth unemployment.

A number of studies point out that the employment circumstances of immigrants and their children are an important dimension of their integration and adaptation into the host societies (Bevelander, 1999, 2000; Bisin, Patacchini, Verdier, & Zenou, 2011). Most of the literature in which employment outcomes of immigrants is evaluated, and sometimes compared with natives, concerns Europe. For the most part, a

Table 2.3 Comparison of employment and unemployment between Australian Muslims and non-Muslims, by age

Age range (years)	Muslims					Non-Muslims				
	Employed	Unemployed	Total	% Employed	% Unemployed	Employed	Unemployed	Total	% Employed	% Unemployed
0–14	0	0	0	0	0	0	0	0	0	0
15–19	7011	2769	9780	72	28	534,591	101,183	635,774	84	16
20–24	19,309	4434	23,743	81	19	916,398	95,355	1,011,753	91	9
25–29	26,482	3760	30,242	88	12	1,046,914	62,370	1,109,284	94	6
30–34	26,141	3145	29,286	89	11	1,010,001	49,396	1,059,397	95	5
35–39	20,641	2412	23,053	90	10	1,073,122	49,042	1,122,164	96	4
40–44	17,095	1945	19,040	90	10	1,118,411	48,564	1,166,975	96	4
45–49	13,972	1423	15,395	91	9	1,105,178	44,525	1,149,703	96	4
50–54	9585	924	10,509	91	9	1,036,933	38,920	1,075,853	96	4
55–59	5730	523	6253	92	8	822,572	31,849	854,421	96	4
60–64	2867	275	3142	91	9	550,724	22,897	573,621	96	4
65+	1334	94	1428	93	7	311,812	6576	318,388	98	2
Total	150,167	21,704	171,871	87	13	9,526,656	550,677	10,077,333	95	5

review of this literature reveals that in most European countries, immigrants have lower levels of labour market participation rates than members of host societies (Husted, Heinesen, & Andersen, 2009). Husted et al. (2009) also note that immigrant labour market participation is important, as it may increase the nation's aggregate labour supply, economic growth, public finances, and specifically, it may significantly contribute to major demographic problems such as the ageing of the population.

The evidence in the available literature suggests that immigrant participation in the host nation's labour market can affect integration levels and overall wellbeing (Adida, Laitin, & Valfort, 2010). In France for example, Adida et al. (2010) have been able to identify strong levels of religious discrimination against Muslims in accessing the French labour market. They found that over two generations, Muslims performed poorly economically compared to Christians (Adida et al., 2010). This study claims that high youth unemployment poses challenges to Australia as a nation and further argues that high Muslim youth unemployment risks undermining the government's social inclusion policies and de-radicalisation programs. Equally, underemployment is an important element in the integration of minorities. Despite these low levels of employment participation within migrant groups, researchers found that adoption of minorities into the Australian labour market improves over time and equals the non-immigrant cohort of the population (Johnston, Forrest, Jones, Manley, & Owen, 2015). The economic performance of immigrants is not only about employment status but is also about what kind of jobs they hold and in which occupational group they are placed.

Occupational Group and Industry

In Australia, Muslims work within the full spectrum of industries, occupying a great variety of positions in the labour force. Researchers have found that earnings and occupational attainments are equally important indicators of integration (Beach & Worswick, 1993; Tastsoglou & Preston, 2012). Muslims occupy 12% of the recorded managerial

Table 2.4 Count of persons (excluding overseas visitors) by religious affiliation, by occupation, by industry

Industry	Muslim	%	Non-Muslim	%	Total
Managers	13,883	12	1,236,423	16	1,250,306
Professionals	30,439	27	2,042,118	26	2,072,557
Technicians and trade workers	21,834	19	1,345,527	17	1,367,361
Community and personal service workers	14,317	13	921,635	12	935,952
Clerical and administrative workers	17,073	15	1,416,024	18	1,433,097
Sales workers	14,747	13	891,992	11	906,739
Total	112,293	100	7,853,719	100	7,966,012

roles in the labour force, a figure somewhat lower than that of the non-Muslim figure of 16%. However, 27% of Muslims report that they occupy professional positions, whereas the non-Muslim figure of people holding professional positions is 26%. A high percentage of Muslims (19%) report that they are employed as technicians or trade workers, as opposed to 17% of the non-Muslim population. Muslims also have a greater percentage of the population who are working as community and personal service workers, at 13% as opposed to 12% of the non-Muslim population, however they have a lower number of people who are employed as clerical and administrative workers. In consideration of these figures, it is reasonable to assume that Muslims are well-integrated into all facets of Australian life and are working in ordinary jobs, just like most Australians (see Table 2.4).

Average Weekly Income

By looking closely at the 2011 ABS Census data, it is obvious that Muslims do not fare so well in the average weekly income data. For example, with the exception of the three lowest income brackets, "nil income", those earning between $1 and $99 per week, and those earning between $200 and $299 per week, Muslims reported having lower income levels in all other income brackets, as shown in Table 2.5.

Table 2.5 Average weekly income of the Muslim and non-Muslim population in Australia

Weekly individual income	Muslim	%	Non-Muslim	%	Total
Negative income	652	1	26,108	1	26,760
Nil income	7009	11	307,157	6	314,166
$1–199	5845	9	368,045	7	373,890
$200–299	10,138	16	755,408	14	765,546
$300–399	4881	8	690,196	13	695,077
$400–599	5241	8	690,550	13	695,791
$600–799	4384	7	476,819	9	481,203
$800–999	3067	5	341,986	7	345,053
$1000–1249	2479	4	302,956	6	305,435
$1250–1499	1618	3	195,934	4	197,552
$1500–1999	1489	2	229,525	4	231,014
$2000 or more	1688	3	251,604	5	253,292
Not stated	2157	3	144,002	3	146,159
Entered not applicable	12,671	20	440,741	8	453,412
Total	63,319	100	5,221,031	100	5,284,350

The findings on the average weekly income of Muslims compared to that of the non-Muslim cohort of the Australian population merit an investigation into Muslims' levels of home ownership.

Home Ownership

Some studies point to a link between immigrant integration and housing and home ownership (Bolt, Özüekren, & Phillips, 2010; Owusu, 1998; Ray & Moore, 1991; Sinning, 2010). To immigrants, the benefits of home ownership determine the expression of long-term economic progress, wealth accumulation and financial wellbeing, but may also represent better living standards and higher social status (Constant, Roberts, & Zimmermann, 2009). Other researchers go as far as linking immigrant home ownership to psychological health and greater life satisfaction, as well as improved educational, behavioural and social outcomes (Constant et al., 2009). In the Australian context, home ownership is commonly associated with assimilation into the culture of the host society and attainment of the middle class "norm" (Constant et al., 2009). It is also important to understand that home ownership is

Table 2.6 Home ownership* by the Muslim and non-Muslim population in Australia

Weekly individual income	Muslim	%	Non-Muslim	%	Total
Negative income	1275	1	30,750	0	32,025
Nil income	17,390	10	499,670	6	517,060
$1–199	13,640	8	478,272	6	491,912
$200–299	14,617	9	347,600	4	362,217
$300–399	8631	5	333,682	4	342,313
$400–599	11,778	7	549,203	7	560,981
$600–799	11,225	7	631,174	8	642,399
$800–999	8965	5	582,523	8	591,488
$1000–1249	7908	5	613,531	8	621,439
$1250–1499	5211	3	466,789	6	472,000
$1500–1999	5558	3	581,488	8	587,046
$2000 or more	4847	3	529,944	7	534,791
Not stated	4315	3	124,305	2	128,620
Not applicable (c)	52,766	31	1,977,687	26	2,030,453
Total	168,126	100	7,746,618	100	7,914,744

Note *Tenure type: owned with a mortgage (includes rent/buy)

dependent on the average weekly income of individuals and households. For this reason, these two sets of data are interlinked and reveal how many Muslims own their own homes, how many are renters and what their average incomes are in comparison with those of their non-Muslim counterparts.

As the data in Table 2.6 reveal, home ownership by Muslims in Australia is comparatively lower than that of the non-Muslim population. In particular, in most of the average weekly individual income brackets, the percentage of Muslims owning homes with a mortgage (including rent/buy) is significantly lower than within its counterpart non-Muslim population. However, we need to be cautious about drawing any conclusions from this data, as there are a number of variables that can influence these results. There is protracted housing affordability stress in Australia that affects Muslim and non-Muslim groups, as explained by the Australian Housing and Urban Research Institute (AHURI, 2015). It is possible that there may be Muslim individuals who refrain from purchasing a home on a mortgage via a loan from a conventional, interest-based bank. These individuals cite religious reasons for their decisions, notably the prohibition against dealing in usury (*riba*) in the Quran "O those who believe, fear Allah and give up what still remains of the *riba* if you are believers. However, if you do not, then listen to the declaration of war from Allah and His Messenger" (Quran: Al-Baqarah 2:275).

Other factors include the migration stream, the circumstances in the home country and the cultural capital of a group, all of which may influence home ownership amongst immigrant communities (Forrest, Johnston, & Poulsen, 2014). For example, many Muslim groups migrate to Australia from war-torn countries, including Iraq, Afghanistan and Somalia. Some of these migrants arrive in Australia under the refugee and humanitarian program and may not have the necessary language and technical skills to be able to enter the labour market quickly, thus impeding any aspiration to purchase their own homes during their early years of resettlement. Even those with previous qualifications face the dilemma of difficulties posed by the Australian authorities' recognition of their prior qualifications. Some studies point out the difficulties that new immigrants face in the recognition of the credentials they have gained in their home countries, and the effect this has on their participation in the labour market (Andersson & Uthman, 2008; Guo, 2009; Wagner & Childs, 2006).

In contrast to the previous group, there are also Muslim groups who have migrated to Australia under its business and skills migration program. These are mainly Muslims from India, Pakistan and from the Southern African region including South Africa, Zimbabwe and Zambia. Evidently, the migration streams, the circumstances in the home country and the social capital of this latter group differ from the above-mentioned group. The importance of these variables is demonstrated by research undertaken in several immigrant communities across Europe, Canada and Australia. For example, studies into Polish and Somali refugees in Toronto, Canada, found that Poles have been more successful than Somalis in establishing home ownership (Murdie, 2002). The study further asserts that the reasons for this difference were mainly related to socio-economic status, household size, community resources and the migrants' housing situations before migrating to Canada. It is likely that Muslim migrants from India and Pakistan and those from the southern African region will have the necessary human capital and knowledge to access the labour market and, if they so desire, to establish small or medium-size businesses in Australia. However, Muslim groups who come to Australia on refugee and humanitarian visas, such as those from Afghanistan, Iraq and Somalia, may not have the same levels of human and financial capital as the previous cohort.

The tables give a snapshot of Muslims in Australia and their socio-economic circumstances. While this is not an exhaustive summary, it does give a clear indication of how Muslims are integrating into the wider Australian society. Quite often, issues of migrant integration are directly linked to their participation in the host country's economic and social fabric. On this basis, it is considered that the information in this book sheds considerable light on issues relating to Muslim migrant integration. However, it would be misleading to generalise and to claim that there is uniformity in how Muslims integrate into Australia and other Western societies. In fact, it is imperative to acknowledge that Muslims in Australia are different in their adaptability and resilience in adjusting to their new home. This is generally because of the diverse nature of their experiences and life journeys, including the circumstances which led them to migrate to Australia. This apparent diversity in the Muslim community in Australia must, therefore, be an integral part of the debates about Muslim migrant integration.

References

Adida, C. L., Laitin, D. D., & Valfort, M. A. (2010). Identifying barriers to Muslim integration in France. *Proceedings of the National Academy of Sciences, 107*(52), 22384–22390.

Ager, A., & Strang, A. (2004). *Indicators of integration.* London: Home Office, Research, Development and Statistics Directorate.

Akbarzadeh, S., & Saeed, A. (Eds.). (2001). *Muslim communities in Australia.* Sydney: University of New South Wales Press.

Ali, J. A. (2012). *Islamic revivalism: Encounter the modern world (A study of the Tabligh Jama 'at).* New Delhi: Sterling Publishers.

Andersson, P., & Uthman, A. (2008). Recognition of prior learning as a practice for differential inclusion and exclusion of immigrants in Sweden. *Adult Education Quarterly, 59*(1), 42–60.

Australian Bureau of Statistics. (2011). *Australian Standard Classification of Countries* (SACC). Retrieved from http://www.abs.gov.au/ausstats/abs@.nsf/Lookup/1269.

Australian Housing and Urban Research Institute. (2015). *Addressing recurring or protracted episodes in housing affordability stress 2001–11*. Melbourne: AHURI.

Beach, C. M., & Worswick, C. (1993). Is there a double-negative effect on the earnings of immigrant women? *Canadian Public Policy/Analyse de Politiques, 6*, 36–53.

Bevelander, P. (1999). The employment integration of immigrants in Sweden. *Journal of Ethnic and Migration Studies, 25*(3), 445–468.

Bevelander, P. (2000). *Immigrant employment integration and structural change in Sweden, 1970–1995*. Doctoral dissertation, Lund University.

Bisin, A., Patacchini, E., Verdier, T., & Zenou, Y. (2011). Ethnic identity and labour market outcomes of immigrants in Europe. *Economic Policy, 26*(65), 57–92.

Blanchard, C. M. (2005). *Islam: Sunnis and Shiites*. Washington, DC: Congressional Research Service (Library of Congress).

Bolt, G., Özüekren, A. S., & Phillips, D. (2010). Linking integration and residential segregation. *Journal of Ethnic and Migration Studies, 36*(2), 169–186.

Bouma, G. D. (1994). *Mosques and Muslim settlement in Australia*. Canberra: Australian Government.

Brasted, H. V., & Khan, A. (2012). Islam and the 'clash of civilizations'? An historical perspective. In S. Akbarzadeh (Ed.), *Routledge handbook of political Islam* (pp. 273–301). Abingdon: Routledge.

Campese, G. (2012). The irruption of migrants: Theology of migration in the 21st century. *Theological Studies, 73*(1), 3–32.

Cleland, B. (2002). *Muslims in Australia: A brief history*. Melbourne: Islamic Council of Victoria.

Constant, A. F., Roberts, R., & Zimmermann, K. F. (2009). Ethnic identity and immigrant homeownership. *Urban Studies, 46*(9), 1879–1898.

Convy, P., & Monsour, A. (2008). *Lebanese settlement in New South Wales*. Retrieved from http://www.migrationheritage.nsw.gov.au/mhc-reports/ThematicHistoryOfLebaneseNSW.pdf.

Cruz, G. T. (2008). Between identity and security: Theological implications of migration in the context of globalization. *Theological Studies, 69*(2), 357–375.

Deen, H. (2011). *Ali Abdul v The King: Muslim stories from the dark days of White Australia*. Crawley: University of Western Australia.

Department of Immigration and Citizenship. (2009). *The Australian journey: Muslim communities.* Report Retrieved from https://www.dss.gov.au/sites/default/files/documents/01_2014/australian-journey-muslim-communities.pdf.

Entzinger, H. B., & Biezeveld, R. L. (2003). *Benchmarking in immigrant integration.* A report by the European Research Centre on Migration and Ethnic Relations (ERCOMER, pp. 1–50). Rotterdam, The Netherlands: Erasmus University Rotterdam.

Forrest, J., Johnston, R., & Poulsen, M. (2014). Ethnic capital and assimilation to the great Australian (homeownership) dream: The early housing experience of Australia's skilled immigrants. *Australian Geographer, 45*(2), 109–129.

Ganter, R. (2012). Remembering Muslim histories of Australia. *The La Trobe Journal, 89,* 48–62.

Guo, S. (2009). Difference, deficiency, and devaluation: Tracing the roots of non-recognition of foreign credentials for immigrant professionals in Canada. *Canadian Journal for the Study of Adult Education, 22*(1), 37–52.

Hassan, R. (2009). Social and economic conditions of Australian Muslims: Implications for social inclusion. *National Centre of Excellence for Islamic Studies, 2*(4), 1–13. Retrieved from http://www.nceis.unimelb.edu.au/sites/nceis.unimelb.edu.au/files/NCEIS_Research_Paper_Vol2,No4_Hassan.pdf.

Hassan, R. (2010). Socio-economic marginalization of Muslims in contemporary Australia: Implications for social inclusion. *Journal of Muslim Minority Affairs, 30*(4), 575–584.

Humphrey, M. (2001). Muslim Lebanese. In J. Jupp (Ed.), *The Australian people* (pp. 564–567). Cambridge, UK: Cambridge University Press.

Husted, L., Heinesen, E., & Andersen, S. H. (2009). Labour market integration of immigrants: Estimating local authority effects. *Journal of Population Economics, 22*(4), 909–939.

Jacobson, J. (2006). *Islam in transition: Religion and identity among British Pakistani youth.* London: Routledge.

Johnston, R., Forrest, J., Jones, K., Manley, D., & Owen, D. (2015). The melting-pot and the economic integration of immigrant families: Ancestral and generational variations in Australia. *Environment and Planning A, 47*(12), 2663–2682.

Jones, G. W. (1993). Is demographic uniformity inevitable? *Journal of the Australian Population Association, 10*(1), 1–16.

Jones, P. G., & Kenny, A. (2007). *Australia's Muslim cameleers: Pioneers of the inland, 1860s–1930s.* Mile End, SA: Wakefield Press.

Jupp, J. (2002). *From White Australia to Woomera: The story of Australian immigration.* Cambridge, UK: Cambridge University Press.

Kabir, N. A. (2004). *Muslims in Australia: Immigration, race relations and cultural history.* London, UK: Routledge.

Kundnani, A. (2012). Multiculturalism and its discontents: Left, right and liberal. *European Journal of Cultural Studies, 15*(2), 155–166.

Minkenberg, M. (2008). Religious legacies, churches, and the shaping of immigration policies in the age of religious diversity. *Politics and Religion, 1*(3), 349–383.

Murdie, R. A. (2002). The housing careers of Polish and Somali newcomers in Toronto's rental market. *Housing Studies, 17*(3), 423–443.

Northcote, J., & Casimiro, S. (2010). Muslim citizens and belonging in Australia: Negotiating the inclusive/exclusive divide in a multicultural context. In S. Yasmeen (Ed.), *Muslims in Australia: The dynamics of exclusion and inclusion* (pp. 141–161). Carlton, VIC: Melbourne University Press.

Owusu, T. Y. (1998). To buy or not to buy: Determinants of home ownership among Ghanaian immigrants in Toronto. *The Canadian Geographer/Le Géographe Canadien, 42*(1), 40–52.

Peschke, D. (2009). The role of religion for the integration of migrants and institutional responses in Europe: Some reflections. *The Ecumenical Review, 61*(4), 367–380.

Peucker, M., & Akbarzadeh, S. (2014). *Muslim active citizenship in the West.* Abingdon-on-Thames, UK: Routledge.

Pew Forum. (2009). *Mapping the global Muslim population.* http://www.pewforum.org/2009/10/07/mapping-the-global-muslim-population/ accessed12/05/2014.

Phillimore, J., & Goodson, L. (2008). Making a place in the global city: The relevance of indicators of integration. *Journal of Refugee Studies, 21*(3), 305–325.

Poynting, S., & Mason, V. (2007). The resistible rise of Islamophobia anti-Muslim racism in the UK and Australia before 11 September 2001. *Journal of Sociology, 43*(1), 61–86.

Ramadan, T. (2003). *Western Muslims and the future of Islam.* Oxford: Oxford University Press.

Ramli, M. A. (2013). Postmodernism approach in Islamic jurisprudence (fiqh). *Middle-East Journal of Scientific Research, 13*(1), 33–40.

Ray, B. K., & Moore, E. (1991). Access to homeownership among immigrant groups in Canada. *Canadian Review of Sociology/Revue canadienne de sociologie, 28*(1), 1–29.

Saeed, A. (2003). *Islam in Australia.* Crows Nest, NSW: Allen & Unwin.

Saeed, A. (2004). *Muslim Australians: Their beliefs, practices and institutions.* Melbourne: Department of Immigration and Multicultural and Indigenous Affairs and Australian Multicultural Foundation.

Saeed, A. (2007). Trends in contemporary Islam: A preliminary attempt at a classification. *The Muslim World, 97*(3), 395–404.

Samani, S. (2007). Rhetoric and realities of multiculturalism: The perpetuation of negative constructions of Muslims in Australia. *International Journal of Diversity, 7*(2), 113–119.

Sinning, M. (2010). Homeownership and economic performance of immigrants in Germany. *Urban Studies, 47*(2), 387–409.

Spoonley, P., Peace, R., Butcher, A., & O'Neill, D. (2005). Social cohesion: A policy and indicator framework for assessing immigrant and host outcomes. *Social Policy Journal of New Zealand, 24,* 85–110.

Tastsoglou, E., & Preston, V. (2012). Gender, immigration and labour market integration: Where we are and what we still need to know. *Critical Studies in Gender, Culture & Social Justice, 30*(1), 46–59.

Wagner, R., & Childs, M. (2006). Exclusionary narratives as barriers to the recognition of qualifications, skills and experience—A case of skilled migrants in Australia. *Studies in Continuing Education, 28*(1), 49–62.

Yasmeen, S. (2008). *Understanding Muslim identities: From perceived relative exclusion to inclusion.* Canberra: Department of Immigration and Citizenship.

3

Problematic Conceptions of Integration

A perceived notion of problematic Muslim integration is gaining interest in Australia, creating an intense political and intellectual debate regarding Muslim immigrants' ability and willingness to integrate. In the aftermath of the 2005 Cronulla riots, it is clear that these heated debates are steered mainly by media stereotypes, sensationalism or political statements (Poynting, 2006). Samani (2007, p. 113) noted that the events of 11 September 2001 and the Cronulla riots have created a "... present waxing and waning of anti-Islamic sentiment in many Western nations". Other scholars such as Portes, Rumbaut, Fernandez-Kelly, and Haller (2006) point out that, "Public hostility towards Islam reached a climax after the coordinated attacks against the World Trade Centre and the Pentagon in September 2001, and it has been kept at a high pitch ever since" (p. 336). There appear to be a number of other studies that support this opinion. For example, the study by Celermajer, Yasmeen, and Saeed (2007) finds that the post-September 11, 2001 period only added to problems which had been experienced by Australian Muslims in the past. The media and opportunistic politicians have taken advantage of these circumstances. For example, Aly (2007) notes how the Australian media identify Muslims both explicitly and implicitly as the "other" and equate Muslims with a threat to the wider society (p. 33).

© The Author(s) 2018
A. Hersi, *Conceptualisation of Integration*, Palgrave Politics of Identity and Citizenship Series, https://doi.org/10.1007/978-3-319-91235-6_3

Similarly, the work of Dunn, Forrest, Burnley, and McDonald (2004) is particularly important. A telephone survey they undertook in 2004 of 5056 residents in Queensland and New South Wales, asked respondents to identify whether there were any cultural or ethnic groups that did not fit into Australian society and to nominate three such groups. "The results overwhelmingly indicate the outsider status of Muslims, as well as Australians of Middle-Eastern origin and, less so of Asian origin" (Dunn et al., 2004. p. 414). There appears to be a renewed interest in this subject and in social inclusion generally, as evidenced by an increase in debates about the integration or the lack of integration of Muslims in Australia. For instance, Saeed (2003, p. 186) states that "both global and local events have contributed to the negative image of Islam and Muslims in general, and while there are many Australian journalists who have provided positive constructions of Islam and Muslims, a significant section of media (particularly some of the tabloid newspapers and talkback radio) focused on a negative representation of Islam".

In modern Australia, Muslims are undeniably part of the wider mix of Australia's diverse multicultural society. Research into the incorporation of Muslim immigrants is relatively new. Muslims as a distinct faith group face the challenge of living with their religious loyalty. As a result, their integration into the wider society is often questioned. Despite the absence of any clear understanding regarding what integration might mean and whether or not it can be measured, either subjectively or objectively, there seems to be an emerging body of literature that casts doubt on whether or not Muslims in Australia are integratable (Aly, 2007; Samani, 2007).

Despite being a key policy objective for the governments of a number of states in an attempt to resettle their new immigrant groups, to date integration remains the subject of a significant level of controversy, both in Australia and the rest of the world. It is a fact that in some Western nations including Australia, the character and integrability of Muslims has become central to debates about integration. In these debates, negative perceptions about the integration of Muslims is evident in parts of Europe such as Britain, Germany, France and the Netherlands (Bloemraad, Korteweg, & Yurdakal, 2008).

Numerous studies into immigration focus on the problematic integration of Muslim communities, and government strategies for improving integration policies (Bloemraad et al., 2008, p. 169).

In the case of Australia, a number of studies suggest that there is perceived to be a problem regarding the integration of Muslims into the society (Celermajer et al., 2007; Dunn et al., 2004). While notions of integration have been integral to public debates around migration and settlement, there is often little consensus about what integration means practically, and how different social communities within Australia understand it.

Proliferated Meanings of Integration

To date, what integration means to Muslims themselves has notably been absent from the debate. This book addresses an important issue that has not been specifically addressed in the larger body of literature examining Australian Muslims and citizenship, that of Muslim interpretations and conceptions of integration. A discussion of the practices and perceptions of integration advanced by Muslims in Australia will certainly make an important contribution to the research into the debates of immigrant integration. An examination of immigrant incorporation literature confirms the existence of a variety of perceived meanings of integration. The apparent interchangeable use of the terms "integration" and "incorporation" perhaps produced some confusion. The words used to describe the processes of migrant incorporation include "absorb", "assimilate", "acculturate", "adopt" and "integrate". The presence of these diverse terms to describe integration shows the level of complexity, ambiguity and contention in the subject (Weiner, 1996).

Variations in the way integration is conceptualised by different groups in society needs to be explained. For instance, members of the dominant host community's views of integration differ somewhat from the way integration is conceptualised by immigrants and newcomers. For example, there is a widespread view among the members of many host societies, in particular that of America, that having a distinct cultural and ethnic identity undermines unity and social integration (Portes et al., 2006). This is despite the fact that some countries are actively encouraging new migrants to retain aspects of their local cultures and traditions. The contrasting viewpoints advanced in these debates appear to be between assimilationist versus pluralist modes of integration, as well as preferences for cultural integration over socio-economic integration, and vice versa. Nevertheless, Doomernik and Knippenberg (2003) conclude that "Integrationist models of immigrant incorporation appear to be superior to assimilationist models because of their culturally-pluralistic basis" (p. 46).

Integration is defined as, "The participation of ethnic and religious minorities, individually and as groups, in the social structure of the host society while having possibilities to retain the distinctive aspects of their culture and identity" (Shadid, 1991, p. 362). Shadid's definition is closer to the multicultural meaning of integration, but there are other definitions that emphasise participation in the social and economic fabric, disregarding the retention and practice of ethnic culture (Portes et al., 2006). Successful integration means more than economic activity and social participation and may include belonging and showing allegiance to one's country, language proficiency and commitment to liberal values (Goodman, 2010, p. 754). As a result, meanings of integration that emphasise civic engagement through cultural commitment are becoming prevalent in Europe, North America and Australia (Goodman, 2010; Joppke, 2007; Kostakopoulou, 2010). For example, in the case of the Netherlands, de Leeuw and van Wichelen (2012) explain how sexual freedom, gender equality, freedom of speech and individuality, are identified as symbols of Dutchness, however, the authors agree that the adaptation of these dominant liberal and secular virtues ignores the cultural and religious diversity of the Dutch community. In fact, the Dutch model of civic integration that emphasises culture over all other determinants of integration has been implemented by many other European and non-European countries, including Australia (Joppke, 2007; Löwenheim & Gazit, 2009).

An interpretation of multiculturalism that signifies integration has gained momentum in Canada, Australia and parts of Europe (Meer, Dwyer, & Modood, 2010; Meer & Modood, 2009), and a considerable body of literature written by Australian multicultural theorists contributes to this interpretation (Castles, 1992; Colic-Peisker, 2011; Jakubowicz, 2011; Kalantzis & Cope, 1988, 1999) by examining Australia's multicultural interpretation of integration. The concept of multiculturalism has prevailed as an alternative to the traditional assimilationist discourses which demand that migrants shed some of their past cultures and embrace the dominant society's cultures (Shadid, 1991). Multiculturalism was institutionalised in the 1970s in parts of Western migrant-receiving countries but fell out of favour during the 2000s (Colic-Peisker & Farquharson, 2011, p. 579). A considerable body of recent work examines the perceived retreat of multiculturalism in Australia. Colic-Peisker and Farquharson (2011, p. 582) assert that the Australian government's treatment of asylum seekers is an important litmus test of a real—and not just declarative—commitment to multiculturalism.

Multiculturalism as a concept and as a policy has come under scrutiny recently, and a body of literature suggesting "the retreat of multiculturalism" has emerged (Banting & Kymlicka, 2013; Kymlicka, 2010; Tip et al., 2012). This perceived retreat is explained by a lack of public support for the concept, failed multicultural policies and the assertiveness of the liberal state in imposing liberal principles (Joppke, 2004). Another reason claimed to be causing a retreat from multiculturalism is the perceived threat felt by members of the dominant society about the implacability of newcomers in maintaining their home culture (Tip et al., 2012). The social mobility of "ethnics" and their increased visibility is also claimed to be causing this perceived retreat (Colic-Peisker & Farquharson, 2011, p. 581). However, the way in which the debate about the retreat away from multiculturalism has been carried out differs between Europe and Australia. In general, the position of most European scholars is that there is a retreat from multiculturalism (Joppke, 2004; Koopmans, 2013; Poynting & Mason, 2008; Vertovec & Wassendorf, 2009). As an exception to this trend in thought is the work of Lenard (2012), who claims that the retreat of multiculturalism is grossly exaggerated, declaring that the death of the concept is premature (p. 194). Kundnani's (2012, p. 155) contribution to the debate is also invaluable, summarised as follows, "Attacks on multiculturalism from across the political spectrum reduce the complex history of settlement and interaction in the United Kingdom to a simple narrative of excessive British tolerance and increasingly disruptive immigrant communities."

In Europe the debate seems to be polaris ed and tense, with claims that multiculturalism poses a core challenge to liberal democracies (Goodman, 2010, p. 754). The predominant view in Europe is that there is a crisis of multiculturalism despite the absence of empirical evidence (Lentin & Titley, 2012). In response to these public debates about integration and multiculturalism, many of Europe's leaders have weighed in. For example, senior political figures in Germany, such as Chancellor Angela Merkel, openly state that multiculturalism is a failed policy (Weaver, October, 2010). Similarly, former British Prime Minister David Cameron claims that multiculturalism has failed, as reported by the British Broadcasting Corporation (Kuenssberg, 2011). The emergence of this considerable body of literature about the retreat away from multiculturalism (Colic-Peisker & Farquharson, 2011; Joppke, 2004; Poynting & Mason, 2008; Tilbury, 2007) arguably takes us back to the failed assimilationist model of incorporation.

There is an argument which suggests that the debate about the retreat of multiculturalism paved the way for the introduction of interculturalism as a new, more plural and alternative concept of an ideal immigrant integration model. The Council of Europe promoted the concept as a mode of integration preferable to multiculturalism (Meer & Modood, 2013, p. 30). Despite this endorsement, interculturalism as a model faced its own challenges in distinguishing itself from multiculturalism. Serious doubts were raised about whether or not interculturalism means the same as multiculturalism. Some scholars have struggled to differentiate between the two concepts, and have explained that they should be considered to be complimentary (Meer & Modood, 2012). Putting forward their suggestions Meer and Modood (2013, pp. 30–33) explain the following four ways in which interculturalism can differentiate itself from multiculturalism:

1. its emphasis on beyond multicultural co-existence,
2. the fact that it is less groupist and culture-bound,
3. its strong sense of whole, and
4. its illiberalism and culture.

A move away from multiculturalism is evident in the scholarly literature even if interculturalism is not fully embraced. Throughout Europe and Australia, integration policies are now shifting towards a model of civic integration (Goodman, 2010, p. 753) where immigration and naturalisation are conditional on learning local history, language and value commitments. This new shift towards civic integration means attaching mandatory integration requirements such as citizenship test s to status acquisition (Goodman, 2010, p. 753). Placing the emphasis on gaining citizenship after successfully completing a number of citizenship tests may seem to be creating a vetting process to deny citizenship for some, or to ensure that their conformity to the mainstream is enforced.

However, there are stark differences between the policies of Europe and Australia, mainly in the areas of social integration policy. The issues of how best to integrate migrants are vigorously debated in Europe, and a review of the extant literature shows that the bulk of academic studies concerning immigrant integration is Europe-based. In Europe, there is a Migrant Integration Policy Indicator Index (MIPEX) in which specific countries are ranked and rated against seven integration policies adopted by those countries, namely labour market mobility, family reunion, education, political participation, long-term residence, access to citizenship and anti-discrimination laws (MIPEX, 2013). Australia joined this index only in 2010 and is faring well across all the migrant integration policy index rankings. Despite the absence of any clear understanding of what integration might mean and whether or not it can be measured at all, there seems to be an emerging body of literature that doubts whether Muslims can be integrated into Australian society.

Absence of Agreed Indicators of Integration

Like the meanings of integration discussed above, there are a multiplicity of migrant integration indicators used by nation-states to measure the integration of their immigrant populations. In the academic literature about migrant integration there is not a single agreed measure of integration among the indicators which ranged from social, political and economic measures. Measures used to evaluate levels of migrant newcomer integration include socio-economic, legal, political and cultural dimensions (Entzinger & Biezeveld, 2003; Waldrauch & Hofinger, 1997). Other measures used include employment status, education and income levels (Phillimore & Goodson, 2008). A study commissioned by the Home Office of the United Kingdom (UK) also cites housing, employment, education and health as markers and means of integration, but more importantly found that relationships (social bonds) are the key to both the definition and achievement of integration (Phillips, 2006).

Public discussions of the indicators of integration seems to range between two competing camps: one which uses functional indicators which mainly focus on the immigrant's educational attainment, employment access, absence of discrimination and rate of inter-marriage, against a camp that uses the host nation's institutional modes and policies as determinants of integration (Soysal, 1994). Nevertheless, there have been attempts to measure integration, and Ager and Strang (2004) suggest functional indicators of immigrant integratio n that mainly emphasise employment, housing, education and health. Similarly, other studies suggest that immigrant integration should be benchmarked against the following four dimensions: socio-economic status, spatial concentration, language assimilation and intermarriage (Waters & Jiménez, 2005). Using the level of intermarriage between immigrants and members of the host society, as an indicator, Furtado and Theodoropoulos (2009) stress the role human capital plays in the social integration of immigrants. Interaction between the functional dimensions of integration and social integration is emphasised by some researchers, for example, Phillimore and Goodson (2008). The harmonisation of these two opposing views becomes important in the integration of Muslims in Europe. For example, in the Dutch society:

> The accomplished changes in the Dutch regulations and guidelines in favour of Muslims indicate a dis-balance between the pace of integration in the juridical sphere on the one hand and in the socio-economic sphere on the other. However, socio-economic integration of Muslims in the Dutch society is impeded by the existing prejudice and discrimination. (Shadid, 1991, p. 355)

Similarly, the Islamic community in Austria follows a policy of integration through participation, which it is claimed contributed to a social climate between the Muslim minority and the non-Muslim majority which is largely devoid of tension and conducive to inter-cultural and inter-religious dialogue (Abid, 2006, p. 263). One reason cited for this positive relationship is that Muslims in Austria are officially recognised as a religious community, have equal access to the labour market and enjoy an absence of various forms of discrimination. Throughout Europe, Austria is referred to as by far the most accommodating country (Abid, 2006, p. 263). The assertion may be disputed, but evidently, Austria's long harmonious relationship with Muslims from the former Yugoslavia and Turkey helps alleviate tensions between its citizens. In the wider debates concerning the indicators of integration, there is a body of literature that looks at the subjective indicators of integration. In particular, the work of Maxwell (2010) refers to subjective integration factors such as the migrant's feelings of satisfaction with life in the host community (p. 25). Maxwell examines abstract notions of integration such as the trust migrants have in their parliament, individuals' concerns about the government's legitimacy and allegiance to their host country or their homeland. This is in line with an emerging body of literature that links the Islamic women's veil or *burqa* to the integration debate, which claims that the *burqa* is a barrier to integration (Ajrouch, 2007; Freedman, 2004; Hamel, 2002).

Further to these public and academic discussions about the indicators and measures of integration, are studies that assert that it is impossible to set standards for an "ideal" integration process due to the immense diversity of immigrants and host societies (Entzinger & Biezeveld, 2006). Some studies have even questioned whether integration is quantifiable at all, citing the perpetrators of the 7th July 2005 London bombing as being reasonably well-adjusted men, born and bred in the United Kingdom (Kolig & Kabir, 2008). Contrary to this widely held negative perception of Muslim integration, the findings from studies in Australia and successive ABS Census data reveal that Australian Muslims are integrating successfully, for example in the areas of "English language skills, citizenship uptake, home ownership, and university qualifications" (Saeed, 2006, p. 12). If Muslims are benchmarked against these key indicators, their integration is not so problematic.

Perceptions and Suspicions

While there is no shortage of literature questioning the levels of Muslim integration, notably absent from the debates about immigrant integration is the question of how Muslims themselves understand the meaning of integration. Muslims in Australia are increasingly becoming a visible minority group within the wider society. Despite their diverse cultures, languages, ethnicities and nationalities, they share a common religious identity. As a minority religious group, Muslims are subject to both public and policy discussions about their integration into the community. Thus, an understanding of how Muslims' conceptions of integration are similar or different from the accepted definitions of integration in the broader scholarly literature becomes important. Muslims are one of the many large groups of immigrants that have made Australia home since the Second World War, and until recently, concerns raised about their integration related to welfare (Cox, 1983) and labour market participation (Harrison, 1984; Tran-Nam & Neville, 1988).

The findings of four focus groups from interviews conducted with Muslim communities in the South East Queensland region of Australia are drawn upon in this research. The objective is to identify how Muslims understand and define integration. In other words, what do Muslims identify as successful integration and barriers to integration?

A total of 31 persons of Muslim faith participated in four focus groups consisting of 20 males and 11 females of various ages, occupational and educational backgrounds. The median group size was seven participants per focus group. Discussions for each group lasted 90 minutes and sessions were tape-recorded. Details of the four focus groups are shown in Table 3.1.

Table 3.1 Focus groups and participants

Date	Location	Participants	Number
5/3/2011	Gold Coast	Men	7
20/11/2010	Brisbane	Men/Women	7
13/11/2010	Brisbane	Men/Women	11
6/11/2010	Brisbane	Men/Women	6

The participants of the focus group discussions included Muslims of all ages and occupational backgrounds. The following is a summary of the social profiles of the four focus groups:

1. 'Regional city' was a group of males living in a coastal city about 60 km south of Brisbane. Participants included those born in Australia and overseas, were mainly young and the majority were blue collar workers such as labourers. One member of the group had a degree and the remainder had lower levels of education, including completing either year 10 or year 12.
2. 'Urban city #1' was a group of mixed males and females living in Brisbane. Amongst the female group, some covered their hair, others did not and some wore a *burqa*. Participants were a mix of Australian born, overseas-born, young and old and were both blue and white-collar employees. One member of the group is a fourth generation Australian.
3. 'Urban city #2' was a group of mixed males and females living in Brisbane. Participants were both Australian born and overseas-born, young and old, and were in blue and white-collar occupations. Amongst the overseas-born was a non-English-speaking background participant who came to Australia under the refugee and humanitarian programme.
4. 'Urban city #3' was a group of mixed males and females living in Brisbane. Some participants were born in Australia, others overseas, they were of various ages and the majority were in white-collar occupations. One member of the group was an academic and medical specialist.

The study claims that the diversity found in this small sample is illustrative of Muslim communities in Queensland only, and an effort was made to make the focus group participants reflect the ethnic and religious sect diversity that is apparent in this community. The study used the 2011 ABS Census data as a guide for recruiting a representative sample of the Muslim communities in the Southern Queensland region. As a guide, it has also used the ABS Standard Classification of Countries (SACC), which groups countries in the world in the

Table 3.2 Participant country of origin

Country of origin	Number	Percentage
Middle East	7	24.1
Australia	7	24.1
Sub Saharan Africa	5	17.2
Southern Africa region	4	13.7
South Asia	5	17.2
Europe	1	3.4

Two people chose not to answer the country of origin question and therefore were not included in the country of origin data table

following regional blocks: Oceania and Antarctica, North West Europe, Southern and Eastern Europe, North Africa and Middle East, South East Asia, North East Asia, Southern and Central Asia, the Americas and sub-Saharan Africa (ABS, 2011). Regional blocks relating to patterns of representations of Muslims in Queensland, Australia were then chosen. The regional origins of the groups represented in the study are shown in Table 3.2.

Before presenting the findings of how Muslims understand and define integration, it is noteworthy to first discuss the general Muslim response to the integration debate. The participants in our study tend to regard the integration debate with suspicion and see it as slanted against Muslim communities. The reservations that Muslim participants have about the term *integration* are a clear discussion thread in all four focus groups. The core of the participants' concerns was that they understood the call for integration to be a demand for the abandonment of their culture and religion. The following are the comments of a 25-year-old Muslim male in response to the question "what does integration mean to you?"

I think that the meaning of integration from the Western perspective regardless of how they are portraying it to be is that we end up accepting and respecting their way of life and ultimately perhaps integrating in a way adopting their way of life as our own. That's what I believe integration means from the Western perspective.

A 32-year-old female respondent attempts to highlight how she is sceptical of certain interpretations of integration by some in the wider society and offers a counter interpretation of integration.

Actually my understanding of integration is this. You work hard in Australian society, whatever you work in whatever your job is, you do it honestly, pay taxes and so on. We take part in developing this beautiful country. To me that is my understanding and there is another misunderstanding from the government's point of view or from the people's point of view, they think integration means we dress like them, we eat the way they eat, they do many things we can't, so I think it is best for them to respect us and we can tell them, our understanding about integration is this, we will be contributing to this society, but there are a few personal things that we cannot negotiate.

The suspicions Muslim participants express about what integration means may have occurred as a result of one or more of the following possible reasons: the general perceived anti-Islamic sentiments, termed Islamophobia, experienced by Muslims may be influencing some Muslims to be suspicious about the calls for integration. Tufail and Poynting (2013) make a link between the new post-multiculturalism integrationism concept that changes meanings of integration from acceptance and accommodation to punishment and blame and the phenomenon of Islamophobia. Feelings of "othering" and constantly being referred to as foreigners may be factors that have led some Muslim participants to be suspicious of meanings of integration (Tufail & Poynting, 2013). Constant and ever-present negative representations of Islam and Muslims by hostile media outlets could be another factor for suspicions about the term *integration* (Gardner, Karakaşoğlus, & Luchtenberg, 2008).

Other important factors which increase this sense of suspicion among Muslim participants are the general controversies about immigrant integration in Europe, Australia and beyond. The immigration and integration of migrants are becoming highly topical issues and extremist elements in various parts of Europe blame migrants, including Muslims, for failing to integrate (Norris & Inglehart, 2012). These public discussions are also occurring at a time when the Muslim population is increasing, and Muslims are becoming more visible in the public sphere of many European and Australian communities (Ajrouch, 2007; Freedman, 2004; Hamel, 2002). The increasing visibility of the Islamic religion and Muslims in the public space has sparked deep discussions.

Controversy is rising about an individual Muslim's preferred allegiance to his or her adoptive country or ancestral home, the wearing of the veil for women (Ajrouch, 2007; Hamel, 2002) and the existence, and building of new mosques and Islamic schools (Verkaaik, 2012).

Similarly, the frequency and heightened pitch of public discussions about integration may have led many Muslims to be somewhat suspicious about what is meant by integration. Muslim participants in this study conveyed that, despite their personal efforts to integrate linguistically and in matters relating to appearance and dress code, some members of the wider society continue to cast doubt about whether they are integratable at all. As a 36-year-old Muslim male participant conveyed:

> This guy came to me where I was praying and he started talking to me about how we guys haven't integrated, and I said, 'What are you talking about, integration, I am speaking the language, I am dressed like you, I am sitting here saying hi to you, what more do you want, what else do you want more than integration?'

Suspicions about what integration might mean appear to be held by both male and female participants in the focus group discussions. One Australian-born Muslim female participant confirmed suspicions that integration means something different to some members of the wider society than to how she conceptualises it. For instance, this participant explains that Muslims are asked to conform rather than integrate. She challenges the unwillingness on the part of some in the wider society to accept that Muslims as a group are different.

> My father was in the Air Force for thirty-two years, so he is a military man, so you can understand exactly where he comes from, America, US all the way, he went to Vietnam and all that stuff. It has taken him a long time to accept that he has got Muslim grandchildren that don't have English names. I don't mean that it has taken him a really long time, but is it something that he's had to stomach. But that being the case I think that the average Australian probably simply wants Muslims to be like them. Not look physically different, don't do things different, just be like us. Without actually saying what it is that you should do, just somehow don't be different. Which I think ultimately is what Pauline Hanson's

message was. I'm not saying we have to agree with it and I don't, but I think that's what Australian people believe. When they are saying that Muslims don't integrate, what they are saying is that Muslims aren't like me, they don't look like me, they don't act like me, they don't do what I do. Therefore, you're not Australian.

A Muslim convert who was born and bred in Australia advanced a similar argument. He explains that he faces the dilemma of not being acknowledged as being integrated by his family members simply because he embraced the Muslim faith. As he states:

Convert 2: It wasn't my parents, it was my sister maybe, she could not explain it. I have been in the military, I have been shot at, blown up in defence of Australia, I've gone to Australian schools, I've worked in Australia, paid taxes in Australia but she still can't explain to me why I'm not Australian.

The above sentiment suggests that there is a perception that some citizens are not accepted simply because of their Muslim faith even if they consider themselves to be part of an "in-group" apart from their religion. Possibly this perception caused some Muslims to respond to the question of integration with suspicion.

The findings of this study also show that Muslims themselves make a distinction between integration and assimilation. In fact, when they are asked what integration means to them, their responses to the research questions generally referred to what integration is not, rather than what it is. From the focus group data, it is clear that Muslims consistently understood that the concept of integration did not mean assimilation.

The first thing I would say is that there's a big difference between assimilation and integration. A lot of people tend to mix these two terms and use them together in the same sentence even though they have two very different definitions to me. Assimilation is totally different, assimilation is when you're expected to change the whole way of life that you live according to your culture, your beliefs, your values, just to integrate with the society that is a totally different context.

The vagueness implanted in the meanings of the concept of integration discussed at great length above further justifies participants' suspicion of its true meanings. It is evident in the literature that, at times, calls for integration might mean assimilation (Bowskill, Lyons, & Coyle, 2007). For example, Bowskill et al. (2007, p. 805) argue that, "Integration was often used synonymously with a privileging of assimilative outcomes, while assimilation itself was never directly oriented to. Typically, this was predicted on an implicit rendering of insider and outsider status". The very fact that Muslims are called upon to integrate suggests that they are positioned as outsiders and are not considered an in-group.

Respondents providing explanations of differences between the meanings of integration and assimilation were a common thread throughout the discussions. In responding to the question of what integration means to them, one of the study participants commented as follows:

> The term integration is very loose and I don't think it can be defined but it has implications, there is a very thin line as to what you see integration is, what's outside of what is integration, what's the difference between assimilation and integration. However, assimilation is when you adopt the morals, adopt the values, adopt the entire … basically copy, identically copy the popular culture, the popular beliefs and popular political methodology and ideology of Australia.

The comments above are perhaps a bit exaggerated but show the level of scepticism some Muslim participants have of what is meant by integration. These inflated Muslim definitions of integration were not uncommon throughout the group discussions. Another Muslim respondent commented:

> I personally have always said that when we speak of integration people usually confuse it with assimilation, which if you look, there is a fine line between integration and assimilation. In the sense that when you say assimilation is that you accept other people, not only their way of life, but also their values and their entire being, whatever they do you tend to do as well, and it becomes something that looks good, that's something

that makes you happy to be part of that community. For example, if you look at the French colonial system, that's what it was based on, that the people should act like the French, they should eat like the French, they should have freedom like the French, while the English system was different, they were colonising people but they had to stick to their own values and all that, so in my own view, integration doesn't mean assimilation.

In their rejection of assimilation, Muslim participants in the focus group discussions also state that issues relating to their appearance, mode of dress and how they look should not be used as measures of their levels of integration. In particular, strong references were made to the Muslim women's veil, the male Muslims' *jalabiya* and the growing of the beard. A middle-aged Muslim male convert participant referred to these issues as being superficial:

Some might say that because I wear a scarf I'm not integrated but some others might say that because I speak English and I have a job that I am integrated. It depends how we individually want to look at that, whether we are going to individually integrate ourselves or whether we are waiting for acceptance of others if we're integrated or not.

The Muslim convert participant also confirms that members of the wider society judge Muslims on their appearance, and explains how he personally makes an effort to lessen this perceived pressure from the wider society. His comment on this matter is as follows:

I tell my wife don't scare the white folks, just dress in lighter colours today, not that I am saying don't wear what you want to wear, but just by wearing a colourful scarf and just by wearing a lighter colour straight away they are disarmed. One day she wore all black and she came home and she said you're right, no one waved or looked at me today, it happens.

Similarly, others argued that Muslims are judged on their appearances unfairly when compared with the wider society. A young Australian-born Muslim participant also highlights how changing your appearance does not increase or decrease your level of integration. As he explains:

Just on the point of clothing and stuff like that, again it is one of these fake issues that people have brought up. Somebody can be the gothic or emo type or all of the weird piercings and all of that and nobody will say they're multi-integrated into the Australian society but from the history as well that happened with the Aboriginal people on all of the missions. They took them from wearing nothing in their sense and shoved them into Western clothes but it was still another forty-fifty years for them to be granted Australian citizenship. So even if you look the part it doesn't mean that the wider white population are going to accept you or allow you to integrate anyway, so I think that people who bring up this as an objection, Muslims don't integrate because they look different, well you don't integrate because you've got red hair. So I don't buy it, I think that physical appearance is irrelevant.

In addition to the perceptions that Muslims had about the meanings of the term *integration*, they also indicated that the extent to which they believe in their religion plays a role in how they understand integration. The slippery nature of the term *integration* has allowed Muslim participants to come up with a compromise definition of integration that fits their personal circumstances as a distinct faith group. Some the participants stressed the significance of maintaining their belief systems while integrating successfully into the wider society. In this next section, responses provided by Muslim participants about integration and maintaining their belief system and how that aligns with the scholarly literature are discussed.

References

Abid, L. J. (2006). Muslims in Austria: Integration through participation in Austrian society. *Journal of Muslim Minority Affairs, 26*(2), 263–278.

Ager, A., & Strang, A. (2004). *Indicators of integration*. London: Home Office, Research, Development and Statistics Directorate.

Ajrouch, K. J. (2007). Global contexts and the veil: Muslim integration in the United States and France. *Sociology of Religion, 68*(3), 321–325.

Aly, A. (2007). Australian Muslim responses to the discourse on terrorism in the Australian popular media. *Australian Journal of Social Issues, 42*(1), 27–40.

Australian Bureau of Statistics. (2011). *Australian Standard Classification of Countries* (SACC). Retrieved from http://www.abs.gov.au/ausstats/abs@.nsf/Lookup/1269.

Banting, K., & Kymlicka, W. (2013). Is there really a retreat from multiculturalism policies & quest: New evidence from the multiculturalism policy index. *Comparative European Politics, 11*(5), 577–598.

Bloemraad, I., Korteweg, A., & Yurdakal, G. (2008). Citizenship and immigration: Multiculturalism, assimilation, and challenges to the nation-state. *Annual Review of Sociology, 34*(1), 153–179.

Bowskill, M., Lyons, E., & Coyle, A. (2007). The rhetoric of acculturation: When integration means assimilation. *British Journal of Social Psychology, 46*(4), 793–813.

Castles, S. (1992). The Australian model of immigration and multiculturalism: Is it applicable to Europe? *International Migration Review, 26*(2), 549–567.

Celermajer, D., Yasmeen, S., & Saeed, A. (2007). Introduction special edition: Australian Muslims and secularism. *Australian Journal of Social Issues, 42*(1), 1–5.

Colic-Peisker, V. (2011). A new era in Australian multiculturalism? From working-class "ethnics" to a "multicultural middle-class". *International Migration Review, 45*(3), 562–587.

Colic-Peisker, V., & Farquharson, K. (2011). A new era in Australian multiculturalism? The need for critical interrogation. *Journal of Intercultural Studies, 32*(6), 579–586.

Cox, D. R. (1983). Religion and the welfare of immigrants. *Australian Social Work, 36*(1), 3–10.

De Leeuw, M., & Van Wichelen, S. (2012). Civilizing migrants: Integration, culture and citizenship. *European Journal of Cultural Studies, 15*(2), 195–210.

Doomernik, J. M. J., & Knippenberg, H. (2003). *Migration and immigrants: Between policy and reality: A volume in honor of Hans van Amersfoort.* Amsterdam: Aksant.

Dunn, K. M., Forrest, J., Burnley, I., & McDonald, A. (2004). Constructing racism in Australia. *Australian Journal of Social Issues, 39*(4), 409–430.

Entzinger, H. (2006). Changing the rules while the game is on: From multiculturalism to assimilation in the Netherlands. In Y. M. Bodemann & G. Yurdakul (Eds.), *Migration, citizenship, ethnos: Incorporation regimes in Germany, Western Europe and North America* (pp. 121–144). New York, NY: Palgrave Macmillan.

Entzinger, H. B., & Biezeveld, R. L. (2003). *Benchmarking in immigrant integration. A report by the European Research Centre on Migration and Ethnic Relations* (ERCOMER, pp. 1–50). Rotterdam, The Netherlands: Erasmus University Rotterdam.

Freedman, J. (2004). Secularism as a barrier to integration? The French dilemma. *International Migration, 42*(3), 5–27.

Furtado, D., & Theodoropoulos, N. (2009). *Intermarriage and immigrant employment: The role of networks* (Discussion Paper Series 06/09). London, UK: Centre for Research and Analysis of Migration.

Gardner, R., Karakaşoğlus, Y., & Luchtenberg, S. (2008). Islamophobia in the media: A response from multicultural education. *Intercultural Education, 19*(2), 119–136.

Goodman, S. W. (2010). Integration requirements for integration's sake? Identifying, categorising and comparing civic integration. *Journal of Ethnic and Migration Studies, 36*(5), 753–772.

Hamel, C. E. (2002). Muslim diaspora in Western Europe: The Islamic headscarf (hijab), the media and Muslim's integration in France. *Citizenship Studies, 6*(3), 293–308.

Harrison, D. S. (1984). The impact of immigration on a depressed labour market: The South Australian experience. *Economic Record, 60*(1), 57–67.

Jakubowicz, A. (2011). Chinese walls: Australian multiculturalism and the necessity for human rights. *Journal of Intercultural Studies, 32*(6), 691–706.

Joppke, C. (2004). The retreat of multiculturalism in the liberal state: Theory and policy. *The British Journal of Sociology, 55*(2), 237–257.

Joppke, C. (2007). Transformation of immigrant integration: Civic integration and antidiscrimination in the Netherlands, France, and Germany. *World Politics, 59*(2), 243–273.

Kalantzis, M., & Cope, B. (1988). Why we need multicultural education: A review of the 'ethnic disadvantage' debate. *Journal of Intercultural Studies, 9*(1), 39–57.

Kalantzis, M., & Cope, B. (1999). Multicultural education: Transforming the mainstream. In S. May (Ed.), *Critical multiculturalism: Rethinking multicultural and antiracist education* (pp. 245–276). London, UK: Falmer Press.

Kolig, E., & Kabir, N. (2008). Not friend, not foe: The rocky road of enfranchisement of Muslims into multicultural nationhood in Australia and New Zealand. *Immigrants & Minorities, 26*(3), 266–300.

Koopmans, R. (2013). Multiculturalism and immigration: A contested field in cross-national comparison. *Annual Review of Sociology, 39*, 147–169.

Kostakopoulou, D. (2010). The anatomy of civic integration. *The Modern Law Review, 73*(6), 933–958.

Kuenssberg, L. (2011, February). State multiculturalism has failed, says David Cameron. *BBC News*.

Kundnani, A. (2012). Multiculturalism and its discontents: Left, right and liberal. *European Journal of Cultural Studies, 15*(2), 155–166.

Kymlicka, W. (2010). The rise and fall of multiculturalism? New debates on inclusion and accommodation in diverse societies. *International Social Science Journal, 61*(199), 97–112.

Lenard, P. (2012). The report of multiculturalism's death are greatly exaggerated. *Politics, 32*(3), 186–196.

Lentin, A., & Titley, G. (2012). The crisis of 'multiculturalism' in Europe: Mediated minarets, intolerable subjects. *European Journal of Cultural Studies, 15,* 123–138.

Löwenheim, O., & Gazit, O. (2009). Power and examination: A critique of citizenship tests. *Security Dialogue, 40*(20), 145–167.

Maxwell, R. (2010). Evaluating migrant integration: Political attitudes across generations in Europe. *International Migration Review, 44*(1), 25–52.

Meer, N., Dwyer, C., & Modood, T. (2010). Embodying nationhood? Conceptions of British national identity, citizenship, and gender in the 'veil affair'. *The Sociological Review, 58*(1), 85–111.

Meer, N., & Modood, T. (2009). The multicultural state we're in: Muslims, 'multiculture' and the 'civic re-balancing' of British multiculturalism. *Political Studies, 57,* 473–497.

Meer, N., & Modood, T. (2012). For 'Jewish' read 'Muslim'? Islamophobia as a form of racialisation of ethno religious groups in Britain today. *Islamophobia Studies Journal, 1*(1), 36–55.

Meer, N., & Modood, T. (2013). *Interculturalism, multiculturalism, or both?* European University Institute Robert Schuman Centre for Advanced Studies, RSCAS Policy Paper 2013/18.

Huddleston, T., Niessen, J., Ni Chaoimh, E., & White, E. (2011). *Migrant Integration Policy Index III.* Brussels, Belgium: British Council and Migration Policy Group. Retrieved from http://www.mipex.eu/.

Norris, P., & Inglehart, R. F. (2012). Muslim integration into Western cultures: Between origins and destinations. *Political Studies, 60*(2), 228–251.

Phillimore, J., & Goodson, L. (2008). Making a place in the global city: The relevance of indicators of integration. *Journal of Refugee Studies, 21*(3), 305–325.

Phillips, D. (2006). Moving towards integration: The housing of asylum seekers and refugees in Britain. *Housing Studies, 21*(4), 539–553.

Portes, A., Rumbaut, R. G., Fernandez-Kelly, P., & Haller, W. (2006). *Religion: The Enduring Presence.* Unpublished manuscript.

Poynting, S. (2006). What caused the Cronulla riots? *Race and Class, 48,* 85–91.

Poynting, S., & Mason, V. (2008). The new integrationism, the state and Islamophobia: Retreat from multiculturalism in Australia. *International Journal of Law, Crime and Justice, 36,* 230–246.

Saeed, A. (2003). *Islam in Australia*. Crows Nest, NSW: Allen & Unwin.

Saeed, A. (2006). *Islamic thought: An introduction*. London: Routledge.

Samani, S. (2007). Rhetoric and realities of multiculturalism: The perpetuation of negative constructions of Muslims in Australia. *International Journal of Diversity, 7*(2), 113–119.

Shadid, W. A. (1991). The integration of Muslim minorities in the Netherlands. *International Migration Review, 25*(2), 355–374.

Soysal, Y. N. (1994). *Limits of citizenship: Migrants and postnational membership in Europe*. Chicago: University of Chicago.

Tilbury, F. (2007). *The retreat from multiculturalism: The Australian experience*. Paper presented at Pluralism, Inclusion and Citizenship, 3rd Global Conference, Interdisciplinary.net, Salzburg, November. Available at http://www.inter-disciplinary.net/ati/diversity/pluralism/pl3/Tilbury%20paper.pdf.

Tip, L. K., Zagefka, H., Gonzalez, R., Brown, R., Cinnirella, M., & Na, X. (2012). Is support for multiculturalism threatened by ... threat itself? *International Journal of Intercultural Relations, 36*, 22–30.

Tran-Nam, B., & Neville, J. W. (1988). The effects of birthplace on male earnings in Australia. *Australian Economic Papers, 27*(50), 83–101.

Tufail, W., & Poynting, S. (2013). A common 'outlawness': Criminalisation of Muslim minorities in the UK and Australia. *International Journal for Crime, Justice and Social Democracy, 2*(3), 43–54.

Verkaaik, O. (2012). Designing the 'anti-mosque': Identity, religion and affect in contemporary European mosque design. *Social Anthropology, 20*(2), 161–176.

Vertovec, S., & Wassendorf, S. (2009) *The multiculturalism backlash: European discourses, policies and practices* (e-book). London: Routledge.

Waldrauch, H., & Hofinger, C. (1997). An index to measure the legal obstacles to the integration of migrants. *Journal of Ethnic and Migration Studies, 23*(2), 271–285.

Waters, M. C., & Jiménez, T. R. (2005). Assessing immigrant assimilation: New empirical and theoretical challenges. *Annual Review of Sociology, 31*(1), 105–125.

Weaver, M. (2010, October 17). Angela Merkel: German multiculturalism has utterly failed. *The Guardian*. Retrieved April 22, 2016, from http://www.theguardian.com/world/2010/oct/17/angela-merkel-german-multiculturalism-failed.

Weiner, M. (1996). Determinants of immigrant integration: An international comparative analysis. In S. Vertovec (Ed.), *Migration and social cohesion*. Northampton, MA: Edward Elgar.

4

Determinants of Integration

This book provides the Australian Muslim conceptions of integration, which have until now been noticeably absent from the debate, however, the ways in which Muslims conceptualise integration is discussed in line with the diverse debates about Muslim integration taking place in Australia and parts of Western Europe today. At the core of the integration conceptualisation of Australian Muslims is their belief system, and Muslims openly link aspects of their integration to their religion. Responses to research focus group questions reveal a wide range of definitions of integration, with the majority of participants mentioning Islam, religion and spirituality related terms in their definition. The extent to which Australian Muslim participants in this study linked their integration to their belief system was evident in the focus group discussions. While conceptualising integration with similar definitions to those prevalent in the scholarly literature on integration, Muslims emphasise that their faith limits some aspects of the wider society's culture into which they may be able to integrate. Muslim participants expressly reject activities and behaviours they perceive to compromise their faith. In particular, across all the four focus group discussions, Muslims identified practising the cultures of the social drinking of

© The Author(s) 2018
A. Hersi, *Conceptualisation of Integration*, Palgrave Politics of Identity
and Citizenship Series, https://doi.org/10.1007/978-3-319-91235-6_4

alcohol and attending nightclubs as areas in which they would be in breach of their faith. A 29-year-old Muslim male participant explained the issue in this way:

> You can't get more Australian than the, you know, beach, kabana, VB, you know, being Muslim I'm outta that, coz I can't eat the sausage or it has to be *halal*, just like a Jew won't eat it, wants kosher. I don't drink alcohol.
>
> I think the value of choosing how to live your life, social life. Like some, if we have to integrate like non-Muslims and they choose on the weekend to go to nightclubs and things like that, I mean that is fine because that is how they choose to live their life but at the same time they should accept that we can't do that to be able to friends with them, have that continuous relationship with them.

The comments above illustrate how specific spheres of a Muslim's everyday life, such as going to the mosque, interrelate with aspects of identity and integration. The comments also highlight the importance of the key requirements of adoptability and flexibility in intercultural relations. In the above-mentioned comments, it is also clear that of particular concern to Muslims was the social space of the wider society, and in particular, the culture of social drinking of alcohol and going to bars and nightclubs which are understood not to be permitted in the Islamic faith. The above comment suggests that it is explicitly demanded of Muslims that they accept the social drinking of alcohol to show they are integrated into the society. This claim is highly questionable and there is no evidence to show that this is the case.

The comments of members of the focus group misleadingly suggest that identified social and cultural drinking is specific to non-Muslims. In fact, the comments of some of the respondents above implying that drinking and going to nightclubs does not happen in a Muslim majority country, are false. Although on a lower scale and less acceptable to wider Muslim majority communities, social drinking and going to nightclubs still happen in those countries. It is generally the case that, over time, individual Muslims might adopt the host society's accepted norms and cultures. Social drinking is one of Australia's accepted popular cultures. Muslim youth may be more susceptible than older Muslims to adopting the culture of social drinking and going to nightclubs.

It is expected that participants in a group discussion do what they say they do, and that how they say they feel might be different from what happens in private. Respondents may have specifically mentioned activities prohibited by Islam as a result of social desirability. They may have made comments that they perceived to be appropriate within the group. This limitation of the focus group discussions is addressed by conducting in-depth one-on-one interviews with key Muslim community leaders (see Chapter 6). Nevertheless, it can be argued that Muslim respondents' suspicions of integration are dictated by a set of unpleasant external factors that are generally unsympathetic to their presence in the newly adopted land.

In general, a number of participants stress that there should be no contradictions between being a Muslim and being integrated into Australian society, as in the comment below, from a 56-year-old Muslim female:

> I think integration probably means when Muslims, particularly Muslims come to this country, Muslim migrants, they don't have to accept the way of life of the average Aussie, which is contrary to Islam. And if a person is more religious than another person that doesn't necessarily mean they are not integrating, if anything a religious man who goes to the mosque, but then goes to, you know he's at work and he is doing the exact things we spoke about, just living his life as a Muslim is supposed to, that's integration, whereas if a person believes in confining himself in that mosque and not mixing with the wider society, that's not integration, so his religiosity does not impact on a person's ability to integrate or not.

Despite the above-mentioned conditions, Muslim participants in the study showed a willingness to integrate, and even to assimilate with aspects of local culture and values, where common fundamental principles of their faith match with that of the wider society. As a 20-year-old Muslim male participant comments:

...the Islamic principles are that whatever good is happening outside, like the Christians are doing good for the homeless, it is encouraged that the Muslims support that because it is good for the general community, but in terms of them wanting us to go and drink alcohol and stuff, no, no that's not my principle.

Questions of whether or not high levels of religiosity help individuals to integrate or impede integration are not well explored. Debates about whether or not faith is a determinant or a detractor of integration are neglected. Mogahed and Nyiri (2007) found that there is an assumption in the public, political and media discourse that Muslim religiosity is both an impediment to integration and a threat to Western society. However, other studies conducted in the UK find that strong religious identity has not impeded the integration of Muslims. Rather, higher levels of income and job qualification were found to be closely linked to strong religious identity and integration (Bisin, Verdier, Pattachini, & Zenou, 2008). This study finds that Muslims exclusively framed their responses to the meanings of integration in terms of what is acceptable within their faith. However, in explaining what integration means, 116 references to religion and faith were recorded from the four focus group discussions. The significance of this is the number of times in which participants referred to faith and religion in defining integration. As a result, the implications might be that Muslim participants in this research are agreeable to integration in the wider society as long as it did not mean comprising their faith.

It was apparent from the focus group data that Muslims were more likely to consider that they were integrated only where it did not compromise their faith. Some study participants stated that they do not wish to do certain things that are not endorsed by the Muslim faith, even though some in the wider society see these things as being a sign of Muslim participation in social life in Australia. Importantly, Bisin et al. (2008) found that religiosity is not a factor in respect to support for integration. Previous research such as that by Dunn, Forrest, Burnley and McDonald (2004), asserts that religiosity does not suggest a lack or a slow down in integration. Similarly, Rane, Nathie, Isakhan and Abdalla (2011, p. 10) observe that "strong retention of cultural (religious) mores does not weaken feelings of association with Australia". However, there are also studies which show that other variables, including unemployment and inequality, play an integral role in immigrants' integration and affect their levels of religiosity (Van Tubergen & Sindradottir, 2011). These studies have demonstrated that income inequality and a higher level of unemployment are positively related to higher levels of religiosity in the general population.

Any discourse about the possible interactions between religion and integration appears to have been understudied. However, a few studies have looked at this matter, including that by Bisin et al. (2008), who, using the probability of having a strong religious identity as a measure, found that in the UK Muslims integrate less and more slowly than non-Muslims. Notable is also the work of Kastoryano (2004) in which he discusses the incorporation of religious groups into the secular systems of government in Germany and France. However, contrary to the assumptions which declare that Muslim religiosity somewhat threatens the existence of Europe (Mogahed & Nyiri, 2007, p. 14), the participants in this research did not see that their religion impeded their level of integration. Peschke (2009) states that the relationship between religion and integration is one that centres around discussions of whether or not religion is a factor of integration or disintegration. The cultural and religious diversity of new immigrant groups seems to have been attributed to this link between religion and integration. Researchers who studied the religiosity levels between immigrant communities and members of host society members in 27 European countries found that, on average, immigrants are more religious than the native-born population (Van Tubergen & Sindradottir, 2011). They also found that higher numbers of immigrants attend religious services at least weekly, that is, 18.02% compared to 16.86% of the native-born population (Van Tubergen & Sindradottir, 2011). Leaving aside the apparent differences in religiosity of immigrant groups and host societies, it is imperative to understand how these differences play out in the sphere of immigrant integration.

The role which religion plays in immigrant integration is viewed differently in different nation-states. For example, in the USA, the religious views of immigrants are viewed in a positive light, and are thought to promote ethnic and socio-economic integration and to facilitate the incorporation process (Portes, Rumbaut, Fernandez-Kelly, & Haller, 2006). On the other hand, in Western Europe, the religiosity of immigrants is seen rather as an impediment to integration, and is associated with inherent conflict, discrimination and social distance (Diehl, Koenig, & Ruckdeschel, 2009; Kalmijn & Van Tubergen, 2006; Van Tubergen & Sindradottir, 2011). Muslim integration is linked to Muslim religiosity, and Muslim religiosity is claimed to be a phenomenon that perhaps undermines effective integration and one that raises fears about potential radicalisation (Abbas, 2007; Casanova, 2006; Foner & Alba, 2008).

One of the most pervasive assumptions in the discourse of European Muslim integration is that Muslim religiosity threatens the survival of Europe (Mogahed & Nyiri, 2007). Those who believe in the irreconcilability of Western and Muslim identities generally argue that Muslim piety, expressed in religious symbols and moral conservatism, contrasts with an increasingly secular and sexually liberal Europe, and is a recipe which will increasingly insulate Muslim communities and create profound alienation from the current European national identity (Mogahed & Nyiri, 2007, p. 14). However, these believers are somewhat blind to the fact that religious pluralism is a key feature of Australia's democracy and is an undeniable part of the fabric of its society. As the numbers of Muslims in Australia increase, Islam becomes more visible, and interaction with Australians of other faiths is unavoidable. The notion that migrants' religious identities would successively disappear as they acculturated to the values of liberal democracy is falsified by the increasing visibility of Islam in the public sphere (Koenig, 2007, p. 911).

The debates about Muslim women wearing the *hijab* or veil are part of the discourses about the interplay between religion and integration. Amongst the top unique identifiers of a Muslim female in the public space is the headscarf, which has created controversy in some parts of Europe (Ajrouch, 2007; Freedman, 2004; Hamel, 2002). However, contrary to the notion that strict observance of a religion, Islam in particular, is a hindrance to integration, it is argued that France's focus on secular ism, for example, banning the veil, is a barrier to integration and decreases the strength of the right to differ (Freedman, 2004, p. 2). Modood (2013) suggests that there is an apparent contradiction between the secular thinking of some Western countries and their support for religion. Most governments in Europe state openly that Christianity is Europe's cultural marker. In Australia currently, there is a constant decline in the number of people identifying themselves as Christians.

According to the Australian Bureau of Statistics, 96% of Australians identified themselves as Christians in 1911 whereas in the last Census of population figures, this number had decreased to 61% (ABS, 2011). If, as suggested, this proposition is accepted, integration needs to be redefined as a process, based less on ideas of cultural conformity, and more on having shared goals and commitment (Mogahed & Nyiri, 2007). However, it is not only about religion, because just as Muslim participants conditioned meanings of integration to what is acceptable within their faith, similarly they advanced the argument that integration does not equal assimilation. So, what then does integration mean to Muslims? In their responses to the research questions, the participants in this study have described some practices that they perceive to be determinants and/or detractors and barriers to integration.

In the focus group discussions, it was revealed that there are certain practices that Muslim participants determine as meaning integration. Similarly, they identified other practices that they deemed to be detractors from their full integration. In this context, determinants are practices, behaviours and actions that aid and/or influence integration, whereas detractors are practices, behaviours and actions that impede integration. In analysing the focus group data, Muslim participants' conversations were coded along these thematic lines. In the following sections, the meanings of integration, that is, practices, determinants and detractors as advanced by the Muslim participants in the study are discussed in detail.

Within all four focus groups, there were 161 references to factors perceived to be determinants of integration. These 161 items were grouped into eight top-ranking categories as follows (see Table 4.1):

Table 4.1 Determinants of integration

Determinants of integration	No. of groups	Mentions	Percent (%)
Participation	4	44	21.6
Contribution	4	38	17.8
Belonging	4	36	16.9
Employment	4	26	12.2
English language	3	20	9.3
Sport	3	20	9.3
Education	4	15	7.04
Political participation	3	14	6.5
Total	**N/A**	**213**	**100**

1. participation in mainstream society's social, economic and leisure activities (44 mentions);
2. contribution to activities within the wider society (38 mentions);
3. being accepted and feelings of belonging (36 mentions);
4. participation in the labour market (26 mentions);
5. playing sport (20 mentions);
6. learning the English language (20 mentions);
7. education (15 mentions); and
8. political participation (14 mentions).

In addition to these eight categories, two others, obeying the law (1.2%) and learning Australian history (1.2%), were mentioned, but far more infrequently than the other categories, and therefore, these were not included in this discussion. In the following discussion of the findings, an examination of the association's participants make with the notion of integration is undertaken, and this is followed by an exploration and presentation of three important themes in the focus group data. These are:

• the meaning of various types of social and civic participation as being emblematic of integration;
• reflections on the relationship between religious faith and values, and their role in shaping people's capacity to integrate; and,
• reflections on the precise character of the meaning of integration, specifically its relational difference to notions of assimilation.

Participation

In their conceptualisation of the meanings of integration, participants emphasised the importance of participation and contribution to the economic and social fabric of Australian society. Noticeably, they conceptualise integration in socio-economic terms rather than cultural terms. Active participation in Australia's economic, political and social fabric was what some Muslim participants of the focus group discussions assigned to the meaning of integration. According to one young participant:

> When we, uhh, when we have elections and we want to see how the economy is going and we try to give each other support in the community, when we are helping the people in need, when we're joining in, like our welfare shop does, we don't discriminate against the Aboriginals, or any other race. (26-year-old professional Muslim female)

Other participants of the focus group discussions echoed similar sentiments. For example, a 31-year-old professional Muslim male also made the following comment:

> We try to help the whole community, the same thing with education, we have open days at the school, we have fetes, we have community events, we even have Crestwalk, anybody can join in, all they have to do is join in. We have a lot of things where anybody can integrate.

The above comments show that Muslim conceptions of integration refer mainly to their desire to participate in the social, economic and political spheres of Australia's multicultural society. Both of these comments are from Muslim professionals of different genders. In the context of Australia, Rane et al. (2011) find a positive correlation between levels of educational attainment and support for integration amongst Muslims. In the scholarly literature, there is disagreement about whether or not religiosity is associated with low or high levels of integration (Peschke, 2009). However, participants in this study suggested that they used their belief systems to influence their levels of integration. They used religion not only as an aspect of the wider society's life that they may be able to integrate, but they also used their religion to justify their belief that Muslims have a faith-based obligation to integrate. As an example, the study finds a middle-aged Muslim participant who referred to a religious text to explain what integration means. In fact, he did not see participation as a determinant of integration only, but also as being a Muslim individual's duty. He commented as follows:

> Being proactive as a Muslim you can't just sit back and think I'm going to take the benefits of the country and just live it and enjoy it without giving back as well. (42-year-old Australian born Muslim male)

Similarly, emphasis on participation in the activities of the wider society was clear from the responses of other participants. A middle-aged Australian-born Muslim participant was critical of the attitudes of some Muslim community members because of their lack of participation in the social and economic fabric of the nation. He provided the following comments:

> I'm not going to get a job because all of the jobs are *haram* (impermissible) and just live off Centrelink payments. It's just these lazy cop-out attitudes that are clear examples of someone not wanting to participate and basically saying that participation with broader society equals integration, so those people who stubbornly refuse to participate are failing to integrate.

These findings correspond with the findings of other research undertaken in the mainly non-Muslim immigrant groups in Europe. For example, in Germany, middle-aged and older post-Soviet immigrants who were long-term unemployed, insisted that the importance of paid work was uppermost in their feelings of integration (Matejskova, 2013). One article about integration incorporated the phrase "one needs to work" in its title (Matejskova, 2013). Adaptation into the labour market of the receiving country is seen to be a major hurdle that many immigrants face in their initial period of settlement. In Israel, for example, former Soviet Union immigrants have shown better coping strategies in overcoming barriers in the Israeli labour market than Ethiopian immigrants (Heilbrunn, Kushnirovich, & Zeltzer-Zubida, 2010). It is important to note though that both of these two groups of immigrants entered Israel based upon their religious affiliation (Heilbrunn et al., 2010) and therefore, no conclusions can be made about how immigrants with no religious affiliation to the receiving society adapt in the receiving country's labour market.

On the other hand, some of the respondents provided examples of participation in Australia's economic, social and political life, including undertaking voluntary activities, education and employment. Amongst the focus group discussants was a 45-year-old Muslim school teacher who explains how engaging in such activities determines integration. He comments as follows:

> Voluntary activities, like recently the floods and the Muslim organisations have got together and gone to various government organisations saying we want to help out, with this aspect of the floods and this type stuff, so we went out and helped, and in that aspect we were integrated.
>
> Yeah for me it's just normal activities, the norm in the society, getting a job, paying your taxes, is a way of integrating.

Participation in the social life of the wider society and having interaction with local populations is rated high in the determinants category. In particular, the emphasis was placed on the interaction with neighbours, and this importance is shown in the following comments:

> When you get accepted, you get invited to their homes and you invite them to your home I think that would suggest that you have been accepted into the society yes.
>
> We have a lot of Australian neighbours in my area and we do invite them to anything. When we had Ramadan we used to take food to them because they could smell the food and they would say it is beautiful food, so we give it to them, next time they bake a cake they will bring it to you.
>
> About ten years ago I was invited to a Muslim South African's home and brought a plate of food for the barbecue. Present there were his white Australian neighbours, a chap by the name of Chris and his wife and kids and so on. He said do what Yusuf has been doing, if all you Muslims

invite your Australian neighbours to your home, let them come and see what type of people you are, you are just like us, you dress like us, you eat like us, you have got the same aspirations for your kids like us, we didn't know that, the impression is that you are some weirdos.

While Muslims generally place emphasis on participation, they rated political participation at the bottom of their list. Even those who commented on political participation were engaging in limited participation in the politics of Australia, namely exercising their right to vote. Political integration is generally measured by political interest and participation (Wright & Bloemraad, 2012). It is not clear why Muslims rate political participation low, but previous studies of minority groups, such as the Lao community in Canada, suggest that the autocratic nature of politics in their home countries may discourage minorities in their participation of politics in their new homeland (Harles, 1997, p. 724). The extent to which this proposition is true regarding Muslims in Australia is not tested in this study. In the case of the Lao community in Canada, the very idea of politics is tainted by the homeland experience (Harles, 1997, p. 724).

Nevertheless, absent from Muslim respondents' comments were any meaningful and deep engagement in politics, such as joining a political party and standing for political office. The importance of the political integration of Muslims is crucial, as previous research suggests increased participation of minorities in the political systems strengthens democracies (Bieber, 2008; Petrusevska, 2009). Consistent with the findings of this study are the realities of low participation of Muslims in the political system in Australia. For example, the Honourable Ed Husic is the first Australian Muslim Federal Member of Parliament and in 2010 was elected on an Australian Labor Party ticket in the safe Labor seat of Chifley. He was since re-elected in 2013 in the same federal seat. In the 2016 federal election, an academic and counterterrorism expert Anne Aly won the West Australian seat of Cowen on a Labor Party ticket and became the second Muslim person elected into the Australian federal parliament. While Muslims in Australia are not fully participating in the politics of the nation, a highly educated Muslim elite is emerging which is proactive and wants to represent Muslim issues on national platforms (Peucker, Roose, & Akbarzadeh, 2014).

Belonging and Acceptance

A sense of belonging is defined as being a subjective feeling of being valued and respected that is derived from a reciprocal relationship to an external referent (the wider society), built on a foundation of shared experiences, beliefs and personal circumstances (Mahar, Cobigo, & Stuart, 2013). A significant number of focus group participants understood the general meaning of integration to be "to belong" and "to be accepted" into the wider society. The Muslim participants in the study rate belonging and acceptance as the third most important determinant of integration. Some of them used phrases, such as "integration is to be part of", "to interact" and "to mingle". Some examples of such statements include:

> Integration is to make Australia a better country, for everyone involved, whatever happens to Australian society happens to us because we're part and parcel of that society, definitely. (Female, 27)
> I think that basically [integration] is that we need to be accepted at all levels. No matter what level, if it is a kid at school, and he does school activities that include sport activities. (Male, 58)
> This is what I think most migrants want, to be accepted in this society, and to be part of the society and to be given equal opportunity. (Female, 22)

In the above comments, Muslim participants stress the importance of the need to feel that they belong to the Australian society. They used words such as acceptance and being part of the wider society. Their conceptualisation of integration, apart from access to opportunities of employment and education and their public expressions of wanting to belong, is evident in their comments. Modood (2013) asserted that sectoral integration (employment, education and housing) is not full integration without some degree of subjective identification with the society or country. In stressing this point, Modood (2013) also cites the work of the Commission on Multi-Ethnic Britain, who called this degree of subjective identification a "sense of belonging" (Commission on Multi-Ethnic Britain [CMEB], 2000).

The concept of belonging is directly related to the meanings of integration. The feelings of belonging, and the way in which collectively shaped individual emotions influence the degrees of success of the integration of migrants, was discussed by the study participants. This is in line with findings of Woodward, Skrbiš, and Bean (2008) who point out that, "A sense of belonging is central to the experience and performance of elementary human sociality and it is derived from the capacity and the need of people to form meaningful attachments" (p. 53). Belonging and membership in the wider society are therefore seen as an important step in achieving full integration. Muslim participants in this study linked integration and their acceptance as being interrelated issues. It is not suggested that Muslims do not feel accepted, but the fact that they mention this more often than other perceived determinants of integration is worth noting. Previous studies undertaken in Australia, such as that by Dunn et al. (2004), have found that over 70% of Muslims felt comfortable in identifying as Australian, and a majority indicated the importance of their children being accepted as being Australian. However, in their conceptualisation, integration is not independent of their belief system and Muslims saw no inconsistency between being a Muslim and being Australian (Dunn et al., 2007).

Overall, the comments made by Muslim participants are positive about how they feel about belonging in Australia. The Australian Muslim participants in the study attempted to demonstrate that they want to belong to the wider Australian community. The subjective sense of belonging and acceptance by the majority that they are full members of society was mentioned a number of times. For instance, in the area of sports in social life, Muslims provided comments about how they felt the majority accepted them. The following are the comments of a 58-year-old Muslim male participant:

> My kids play sports, they play for [...] school, my son is a good cricketer, and in his team are all white kids, if I could use that term, he is the only sort of non-European, he is accepted.

Garbutt (2009), in discussing the sense of local belonging, explains that practices such as regularly engaging in team sports are accepted ways of establishing and maintaining a sense of belonging. However, the facts remain that in any process of integration, there is a group which is not integrated, does not belong or is considered to be outside the in-group. It is the basis of the conceptualisation of social inclusion which places boundaries on being included or excluded in society (Garbutt, 2009). Muslim participants seem to be negotiating local membership during a period in which concepts of national identity, belonging and citizenship pose challenges to the nation-state in a globalised world (Castles, 1999). Furthermore, in the aftermath of the 9/11 events in the United States, the question remains, how could Muslim migrants belong in situations where belonging is denied, discounted or pushed out of reach by host communities (Skrbiš, Baldassar, & Poynting, 2007)? It is therefore apparent from the Muslim participants' comments above that they are attempting to negotiate their membership within the wider society with the expectations of that society, namely the willingness and openness to accepting Muslim communities as in-groups rather than as out-groups.

Hagan (2006) endorses the use of a framework of expectations of immigrant groups to negotiate social membership in contemporary societies. Nevertheless, belonging must not only be the mere membership of a group, but something that is ongoing, practised every day (Garbutt, 2009). The difficulties associated with measuring belonging and acceptance of a group such as Muslims in Australia are acknowledged, and doubtless, there may be variables that make this relative to social and personal circumstances and contexts. It has already been documented that differences in integration contexts, including institutional arrangements in education, the labour market, housing, religion and legislation, can play a role in how someone perceives a sense of belonging and acceptance or vice versa (Crul & Schneider, 2010).

The subjective nature of this concept of belonging and local membership makes it difficult to achieve an agreed conceptualisation. Overall, participants described participation and belonging and acceptance as being key determinants of their integration into Australian society. However, in addition to their conceptualisation of integration, this study asked participants to describe key barriers to their integration. In the next section, participants' responses and conceptualisations of barriers to integration are discussed.

References

Abbas, T. (2007). Muslim minorities in Britain: Integration, multiculturalism and radicalism in the post 7/7 period. *Journal of International Studies, 28*(3), 287–300.

Ajrouch, K. J. (2007). Global contexts and the veil: Muslim integration in the United States and France. *Sociology of Religion, 68*(3), 321–325.

Australian Bureau of Statistics. (2011). *Australian Standard Classification of Countries* (SACC). Retrieved from http://www.abs.gov.au/ausstats/abs@.nsf/Lookup/1269.

Bieber, F. (2008). *Minority participation and political parties.* Skopje: Friedrich Ebert Stiftung.

Bisin, A., Verdier, T. H., Pattachini, E., & Zenou, Y. (2008). Are Muslim immigrants different in terms of cultural integration? *Journal of European Economic Association, 6*(2), 445–456.

Casanova, J. (2006). Religion, European secular identities, and European integration. In T. Byrnes & P. Katzenstein (Eds.), *Religion in an expanding Europe* (pp. 65–92). Cambridge, UK: Cambridge University Press.

Castles, S. (1999). *Challenges to national identity and citizenship: A comparative study of immigration and society in Germany, France and Australia.* Wollongong, NSW: University of Wollongong.

Commission on Multi-Ethnic Britain (CMEB). (2000). *The future of multi-ethnic Britain: Report of the commission the future of multi-ethnic Britain.* London, UK: Runnymede Trust.

Crul, M., & Schneider, J. (2010). Comparative integration context theory: Participation and belonging in new diverse European cities. *Ethnic and Racial Studies, 33*(7), 1249–1268.

Diehl, C., Koenig, M., & Ruckdeschel, K. (2009). Religiosity and gender equality: Comparing natives and Muslim migrants in Germany. *Ethnic and Racial Studies, 32*(2), 278–301.

Dunn, K. M., Forrest, J., Burnley, I., & McDonald, A. (2004). Constructing racism in Australia. *Australian Journal of Social Issues, 39*(4), 409–430.

Dunn, K. M., Klocker, N., & Salabay, T. (2007). Contemporary racism and Islamophobia in Australia racializing religion. *Ethnicities, 7*(4), 564–589.

Foner, N., & Alba, R. (2008). Immigrant religion in the US and Western Europe: Bridge or barrier to inclusion? *International Migration Review, 42*(2), 360–392.

Freedman, J. (2004). Secularism as a barrier to integration? The French dilemma. *International Migration, 42*(3), 5–27.

Garbutt, R. (2009). Social inclusion and local practices of belonging. *Cosmopolitan Civil Societies: An Interdisciplinary Journal, 1*(3), 84–108.

Hagan, J. (2006). Negotiating social membership in the contemporary world. *Social Forces, 85*(2), 631–642.

Hamel, C. E. (2002). Muslim Diaspora in Western Europe: The Islamic head-scarf (Hijab), the media and Muslim's integration in France. *Citizenship Studies, 6*(3), 293–308.

Harles, J. C. (1997). Integration before assimilation: Immigration, multicul-turalism and the Canadian polity. *Canadian Journal of Political Science, 30*(4), 711–736.

Heilbrunn, S., Kushnirovich, N., & Zeltzer-Zubida, A. (2010). Barriers to immigrants' integration into the labour market: Modes and coping. *International Journal of Intercultural Relations, 34*(3), 244–252.

Kalmijn, M., & Van Tubergen, F. (2006). Ethnic intermarriage in the Netherlands: Confirmations and refutations of accepted insights. *European Journal of Population/Revue européenne de Démographie, 22*(4), 371–397.

Kastoryano, R. (2004). Religion and incorporation: Islam in France and Germany. *International Migration Review, 38*(3), 1234–1255.

Koenig, M. (2007). Europeanising the governance of religious diversity: An institutionalist account of Muslim struggles for public recognition. *Journal of Ethnic and Migration Studies, 33*(6), 911–932.

Mahar, A. L., Cobigo, V., & Stuart, H. (2013). Conceptualizing belonging. *Disability and Rehabilitation, 35*(11), 1026–1032.

Matejskova, T. (2013). "But one needs to work!": Neoliberal citizenship, work-based immigrant integration, and post-socialist subjectivities in Berlin-Marzahn. *Antipode, 45*(4), 984–1004.

Modood, T. (2013). Post-immigration 'difference' and integration. *Meritum, revista de Direito da Universidade FUMEC, 8*(1), 389–415.

Mogahed, D., & Nyiri, Z. (2007). Re-inventing integration: Muslims in the West. *Courting Africa, 29*(2), 2–20.

Peschke, D. (2009). The role of religion for the integration of migrants and institutional responses in Europe: Some reflections. *The Ecumenical Review, 61*(4), 367–380.

Petrusevska, T. (Ed.). (2009). *A guide to minorities and political participation in South-East Europe*. Brussels: King Baudouin Foundation.

Peucker, M., Roose, J. M., & Akbarzadeh, S. (2014). Muslim active citizenship in Australia: Socioeconomic challenges and the emergence of a Muslim elite. *Australian Journal of Political Science, 49*(2), 282–299.

Portes, A., Rumbaut, R. G., Fernandez-Kelly, P., & Haller, W. (2006). *Religion: The enduring presence.* Unpublished manuscript.

Rane, H., Nathie, M., Isakhan, B., & Abdalla, M. (2011). Towards understanding what Australia's Muslims really think. *Journal of Sociology, 47*(2), 1–21. https://doi.org/10.1177/1440783310386829.

Skrbiš, Z., Baldassar, L., & Poynting, S. (2007). Introduction—Negotiating belonging: Migration and generations. *Journal of Intercultural Studies, 28*(3), 261–269.

Van Tubergen, F., & Sindradottir, J. I. (2011). The religiosity of immigrants in Europe: A cross-national study. *Journal for the Scientific Study of Religion, 50*(2), 272–288.

Woodward, I., Skrbiš, Z., & Bean, C. (2008). Attitudes towards globalisation and cosmopolitanism: Cultural diversity, personal consumption and the national economy. *The British Journal of Sociology, 59*(2), 207–226.

Wright, M., & Bloemraad, I. (2012). Is there a trade-off between multiculturalism and socio-political integration? Policy regimes and immigrant incorporation in comparative perspective. *Perspectives on Politics, 10*(1), 77–95.

5

Detractors of Integration

Just as they described activities, behaviours and actions that mean integration to them, the participants also described activities, behaviours and actions they deemed to mean lack of integration or detractors from integration. It was observed that the respondents, while stating perceived structural barriers to integration, were also open about the failure of some people to make the effort necessary to integrate. In fact, they were not reluctant to state that certain individual Muslims are not serious about the responsibilities they need to undertake to become integrated into the wider society. In analysing the research data, it was found that participants in the focus group discussions mentioned what they perceived to be barriers to integration 161 times. These entries were grouped into seven top ranking categories (see Table 5.1):

- discrimination (20 times)
- media bias (18 times)
- self-imposed isolation (15 times)
- lack of English language (13 times)
- negative perceptions about host society (9 times)
- religious observance (5 times)
- unwillingness to participate (3 times)

© The Author(s) 2018
A. Hersi, *Conceptualisation of Integration*, Palgrave Politics of Identity
and Citizenship Series, https://doi.org/10.1007/978-3-319-91235-6_5

Table 5.1 Barriers to integration

Barriers to integration	Source	Number of entries	Percent (%)
Discrimination	3	20	24.6
Media bias	4	18	21.6
Self-imposed isolation	4	15	18.0
Lack of English language	3	13	15.6
Negative perception	2	9	10.0
Religious observance	3	5	6.02
Unwillingness to participate	3	3	3.61
Total	N/A	83	100

The barriers listed above can be grouped into two main themes: individual barriers to integration, where the person has some control over what to do about the situation, and institutional barriers to integration where such control is perhaps beyond the individual's capacity. For example, discrimination, media bias and negative perceptions are the structural barriers, whereas self-imposed isolation, lack of English language and unwillingness to participate can all be regarded as individual barriers to integration. It should be acknowledged that the two forms of barriers stated here are not mutually exclusive, and there is a possibility that they may lead to another barrier. The following sections discuss these two main classifications of barriers to integration.

Institutional Detractors

Integration of immigrants is generally understood to be the efforts undertaken in order for their inclusion into the national social and economic fabric of society. Sections of society that are not integrated can be referred to as the excluded. However, *not integrated* could mean that the individual immigrant did not take responsibility for his integration. It could also mean a failure of systems and policies, namely that of governments failing to develop an environment which enables integration. In this, there are two possible contributors to a failure of integration, that is, the institutional, and the individually controlled contributors. In their attempts to define integration, Muslims discussed the reverse of integration or the lack of integration. It is indeed easier to understand if a person knows what it is not. Respondents to this study identified barriers to immigrant integration as being both individually controlled and structural and systematic ones. They categorised self-imposed isolation and lack of English language as "individually controlled" barriers to integration, and discrimination and media bias as two "institutionally controlled" barriers to integration.

However, research participants rate the structural elements of integration, such as discrimination and media bias, highly in their understanding of the barriers to integration. In line with this understanding is the extensive body of available scholarly research that confirms the fact that ethnic minority groups face racism in Western liberal democracies (Bovenkerk, Miles, & Verbunt, 1990). The identification of discrimination as an institutional barrier to integration is not a new finding. Previous studies have documented the effect of institutional racism in ethnic groups (Durey, Thompson, & Wood, 2012; Pettus, 2013; Phillips, 2011; Pilkington, 2011; Trepagnier, 2010). This study reveals that Muslims in Australia view the perceived discrimination they face from sections of the wider society as being an individual barrier to their levels of integration. In particular, they place emphasise on discrimination in the labour market, stereotypes about their dress code, including undesirable opinions about the wearing of the *hijab*. Following are the comments made by some participants:

When we become adults we want to be able to fit into the workplace, as equals and not be discriminated against.

When we get discriminated against for getting jobs, that's failure of integration.

When we get discriminated against promotionally, when you are in a certain job and you can't get promoted because you are a Muslim, that's failure of integration.

I've been with the government for ten years, they don't trust me, and I know that, and I have been working more than the others, and for example my security clearance took 18 months, my colleague in the same position took 2 months, and a lot of questions I had to complete about 28 pages and all these things.

The above quotes from research participants indicate that discrimination is viewed as impeding the efforts of individual migrants to integrate. This discrimination can take the form of unfavourable selection processes, but can also be in the form of affording an already employed person the same promotional opportunities as those given to other employees. Some of the participants consider that these discriminatory practices do not provide them with a level playing field. In fact, it was apparent that Muslims were linking concepts of justice, equality and fairness, which, as their comments show, are important to the process of incorporating immigrants. One participant said:

> So this is what I think most migrants want, to be accepted in this society, and to be part of the society and to be given equal opportunity.

Discussions about discrimination were not gender neutral. While most men made comments relating to unfair treatment and discrimination mainly in workplaces, some of the women participants indicated that they faced discrimination, particularly in the public space, on the basis of their dress. They explained that unfair treatment of Muslim women is a barrier to their integration. As one participant commented:

> The way we get discriminated against on the basis of our dress, if our women are harassed because they have got the *hijab*, that's failure of integration.

However, the research notes that participants stress differences in the barriers to integration between Muslim men and women. They explain that, in addition to their alleged harassment on the streets because of their distinct Muslim dress, some women participants state that discrimination against them takes place in the workplace. They are particularly of the view that some employers deny them opportunities for work by telling them that the kind of clothes they wear are unsuitable for the work that the employer wants to be done. Following is one of these comments:

> I think when some non-Muslims see you in the community, like in the workplace, it does set some boundaries for some women, I mean maybe

not for the men but for the women because we choose to wear *abayas*, or our *hijab*. I remember one sister, she went for an interview and they said, 'well, you can't wear that big *hijab* because in the kind of work field that you want to do it's going to get in the way', and I feel that that made a boundary for her.

In regards to the socio-economic factors of integration, studies (Beckford, Gale, Owen, Peach, & Weller, 2006; Dunn, Forrest, Burnley, & McDonald, 2004; Dunn, Klocker, & Salabay, 2007; Hassan, 2010) all show that Muslims in several Western countries face discrimination in the labour market, thus impeding this core integration criterion. For example, in the Netherlands, the unemployment rate for immigrant Muslims is, as a general rule, higher than the national average, for example, 31 and 24% for Moroccans and Turks, respectively (Cesari, 2007, p. 59). This is despite anti-discrimination being one of the core tenets of multiculturalism. Dunn et al. (2004) conclude, that despite society's strong support for the policy, it is not succeeding in decreasing the discrimination faced by Muslims in Australia. Researchers report an upsurge of discrimination against Muslims in Australia and Britain since the events of 11 September 2001 (Marranci, 2004). Islamophobia was particularly high in countries where multiculturalism is embraced, and where multicultural policies are developed to maintain social cohesion (Marranci, 2004). This begs the question, how effective is multiculturalism in protecting the rights of minority communities?

Contrary to a widely held view that multiculturalism serves ethnic minorities well, it can be argued that multiculturalism does not necessarily address the needs of culturally and religiously diverse groups in Australia, as it has become a superficial concept that merely mirrors the celebration of cultural festivals. The policy of multiculturalism confines the state's responsibility to integrate immigrant groups by providing annual funding grants to sponsor ethnic-specific cultural festivals. Instead, immigrants in general, and Muslims in particular, may be better off demanding full participation in the economic, social and political life of the nation, as opposed to receiving funding for cultural festivals. Joppke (2004, p. 244) cites one of the "…shortcomings of multiculturalism with respect to the inherent socio-economic marginalisation of migrants and their children". In the case of Muslims in Australia, the existence of higher levels of discrimination has been well-documented (Hassan, 2009). The events of 9/11, the war on terror, and the Bali bombings of 2002, all further alienate Muslims as outsiders, and research has indicated that the way terrorism news is reported has inadvertently increased prejudice against out-groups (Das, Bushman, Bezemer, Kerkhof, & Vermeulen, 2009, p. 457).

Participants in this research rated discrimination highly in their discussions of what they understood to be structural barriers to integration. It was observed that the majority of the respondents were keen to comment on this issue during the discussion. Among the most cited discriminatory practices individuals claim they experienced in Australia was racism based on their appearance, their Muslim names in public and in their workplaces. It is obvious that Islam does not constitute one race or ethnic group, as Islam encompasses a variety of racial groups; however, the notion of racism appears to have emerged from the participants' discussions. In fact, being a Muslim is not biologically determined in the same way that biology determines being "black" or being "Asian" (Meer & Modood, 2012). The arguments that link racism to ethnic groups and disregard other forms of group identity are discredited by a number of researchers (Meer & Nayak, 2013; Modood, 2013). These ideas lend some credibility to the argument that the followers of the religion of Islam, that is, Muslims, are "racialised", or that Muslims are turned into an "ethno-religious group" (Modood, Hansen, Bleich, O'Leary, & Carens, 2006). For these and other reasons, gaining an understanding of racism becomes important. Van Dijk (2000, p. 87) defined racism as follows, "A system of social inequal ity in which ethnic minority groups are dominated by a white (European) majority on the basis of origin, ethnicity, or attributed 'racial' characteristics".

In Australia, studies about racism have been pioneered by the work of Kevin Dunn. Some of his writings about racism have an Australian Muslim focus, and discuss public attitudes towards the wearing of the *hijab* (Dunn, 2009), contemporary racism and Islamophobia, racialising religion (Dunn et al., 2007), and repetitive and troubling discourses of nationalism in the local politics of mosque development in

Sydney (Dunn, 2005). Just as comparable immigrant-receiving Western societies struggle with issues of race relations and racism, Australia faces the challenges of incorporating its highly racially diverse immigrant community. In the midst of writing this book, a major, heated debate developed in Australia about the proposed changes to the *Racial Discrimination Act* of 1975. The incumbent coalition government of Australia, comprised of Liberal and National parties, proposed these changes.

The background to these proposed changes relates to a racial vilification court case against Andrew Bolt, a conservative journalist and columnist, undertaken by nine Aboriginal applicants whom Bolt alleged were taking professional advantage from the colour of their skin (Bodey, 28 September, 2011). The Federal Court ruled that Andrew Bolt was in breach of the *Racial Discrimination Act*. The proposed changes to the Act are specifically Section 18c, of which Bolt was found to be in contravention. The proposed laws faced significant public opposition, mainly from ethnic groups. The government invited public submissions, and was inundated with over 5000 submissions from peak ethnic organisations and other interested parties. There was also a reported backbench revolt in the Liberal–National Coalition government against these proposed changes, and in particular, this was the case for members of parliament who held seats with significant ethnic majority votes. The government finally surrendered to the public demand, dropping the changes to the law. However, recently the government was accused of linking the dropping of the changes to the law to its new antiterrorism measures.

In regard to institutionally influenced detractors of integration, Muslims rated the media highly. A significant number of focus group discussants explained how distorted reporting by mainstream media about the place of Muslims in Australia was a barrier to integration. In particular, Muslim focus group participants were concerned about the media's influence on the public perceptions of Muslim immigrant integration. For the most part, participants were of the view that the Australian mass media projects a negative image of Islam and Muslims in this country. One participant explains how the mainstream mass media influences the wider public's views about a number of issues:

I think their (wider society) attitude is like all the brothers said, is mainly controlled by the media, in the sense that 90% of Australians get their information from the mass media and the mass media stigmatises the Islamic community.

The comments above suggest that the wider society receives clues of what integration means from what is reported in the mass media. This is in line with the content analysis of the Australian press coverage of integration as it pertains to Australia's Muslim communities. Rane and Hersi (2012) analysed articles published in *The Australian, The Courier Mail, The Sydney Morning Herald* and *The Age* between 2002 and 2010. The sample of their analysis included editorials, features, opinion pieces, and general news content published in alternate years, specifically 2002, 2004, 2006, 2008 and 2010. Overall, they found that the largest proportion of articles that mention Muslims and integration tended to be reported in the context of terrorism and radicalisation (14%). This selective reporting of integration was particularly a concern for some of the Muslim participants in the focus group discussions. Below is the comment of one participant, accusing mainstream media of selective reporting and bias against Muslims in Australia:

The fact that you can walk on [...] Street or any of these big shops, you'll see idols, Buddhist statues everywhere, and Australian people, majority of them, they don't see any harm with that, they take that in, it doesn't talk to them but they take that in, it's the government rather the media doesn't put any emphasis on this kind of religious or spiritual thinking, of idols and gods and, this is actually promoted I find, but when it comes to Islam, which is undoubtedly from my view is the truth, not false, it's truth, and that becomes then a focus of fear and they cannot have the school at such and such, and Islamic school, it's all about no, no, we don't want it here, but a temple is not a problem, and it's got a lot to do with the media.

Another major concern for some participants was the constant redefinition of integration by the media, based on the political rhetoric of the government of the day. The Australian press coverage frames Muslim integration in terms of cultural and civic indicators, Australian values and English language skills, rather than the broader definitions found in the scholarly literature, which include employment, education, income, legal and political indicators (Entzinger & Biezeveld, 2003; Phillimore & Goodson, 2008; Waldrauch & Hofinger, 1997). Below is a comment by a Muslim participant criticising the mass media for redefining integration and assigning it to meanings that differ from its well-intended objectives:

> Well, their (wider society) swallowing of the media propaganda whole is definitely causing a redefinition, restructuring of the entire integration away from its true meanings, away from its true values it was founded on and based on, into rather what political agenda it's served by, and that's going against integration.

Muslim participants cast doubt on the media's meaning of integration and highlight the reality that the concept can potentially be used to exclude, rather than to include, certain groups of the society. Looking at how the media frames debates about Muslim immigrant integration in Australia, this perception has some substance. The following two comments were made by Muslim participants in the focus group discussion:

> Yes, I think that the media has got a lot to do with this, that they like to keep throwing a little bit of petrol on the fire and letting the wider community know that these Muslims could be a threat to us in the future.
> It has this fear attached to Islam so the information that is provided (by media) to the (community), that is what drives their attitude, so for example, there is something happens, an explosion or whatever, the first thing that comes to their mind is that it must be an Islamic person behind it, regardless of an investigation, so we are... and this hinders integration a lot.

While this criticism of the media fuelling tensions between Muslims and the wider society is hard to corroborate, there are indications that terrorism and Muslim radicalisation feature among the dominant issues concerning Muslims in Australia (Rane & Hersi, 2012). It appears to be the case that the media tends to frame integration as a potential answer to Muslim radicalisation and terrorism, while little attention has been paid to the potential for this discourse to alienate and marginalise Muslims. In particular, because of the current Iraq and Islamic State (IS) stand-off, and previously, the events of the aftermath of 11 September 2001 and the London bombings in 2005, the dominant discourse tends to shift from international jihadists to the threat posed by home-grown Muslims not integrating into society. In fact, it is possible that there is a high risk that the meaning of integration will be distorted and become generalised into the reporting of Muslims in Australia as being a threat to this country. This is a point made by the former Australian Federal Police Commissioner, Mick Keelty, who stated: "In order to avoid terrorism, the country must not marginalise people" (Roberts, 2006, p. 5) meaning that increased vilification of Muslims [in the media] has the potential to foment home-grown terrorism. The focus group participants in the study understood the implications of distorted media reporting and one participant made the following comment:

> They are controlled by the media and what the media does, in the world today, is portray Islam which is the true religion of Allah which goes back to Noah, as a religion of fear and fundamentalism and terrorism, that's the situation, that's what they teach the masses and there is a struggle between truth and falsehood in our societies all over, even in Muslim countries.

Another notable reason why Muslims viewed the media as a barrier to integration is their treatment and depiction of Muslim women. In particular, the issues concerning Muslim women and their head covering were discussed as a significant issue in focus group discussions. A participant in the study made the following comment:

> Could I mention something, I think a good case study, that not Muslims live as an activity but has come up on the news and in the West, is the issue of the *niqab*, the issue of the face veil. And the media and a lot of leading voices in the West consider that Muslim women who are covered from the face down are not integrated into the community.
>
> This word has many different meanings, depending on the agenda. If the agenda is, at the moment we are having an unpopular war overseas and we need to regroup and regain support within the country or we need to increase terrorism laws, they want to raise public hysteria about

the Muslim community. So what do we do? We discuss how they are failing to integrate into the community because of their scary *hijabs* and the media will be used as one of the roles.

It is not surprising that Muslims, rightly or wrongly, criticise the media as being biased, because minorities, and occasionally interest and pressure groups, generally blame the media for their own demise. It can be argued that the media has a role and a responsibility in the formation of a united and socially inclusive nation. However, the relationship between the media and minority groups is a complex one. It is not at all disputed that it is a formidable force as an important source of information of host communities (Mahtani, 2001). However, the extent to which the media is helping to build a socially cohesive nation is in doubt. Researchers have criticised the media for stigmatising minority groups, for example, Boomgaarden and Vliegenthart (2007) found that the media played a crucial role in rising anti-immigrant populism throughout Western Europe.

The abovementioned negative media representations of Muslims in Europe are also experienced by Muslims in Australia (Aly, 2007; Ho, 2007; Poynting & Mason, 2007; Saeed, 2007). This has manifested as, "The construction of Muslims as a homogenous unit which enables the media to create narratives that both reflect and shape the cultural and political assumptions of the wider community vis-a-vis the Australian Muslims" (Aly, 2007, p. 28). Arguably, this could have implications for Muslim immigrant integration and it may be the case that distorted reporting of the debate about Muslim integration may undermine social inclusion. It may also create tensions between "born and bred", immigrants and non-immigrants and Muslims and non-Muslims. Studies have shown that where the media plays a positive and constructive role, it has enhanced the understanding between Muslims and their host societies. For example, in Austria, the media is credited with creating a good relationship between Muslims and members of the wider public. When the headscarf debate was at its height in several European societies, remarkably tensions remained low in Austria (Abid, 2006, p. 270) due to the objectivity of media outlets in their coverage of this debate. Furthermore, any distorted reporting of the debate risks increasing the alienation of Muslims, rather than integrating them. For example, Muslims may create alternative narratives of identity (Aly, 2007, p. 38). For Muslim youth in Australia, this may perhaps undermine state efforts currently underway to develop counter violent extremism programmes.

Individual Detractors

The study reveals that Muslim participants in the focus group discussion engaged in a self-critiquing exercise, and the majority of them viewed imposed self-isolation as a detractor to integration. Participants used their knowledge of their local communities and appeared to be speaking from personal encounters with members of their communities who have isolated themselves from the wider society. They explained that this was a hindrance to the integration levels of those individuals. Following are examples of comments made by some of the participants:

> I think it's (lack of integration) when you make an intention not to inte-grate, and not be part of society. So you will only isolate yourself within the Muslim community, you only shop at the Muslim shop, you only go to the Islamic school, you really just limit yourself in the Muslim commu-nity and almost create, like, a ghetto.
>
> It's (lack of integration) when you just isolate yourself and say look I'm not going to follow the rules of this country, I'm not going to do that I'm not going to mix with anyone, I'm just going to stay in my place, I'm not going to get out of my house because I will see a lot of things that I don't like outside, I think that's when Muslims fail to integrate.

Analysis of the focus group discussions reveals that Muslims were crit-ical of the behaviour of some of their community members who iso-lated themselves from the rest of society. They particularly stressed their objections to isolation where the religion of Islam was used as the reason for the individual's withdrawal from the mainstream society. Participants also observed an apparent contradiction between an indi-vidual's selective withdrawal from society while being keen to accept government handouts and the unemployment benefit. Below are exam-ples of comments made by participants:

Even though there apparently are no ghettos in Australia but you create a ghetto effect whereas the Australian mainstream society is bad, it's bad, it's bad and I'm not going to be tainted by it and I'm not going to be dirtied by it and I'm going to stay within the Muslim community and only mix with Muslims and only communicate with Muslims and only shop at Muslim shops. I think that's a failure of that. But you'll take the benefits of Australian society, whether it be the dole or whatever else, but you don't actually do anything positive for this society at all.

Fair enough for a new Muslim, you do have to spend that time in isolation, but the rest of us, it is very easy and I do it now, to exist between mosque, Islamic school, *halal* butchers, it's very easy just to be in that circle, and you have to step out of that circle, and that's something I am only doing now, and it's been seven years.

Nevertheless, the above sentiments did not go unchallenged in the focus group discussions, and one participant explained the differences between self-imposed isolation and what he describes as "a comfort zone". Here is his comment:

Living in isolation in a bubble is one thing but having a comfort zone is something else. Because every group of people has a comfort zone.

An Australian Muslim convert in the group discussion, who is also a teacher working with young people, describes what he sees as some Muslims having more than a comfort zone, but instead living in a confused situation and in a bubble. Below are his contributions to the discussion:

No matter what their cultural or religious background is, birds of a feather flock together, you know that's normal. But living in a bubble, and I have seen that, and I think that is very, very harmful especially for young Muslims who are trying to develop some form of identity. Their parents for some reason are living in Australia but their heart and soul is still in 'Whereveristan', (related to Afghanistan, Pakistan, etc.) and they want to go back but they don't want to leave Australia and so they are trying to bring up their kid with some, I don't know, values from elsewhere that just don't match with what the experience is for the child, and so the child is becoming very confused they just, all of the general society around them doesn't add up to what they're being told and in the end they just rebel or become nothings and that's the beginning of social problems.

I would say it would only help if the person is able to say to themselves, I am Australian and live here. It doesn't matter that I happen to be different from Johnny that lives next door, but I am Australian. If they have that kind of attitude then there won't be a problem, they will be able to bring up their children as well-rounded, wholesome, but if they're trying to force themselves and their own family to live in an imaginary bubble then they're living in La Land, and they're not going to integrate because they certainly don't want to.

A young participant in the group discussions explains the importance of Muslims becoming engaged in the political systems and addressing their grievances on perceived certain governmental decisions. His comments are as follows:

There are two categories of those who oppose it, there is one category of those who participate within the Australian system to try to change the policy towards the war or bring troops home or whatever, there would be another portion who say to hell with the whole war, to hell with the whole community, I am stepping out. I'd say this person here is not integrated.

A sense of self-reflection and self-evaluation was evident in the responses Muslims provided to define the meanings of integration and barriers to integration. In the determinants of integration, participants highly rated the ability to be able to communicate in English. Similarly, a lack of knowledge of the English language is rated highly in the barriers to integration.

The Muslim participants in the focus group discussions recognised the drawbacks that a lack of English language may have in their successful integration into the host society's many facets of life. A lack of English language proficiency is therefore linked to limited social interaction, and financial and economic survival of the family unit (Hwang, Xi, & Cao, 2010). Immigrant integration is multifaceted, and immigrants must feel integrated in all facets and levels in the society. In the group discussions, there was recognition that English language proficiency can make a difference between a family unit's economic wellbeing or living in poverty. The following are examples of comments by some of the participants:

> And just thinking about my parents, for example, my family migrated from Vietnam to America, my dad is more proficient in English, so he is able to get around, get a job, and stuff like that, but my mother has very limited English, so she relied on her children to be translators for most things.
> I could give you a horror story, I know of one family that is here in Brisbane where the father only speaks Arabic and despite having lived here for almost forty years can't speak English and he has got sons that don't speak any Arabic because they were born here, a completely dysfunctional family where one of his sons left Islam too. So it can be a measure of lack of integration. I have heard of people, outside of Australia though, people from the sub-continent in London who have been there for fifteen years and actually can't speak English, that's going to reflect poorly on us if people can't speak English and it's not that speak English or die, it's not like that, English is just a tool for communication.

Another dimension is the possible link between an immigrant's English language proficiency, labour market integration and economic wellbeing, and researchers report that there is a conditional relationship between English language proficiency and earnings among immigrants. Hwang et al. (2010) acknowledge the importance of English language proficiency for immigrants but explain that this is contingent upon factors which determine the need for intergroup interactions. In using Blau's structural theory (1977), they explain that the language environment in which immigrants live dictates whether or not better language proficiency becomes an advantage in the labour market.

There are some studies that corroborate the effect that lack of local language proficiency has on the economic wellbeing of immigrant groups in many Western countries. Hwang et al. (2010) assert that the ability to communicate in the host community language not only affects an immigrant's social interaction within the wider society but also his economic viability in the labour market. Beyond the economic effects of a lack of proficiency in English language are also the social disadvantages which result from this lack. This is a fact that is well-recognised by some of the major immigrant-receiving countries in Western Europe. For instance, Kaida (2013) states that language training constitutes an integral part of the settlement policies of many immigrant-receiving societies such as Canada and some European countries, for example, France and the Netherlands. In Australia, the government runs and funds the Adult Migrant English Language Program (AMEP), the government's largest settlement program (Department of Industry, 2014). In recognition of the importance of acquiring language skills, the government provides 510 hours of free English language tuition to immigrants eligible under humanitarian grounds.

English language proficiency or its lack is an important part of the debates about immigrant integration. Researchers noted that some anti-immigrant cohorts of the native English-speaking host societies in parts of Western Europe cite lack of English language as an indicator of a failure of integration (Xi, 2013). A number of studies have documented a robust assimilation effect (Alba, Logan, Lutz, & Stults, 2002; Bleakley & Chin, 2010; Chiswick, Lee, & Miller, 2004). However, in the case of the USA, Akresh, Massey and Frank (2014) caution that previous studies focusing on English proficiency lead inevitably to other dimensions of assimilation and suggest that this link is incomplete. Instead, they argue that proficiency is necessary but is an insufficient condition for both cultural and linguistic assimilation (Akresh et al., 2014, p. 209). Muslim participants generally accepted that a lack of proficiency in English impedes integration, but dispute that this is a Muslim specific problem. Some of their comments referred to other non-Muslim immigrant group including Greeks, Italians and Chinese. Below are some of these comments:

> The other thing the language as we mentioned is very important, but some communities, not only Muslims, for example the Italian or Greek community, they been here for fifty, sixty, seventy years and they're still not communicating in English. There are reasons behind that because they have everything there, the shop, the community, they don't need to

communicate with the Australians, they just communicate in their language. Is it possible to have the same, Italian or Greek, we have the same who don't want to learn the language, I know a family in here she was here with the family, she failed the citizenship test though she has been here for ten years she can't communicate in English. She has been for the citizenship test I think ten times. So this is another thing.

Just a really quick example to share which moves away from the Muslim community, I actually worked with a girl who came from a firm within the accounting profession that only spoke Chinese and she moved out of there to go out again but it was totally eye-opening to realise that within Australia we've got companies or firms that operate purely on a different medium. So that would seriously be a lack of integration.

While agreeing on the importance of having English language proficiency, there was no consensus about how much English is necessary for successful communication. Muslim participants in the study recognise the inherent problems in framing successful integration as the sole responsibility of the individual immigrant, and ignoring the systematic discrimination that presents major obstacles to the individual immigrant's incorporation. As one participant noted:

So she, I wouldn't say she integrates much, I mean she gets by, but not as much as she could possibly integrate, because of limited English. So I would say language is a major thing. And you know, you, moving to a country where you don't speak that language, you would be very limited as to what you can do.

It is noted that there is sometimes an overlap between determinants of integration and barriers to integration. For example, while English language proficiency is a determinant and its lack is a barrier to integration, it is arguable that the lack of proficiency in English could lead an immigrant to isolation. However, it is debatable whether this isolation is due to the individual's failure to learn the local language or whether the state failed to assist them in this regard. Researchers found that this predicament is particularly true of older immigrant groups (Treas & Mazumdar, 2002).

Since the events of 9/11, in Australia, parts of Europe and the USA, Muslims have principally become the subject of debates concerning issues of their integration in host societies. However, these debates generally disregard the existence and prevalence of institutional obstacles of integration into the host societies, as opposed to individual obstacles. Muslim participants were asked to explain the barriers to their integration into their host societies. The study found that Muslims identified both individual and institutional barriers to integration. For instance, Muslim participants report self-imposed isolation and lack of proficiency in English as being individual obstacles to integration, whereas they report discrimination and media bias as being institutional obstacles to integration. Overall, Muslim participants' descriptions of barriers to integration are comparable to those prevalent in the scholarly literature on integration, except that little attention has been paid to the institutional barriers to integration, as opposed to the individually based obstacles.

This study has explored the meanings Muslims attribute to the notion of integration. As is evident in the academic literature, and also within public sphere debates about immigration and multiculturalism, the meanings of integration vary greatly. This variation is indeed a product of the diverse life experiences and backgrounds evident in pluralist societies, but it also reflects particular positions of social power and access to power and social resources. This study found that *integration* is a politically charged term. In the case of Muslims, the research finds that the term may provoke some suspicion by its perceived suggestion of the idea that one must "give up" aspects of his or her beliefs and values, specifically their faith. The study found that this perception of giving up something, in particular one's faith, is something that Muslims seem to distinctly resist relating to the meaning of integration. In a particular way, Muslims understand their faith to be a significant element in informing their understandings of integration. For non-Muslims, and also within popular discourses, *integration* can become a polarising term that could be used to blame or exclude other sections of the community.

The results of this study show that Muslims tend to define integration in terms of participation, belonging and contributing to the wider society, conceptualising integration in socio-economic, rather than cultural terms. Faith was found to play a role in Muslims' understanding of integration. Muslims make a distinction between integration and assimilation. The findings of this chapter reveal what behaviours and practices Muslims consider relate to their integration into the wider society. This chapter discussed integration as a social process but a deeper understanding of this dynamic social process requires comprehension of the concept beyond these definitional terms. In Chapter 6 an attempt is made to explore the cognitive dimensions of how Muslims interpret the meanings of integration. In other words, understanding how Muslims negotiate and manage perceptions of membership of the in-group and the out-group.

References

Abid, L. J. (2006). Muslims in Austria: Integration through participation in Austrian society. *Journal of Muslim Minority Affairs, 26*(2), 263–278.

Akresh, I. R., Massey, D. S., & Frank, R. (2014). Beyond English proficiency: Rethinking immigrant integration. *Social Science Research, 45,* 200–210.

Alba, R., Logan, J., Lutz, A., & Stults, B. (2002). Only English by the third generation? Loss and preservation of the mother tongue among the grandchildren of contemporary immigrants. *Demography, 39*(3), 467–484.

Aly, A. (2007). Australian Muslim responses to the discourse on terrorism in the Australian popular media. *Australian Journal of Social Issues, 42*(1), 27–40.

Beckford, J., Gale, R., Owen, D., Peach, C., & Weller, P. (2006). *Review of the evidence base on faith communities.* London, UK: Office of the Deputy Prime Minister.

Blau, P. M. (1977). *Inequality and heterogeneity: A primitive theory of social structure* (Vol. 7). New York, NY: Free Press.

Bleakley, H., & Chin, A. (2010). Age at arrival, English proficiency, and social assimilation among US immigrants. *American Economic Journal: Applied Economics, 2*(1), 165.

Bodey, M. (2011, September 28). Andrew bolt loses racial vilification court case. *The Australian.* Retrieved April 20, 2016, from http://www.theaustralian.com.au/business/media/andrew-bolt-x-racial-vilification-court-case/story-e6frg996-1226148919092.

Boomgaarden, H. G., & Vliegenthart, R. (2007). Explaining the rise of anti-immigrant parties: The role of news media content. *Electoral Studies, 26*(2), 404–417.

Bovenkerk, F., Miles, R., & Verbunt, G. (1990). Racism, migration and the state in Western Europe: A case for comparative analysis. *International Sociology, 5*(4), 475–490.

Cesari, J. (2007). Muslim identities in Europe: The snare of exceptionalism. In A. Al-Azmeh & E. Fokas (Eds.), *Islam in Europe: Diversity, identity and influence* (pp. 49–67). Cambridge, UK: Cambridge University Press.

Chiswick, B. R., Lee, Y. L., & Miller, P. W. (2004). Immigrants' language skills: The Australian experience in a longitudinal survey. *International Migration Review, 38*(2), 611–654.

Das, E., Bushman, B. J., Bezemer, M. D., Kerkhof, P., & Vermeulen, I. E. (2009). How terrorism news reports increase prejudice against outgroups: A terror management account. *Journal of Experimental Social Psychology, 45*(3), 453–459.

Department of Industry. (2014). *Adult Migrant English Program.* Retrieved from http://www.industry.gov.au/skills/AssistanceForIndividuals/AdultMigrantEnglishProgram/Pages/default.aspx.

Dunn, K. M. (2005). Repetitive and troubling discourses of nationalism in the local politics of mosque development in Sydney, Australia. *Environment and Planning D: Society and Space, 23*(1), 29–50.

Dunn, K. M. (2009). Public attitudes towards hijab-wearing in Australia. In T. Dreher & C. Ho (Eds.), *Beyond the hijab debates: New conversations on gender, race and religion* (pp. 31–51). Cambridge, UK: Cambridge Scholars Publishing.

Dunn, K. M., Forrest, J., Burnley, I., & McDonald, A. (2004). Constructing racism in Australia. *Australian Journal of Social Issues, 39*(4), 409–430.

Dunn, K. M., Klocker, N., & Salabay, T. (2007). Contemporary racism and Islamophobia in Australia racializing religion. *Ethnicities, 7*(4), 564–589.

Durey, A., Thompson, S. C., & Wood, M. (2012). Time to bring down the twin towers in poor aboriginal hospital care: Addressing institutional racism and misunderstandings in communication. *Internal Medicine Journal, 42*(1), 17–22.

Entzinger, H. B., & Biezeveld, R. L. (2003). *Benchmarking in immigrant integration.* A report by the European Research Centre on Migration and Ethnic Relations (ERCOMER, pp. 1–50). Rotterdam, The Netherlands: Erasmus University Rotterdam.

Hassan, R. (2009). Social and economic conditions of Australian Muslims: Implications for social inclusion. *National Centre of Excellence for Islamic Studies, 2*(4), 1–13. Retrieved from http://www.nceis.unimelb.edu.au/sites/nceis.unimelb.edu.au/files/NCEIS_Research_Paper_Vol2,No4_Hassan.pdf.

Hassan, R. (2010). Socio-economic marginalization of Muslims in contemporary Australia: Implications for social inclusion. *Journal of Muslim Minority Affairs, 30*(4), 575–584.

Ho, C. (2007). Muslim women's new defenders: Women's rights, nationalism and Islamophobia in contemporary Australia. *Women's Studies International Forum, 30*(4), 290–298.

Hwang, S. S., Xi, J., & Cao, Y. (2010). The conditional relationship between English language proficiency and earnings among US immigrants. *Ethnic and Racial Studies, 33*(9), 1620–1647.

Joppke, C. (2004). The retreat of multiculturalism in the liberal state: Theory and policy. *The British Journal of Sociology, 55*(2), 237–257.

Kaida, L. (2013). Do host country education and language training help recent immigrants exit poverty? *Social Science Research, 42*(3), 726–741.

Mahtani, M. (2001). Representing minorities: Canadian media and minority identities. *Canadian Ethnic Studies, 33*(3), 99–133.

Marranci, G. (2004). Multiculturalism, Islam and the clash of civilisations theory: Rethinking Islamophobia. *Culture and Religion, 5*(1), 105–117.

Meer, N., & Modood, T. (2012). For "Jewish" read "Muslim"? Islamophobia as a form of racialisation of ethno religious groups in Britain today. *Islamophobia Studies Journal, 1*(1), 36–55.

Meer, N., & Nayak, A. (2013). Race ends where? Race, racism and contemporary sociology. *Sociology E-special, 2*, 1–18.

Modood, T. (2013). Post-immigration 'difference' and integration. *Meritum, revista de Direito da Universidade FUMEC, 8*(1), 389–415.

Modood, T., Hansen, R., Bleich, E., O'Leary, B., & Carens, J. H. (2006). The Danish cartoon affair: Free speech, racism, Islamism, and integration. *International Migration, 44*(5), 3–62.

Pettus, K. I. (2013). *Felony disenfranchisement in America: Historical origins, institutional racism, and modern consequences.* Albany, NY: SUNY Press.

Phillimore, J., & Goodson, L. (2008). Making a place in the global city: The relevance of indicators of integration. *Journal of Refugee Studies, 21*(3), 305–325.

Phillips, C. (2011). Institutional racism and ethnic inequalities: An expanded multilevel framework. *Journal of Social Policy, 40*(1), 173–192.

Pilkington, A. (2011). *Institutional racism in the academy: A case study.* Stoke On Trent: Trentham Books.

Poynting, S., & Mason, V. (2007). The resistible rise of Islamophobia anti-Muslim racism in the UK and Australia before 11 September 2001. *Journal of Sociology, 43*(1), 61–86.

Rane, H., & Hersi, A. (2012). Meanings of integration in the Australian press coverage of Muslims: Implications for social inclusion and exclusion. *Media International Australia, Incorporating Culture & Policy, 142*(February), 135–147.

Roberts, J. (2006, October 27). Media blamed for Islam bias. *The Australian,* p. 5.

Saeed, A. (2007). Media, racism and Islamophobia: The representation of Islam and Muslims in the media. *Sociology Compass, 1*(2), 443–462.

Treas, J., & Mazumdar, S. (2002). Older people in America's immigrant families: Dilemmas of dependence, integration, and isolation. *Journal of Aging Studies, 16*(3), 243–258.

Trepagnier, B. (2010). *Silent racism: How well-meaning white people perpetuate the racial divide.* Boulder, CO: Paradigm.

Van Dijk, T. A. (2000). On the analysis of parliamentary debates on immigration. In M. Reisigl & R. Wodak (Eds.), *The semiotics of racism. Approaches in critical discourse analysis* (pp. 85–104). Vienna: Passagen Verlag.

Waldrauch, H., & Hofinger, C. (1997). An index to measure the legal obstacles to the integration of migrants. *Journal of Ethnic and Migration Studies, 23*(2), 271–285.

Xi, J. (2013). English fluency of the US immigrants: Assimilation effects, cohort variations, and periodical changes. *Social Science Research, 42,* 1109–1121.

6

Muslim Frames and Schemas of Integration

As has been discussed extensively in the previous chapters (Chapters 4 and 5), integration is understood to mean a number of things to the Muslim participants in this study. Using the concept of integration as taken from a cognitive psychology point of view, this chapter attempts to gain an understanding of the mental processes undertaken by individual participants, and how they interpret and employ cognitive schemas in their understandings of integration. It is deemed necessary to do so since the participants' experiences play a role in the development of their individual mental life. Unlike the previous chapters in which participants were asked to describe what they understood the meaning of integration to be, this chapter is concerned with the reasons why participants describe integration in a particular way. Despite this difference in approach, this work complements the focus group study presented in Chapters 4 and 5, in which participants described integration only along thematic lines. Before presenting the findings of the schemas Muslims use in their interpretations of the meanings of integration, the next section gives a general overview of the cognitive theory of schema.

Brubaker, Loveman and Stamatov (2004) report that there is an implicit cognitive turn in the study of ethnicity and assert that drawing

© The Author(s) 2018
A. Hersi, *Conceptualisation of Integration*, Palgrave Politics of Identity and Citizenship Series, https://doi.org/10.1007/978-3-319-91235-6_6

on cognitive research in social psychology may extend our under-standing of this subject. Integration is referred to as a crucial concept in the psychology of acculturation (Boski, 2008). Others have pointed out the possible common grounds and convergences that may exist between cultural sociology and psychology (Carley, 1989; Cicourel, 1973; DiMaggio & Markus, 2010). According to Cerulo (2010) how-ever, there is an increase in the number of studies which use cognitive psychology theories. It is cultural sociologists in particular who show interest in engaging research in cognitive psychology (Ignatow, 2007). Inspired by these reported convergences, this chapter utilises the cog-nitive psychology theory of schemata to understand how Muslims in Australia construct cognitive schemas of integration.

The cognitive schemas of integration which Muslims in Australia construct are important to this investigation. An understanding of these schemas enhances the depth of this research, enlarging it from being mere definitional concepts of integration to accessing an individ-ual participant's mental processing of what the term means. Zerubavel (1997, p. 7) contends that the world is experienced not only through senses but also as mental membership in various social groups. Muslim Australians, just like any other citizens, use their frames of reference and schemata to develop their own worldview. As individuals, they con-struct their understanding of the meanings of integration. The schemas and frames they use in interpreting their surroundings are important and may shed light on why they behave in a certain way or conceptu-alise integration in a particular way. The application of schemas is also an appreciation of how cognitive development is situated within a par-ticular social context and is constrained by specific social circumstances (Zerubavel, 1997, p. 15).

While our experiences and personal circumstances may dictate how we perceive others, it is also the case that we employ certain strategies to achieve these mental constructions. Cerulo (2002) calls the strategies and techniques in which human beings organise and sort information "representational constructs" of the brain, and these include concepts, frames, formats and schemas (pp. 113–119). As human beings, we can hardly escape from these representational constructs in our every-day lives. In fact, social psychologists find that our social environment plays a major role in how we interpret things (Zerubavel, 1997, p. 25). Individual in-depth interviews were conducted with ten Queensland Muslim community leaders. The Muslim participants interviewed in this study were found to have employed mental cognitive constructs of the meanings of integration. They appear to have used their own cognitive schemas in their attempts to define what integration means. It has been found that the two main dominant schemata of integration conceptualised by Muslims in Australia are the functional and the cultural framing of integration.

Functional Versus Cultural Schemas of Integration

Throughout the analyses of the responses from the research participants, there were clear indications of the participants' focus when it came to general frames of integration. This data was then unpacked and organised it under these two frames. Respondents provided accounts of different actions, behaviours and values which can reasonably be categorised under these schemas. However, it was also apparent that sometimes these schemas influenced each other and could potentially be classified in both of the general schemas. Table 6.1 is an illustration of these two main schemas of integration.

It is often the case that individual participants emphasised one schema more than another. In the initial analysis of the data, the functional aspects of integration emphasised by the research participants seemed straightforward, but the cultural frames of integration were

Table 6.1 Functional and cultural schemes of integration

Functional	Cultural
Pay tax	Freedom
Study	Respect for the country
Donate blood	Belong to country
Business development	Participate in festivals
English language	Volunteer
Provide services	Good neighbour
	Equality/fair go

not quite as obvious. This apparent difference is because culture is an abstract concept that is normally different to the tangible functional notions of integration. It is perhaps for this reason that cultural studies have become an interesting development in the study of sociology (Kashima, 2014). For instance, Kashima (2014) states that even though culture has become a critical concept in social psychology over the past half-century, its dynamics, its processes, mechanism of formation and maintenance and transformation have begun to be investigated only recently.

In this study, Muslim schemas of integration are approached on the basis that humans are meaning-making animals who create, recreate and exchange information, and then turn this information into a meaningful basis for action (Kashima, 2014). Similarly, on a common-sense level, people construct meaning in relation to their lives. Schmidt (2001) refers to this process as a "constructionist view of knowledge". In analysis of the research data, it is revealed that the meaning Muslims make of the concept of integration align with the four dimensions of integration identified by Heckmann and Schnapper (2003, p. 10) as "Structural integration, cultural integration, interactive integration and identificational integration". It was apparent that the way in which informants conceptualised integration falls under two principal schemas. The following are samples of statements indicating the functional schemas of integration:

Rawda: To contribute positively in your community or be a resourceful person contributing to society; by paying taxes um. It's like it's not really integrating if you're on the dole or you're getting social um, you're just living from hand to mouth.

Noah: So of the Muslims I know, they are posted in the Australian government and some of them are engineers and doctors as well, like uh, providing these kind of services to people.

Uthman: I think a portion of the young Muslim generation, they are not integrating. Um, if they feel they are uh, disenfranchised they are feel they can't get a job; if they feel that um, they are discriminated against uh, regarding name; regarding uh, dress; um, regarding ideas.

Khalid: When there is high unemployment amongst the Muslims, our ability to integrate with the rest of society is drastically reduced. If we are unemployed then our movements in society are from our home to our mosque to the *halal* butcher shop to the *halal* grocery store and back to our homes again; and there is absolutely no integration whatsoever.

The above five sample statements share the perception that to integrate means to have a job, pay taxes and contribute to the society. These respondents conceptualise integration in the more direct sense of having some kind of input into the general wellbeing of society, not becoming a burden on it. Specific fields of functional integration are mainly tangible, measurable and are those that are generally reported by government and policy institutes. For example, employment is the most researched area of integration and it takes a significant space in the scholarly literature (Bisin, Patacchini, Verdier, & Zenou, 2011; Kogan, 2011; Krause & Liebig, 2011). However, it is apparent from the data that how some Muslim individual participants perceived the notion of integration differed significantly, and there are participants who conceptualised integration in cultural terms rather than functional ones. The following are samples of statements indicating the cultural schemas of integration:

Uthman: What belonging to integration is, is to adhere to overarching themes of a society. The overarching themes for Australian society as I said it's the, the country for the fair go, it is the country for the freedom, and it is a hard work place. It is a country for equality. Uh, it is a country for choice. If, if this person maintains, uh, and strongly support the ideas of equality; of freedom of choice; of hard work.

Ali: So I do follow and obey the law of this country. Should I say, I am a valuable member of the community by volunteering; I do volunteer every now and then. When we had the floods I went and volunteered; though we didn't have any floods in Calamvale; but I went, I chipped in you know, I went, I helped people who I don't even know. And that's part of living; you feel part of this place.

Khalid: To behave in a proper manner. To, uh, to be sensitive to the, uh, the values and the mind-set and the culture of the host country, the host people. You know, that everyone should be allowed to be themselves. Um, and everyone should be allowed to move around and to benefit from the country like anyone else. Right? So this to me is integration. Because fundamentally I believe that by following the basic ethics and morals of what Islam teaches us makes you uh, the most reliable, the most professional, the most suitable, um, business partner, employer, work colleague, contractor, that you could possibly be. You honour contracts.

The above three responses also share the schematic perceptions of integration that emphasise the non-functional aspects of integration. They conceptualise integration as being more cultural and value-based than functional and practical-based. The emphasis on the overarching themes of equality, fairness and volunteerism are specific fields of cultural integration that are mainly abstract, not concrete, and are difficult to measure. They are generally based on perceptions and tendencies which are reported in mainstream media in the context of Muslims not fitting in, lacking loyalty, radicalisation and posing a threat of terrorism.

Cognitive schemas used by subjects in the study to conceptualise integration diverged and appeared to emphasise different aspects of the individual's perceptions of integration. For example, Noah's schemata are value-dependent, whereas Uthman conceptualises integration in an identificational sense. However, Rawda's schema is constituted of tangible contributions to society, such as paying taxes. The interesting observation made in analysing the data is that the functional is not independent of the cultural on certain occasions. For example, one needs to have the right attitude of altruism to volunteer, but is functional at the same time by doing voluntary work. Chipping in and volunteering, of course, have something to do with the values of fair go, citizenship and civic duties. In other words, the functional overlaps the cultural and abstract notions of citizenship.

Citizenship Schemas

The introduction of the topic of integration to a private conversation seems to have offered the opportunity for participants to talk about themselves and their understandings of integration. A basic feature of the concept of integration is that participants in the study interpreted it differently based on their individual lived experiences of integration. Their interpretations are wide-ranging, and evidently particular notions of citizenship inform Muslims' understandings of integration. These are generally ideal discourses of citizenship which enlighten ways of seeing people and events. The study found that the most noticeable of these schematic discursive structures that Muslims used are as follows:

- good citizen,
- flexible citizen,
- productive citizen,
- respectful citizen, and
- loyal citizen.

Good Citizen Schema

The frame of good citizen is a dominant feature in the in-depth interviews conducted with the research participants. The way in which people understand themselves as citizens is likely to have a significant impact on their perception of rights and obligations and on whether they participate, in what form and why (Thorson, 2012). Muslims' conceptualisation of citizenship is in line with the other various conceptualisations of good citizen in the general community. In their responses to the research questions, Muslims made some positive statements relating to their conception of what it means to integrate into the wider Australian society. In other words, they attempted to explain what they perceived represented qualities of good citizenship. The series of quotations are from the interview data of study subjects and inform how individuals framed their answers to the question asking what the indicators of successful integration are. A sample of statements indicating the GC schema include:

Hamza: And it doesn't matter what you believe. You know, Christians, Muslims, or Buddhists or something, because all religion tells you not to do any cheating, stealing or crime.

Uthman: If you are a good neighbour; if you help your neighbour; if you care about him; if you talk with him frankly with frank discussion; open discussion; you express your views; he expresses his views; I mean, this is integration in Australia.

Khalid: You are um, you know, you are compassionate towards your employees, when they face difficulties. Uh, and when they cause you grief and cause you inconvenience, uh, you're able to deal with it because of the values that Islam teaches you about being compassionate towards others, being understanding towards others. Um, you are trustworthy, when it comes to business dealings.

Fairuz: But at the moment I'm in Australia, my duty is to produce the good citizen, it is my children, that's my responsibility. So in Australia I will continue to be a good citizen people, educated and all these things.

Rawda: I'm not shy of saying "hello" to a stranger, if we are in a queue, let it be in a bus, in a post office or shop, if they give me a smile I give a smile back.

Muslim participants appeared to describe schemas which they believed constituted good citizenship, and one of these schemas is undertaking a desirable practice such as volunteerism. All the above sample statements are made in relation to what respondents perceived to be qualities of a good citizen. For example, reference to different aspects of good citizenship such as compassion, being a good neighbour, and the simple, everyday greetings to a stranger could be directly related to the individual participant's family and work background. The notion of being a good citizen is translated into being an active and participatory citizen (Bolzendahl & Coffé, 2013). The challenge is that the schema of good citizen is equated to the concept of democracy, which is quite often enacted in a particular context in which positioning, method and motives play an important role (Pykett, Saward, & Schaefer, 2010).

In the sphere of participating in the Australian community's voluntary activism, Muslims appear to be integrating reasonably well, as shown by ABS Census data on good citizenship and volunteerism (see Table 6.2). In particular, the Census reveals the figures on persons (excluding overseas visitors) by religious affiliation, by citizenship and by those undertaking voluntary work. In these areas of altruism and patriotism, Census data shows that Muslims do participate in volunteer activities and are willing to give back to the community. Out of the total of 2,824,250 people who undertook voluntary work for the country in the 2011 Census, 21,461 Muslims are represented as volunteering, which is about 6% as opposed to the 16% of non-Muslims who reported doing some voluntary work in the same Census.

In explanation of this data, it is clear that on one hand, volunteerism is an indicator of participation in unpaid communal services in the nation because in percentage terms, while Australian Muslims constitute only 2.2% of the population (ABS, 2011) the 6% of them involved in voluntary work is a significantly high figure. Assumptions can be made that Muslim participants may be referring to their religious duty of care to the elderly and relatives as voluntary work. The "not a volunteer" category was reported by 58% of Muslims, while 62% of their non-Muslim counterparts reported that they were "not a volunteer". These rather contradictory results could be attributed to different conceptualisations by Muslims and the wider Census population of what is considered to be voluntary work. The fact that there was a strong element of faith in Muslims' conceptualisation of integration lends credibility to this assumption.

Table 6.2 Volunteerism among Muslim and non-Muslim Australian citizens

Citizenship	Voluntary work	Muslim	%	Non-Muslim	%	Total
Australian	Volunteer	21,461	6	2,709,920	16	2,824,250
Australian	Not a volunteer	204,856	58	10,566,147	62	11,241,528
Australian	Not stated	14,018	4	475,436	3	547,500
Australian	Not applicable	112,590	32	3,344,568	20	3,648,529
Australian	Total	352,925	100	17,096,071	100	18,261,807

Overall, the frames of good citizen schemas that Muslim participants used were diverse, and the view is formed here that this could well be true between immigrant groups, and between a group of immigrants and the native population which hosts them. This then necessitates the need for cross-contextual ways in which to judge various claims about the capacities, behaviours and attitudes of good citizens (Pykett et al., 2010). In the scholarly academic literature, the expression of good citizenship arises in different contexts and domains. For instance, Shapcott (2013) used the term *good citizen* to describe a responsible member of a community of nations. Others such as Lawler (2007) used similar expressions to describe countries in their conduct in international affairs. The term is also used in the corporate world to describe a good corporate citizen (Petrovic-Lazarevic, 2010). On a much broader scale than the national, considerable differences were noted in the case of what a "good Europe an citizen" is, and these differences occurred at the levels of the policymakers, civil society and ordinary citizens (Van Deth, 2009). Against this background, it is important to understand Muslims' conceptualisations of being good citizens. It can reasonably be stated that the definition of a good citizen, in this case, is the Muslim view only, and the definition may be different in other groups.

Flexible Citizen

In addition to being a good citizen, study participants suggested that flexibility is another worthy quality of citizenship and integration. Muslim participants' belief in flexibility supports views mentioned in the literature which suggest that existing concepts of citizenship which imply lifelong attachment to one nation-state fail to comprehend the realities of individuals acting in a globalised society (Frey, 2003). Notions of the flexible citizen as suggested by participants varied, and included changing oneself by accommodating others, learning about other cultures and making friends outside the Muslim community. Sample statements relating to these notions of the flexible citizen include:

Rawda: I haven't put my children in Islamic school because I feel that they need to be knowing there are so many different peoples. So for me, I feel, if you only have Muslim friends; you only go to Islamic school; you only live in a Muslim area; you only go to the *masjid*; you don't; it's like you, the only time maybe you go to the shops; but then you only go to the Muslim shops; the *halal* butcher, the Muslim, you're not really, because you're not seeing the wider society.

Najla: Because so long as you still want to cover your face when you are only being asked do you want to drive and do you want to acquire a driving license you should take the covering on the basis of safety or the basis of identification. So, I would not say that the Muslims have integrated.

A key component of this argument is that cultural rigidity was explained to mean lack of integration. However, it is interesting to note the inconsistency inherent in Muslim participants' understanding of integration in this study which calls for flexible citizenship, and the study's findings in the previous chapters (Chapters 4 and 5) where Muslims specifically promoted maintenance of aspects of their religion. Despite these apparent contradictions, some Muslim participants welcome and encourage cultural adjustments into the dominant host culture. Samples of statements relating to this understanding are the following:

Ali: You need to adjust of course. Definitely, when it comes to integration you have to adjust. When you move into another country you need to adjust, you know?

Khalid: You have people, if they come to Australia and they start having barbeques um, and they, you know, they start um, doing things which are considered Australian this is a cultural conformity which is not only harmless, I think it's beneficial.

These seemingly contradictory positions held by Muslim participants are not difficult to explain. For instance, it appears as though Muslims in Australia value the country's diversity, while at the same time making claims that they need to maintain their unique cultural and religious identity. Their views of the flexible citizen are, to some extent, aligned with the shifting and changing meanings of integration and citizenship that were experienced over decades as a result of increasing diversity of citizens within a bounded nation-state territory. Staeheli (2011) asserts that citizenship is "continuously in formation, never static, settled or complete" (p. 398). A body of contemporary scholarly literature also supports Muslims' views of flexible citizenship, which calls for the departure from bounded to flexible citizenship (Benhabib, 2007; Mitchell, 2013; Nyamnjoh, 2008, 2013; Russell & Kleyn, 2013).

In the field of immigrant incorporation, the notion of flexible citizenship has transpired in the form of changing and shifting models of integration which have initially arisen in the form of membership of a community (Bloemraad, 2006). These modes of integration have then moved from post-national (Soysal, 2012) to multicultural citizenship (Kymlicka, 2011) and in the recent past, to cosmopolitan citizenship (Beck, 2014). It was found that the Muslim participants recognised this shift in integration from uniformity to unity in diversity, including religious diversity. The following sample statement describes how Muslims navigate through the dichotomies of solidarity and diversity.

Joseph: So it means that the parent have to give up this almost fantastic, in a fantasy, in a dream situation where life back home was perfect and better in all ways, and then here in Australia, my children, my child is not, has not become what I imagine what they should become. So, there's that level of having to give up, but giving up my entire faith, well, Christians didn't have to do that when they came out to Australia. Christianity is not a native Australian religion.

Arguably, Muslim participants are engaged in a process of negotiating belonging and being different at the same time. In the sense of belonging, they understand that one must participate and interact with fellow citizens in Australia. In explaining what integration means, Rawda takes particular issue with the self-isolating attitudes some Muslims have, simply staying within Muslim circles of socialisation.

Similarly, Joseph's flexible citizen schema is critical of the attitudes of some Muslims who are resisting their children's wishes to adopt and apply parts of their lives and experiences as members of the wider society. Khalid, on the other hand, explains aspects of Australian culture that Muslims should not be afraid to adopt and gives the examples of the proud Australian outdoor culture of barbequing in suburban parks and backyards. However, it is Najla's schematic conception that takes issue with the inflexibility of some Muslims in matters of security and safety significant to the nation; in particular the reports that some veiled Muslim women refuse to uncover their faces for official identification.

While Muslims generally hold strong ideas about flexible citizenship and provided the positive statements above, several of the respondents observed that this notion of flexibility is limited by what is acceptable in Islamic tradition. Samples of statements from Muslim participants who made these observations include:

Rawda: If I go to your house and you have a drink, I'm not going to sit and eat with you; I'm not so strict about those things. If I go to some friend's place and there's you know music, I'm not gonna, I don't want those kind of things.

Khalid: If people come to Australia, like I said, and they go to the beach, go to the beach, and the women are dressed in 'burqini' and they swim with their families on one side, you know, a little bit away from the others, because you know, they feel a little self-conscious, um, I find, I think this is healthy.

Joseph: Well, if somebody said if they don't go to the pub, well yeah, I know a lot of people who don't go to the pub. My nephew's wife doesn't drink alcohol, she's a Christian. She doesn't even drink tea or coffee. So does that mean she needs to be ostracised from Australian society even though her ancestors were sixth generation Australian or something, because she refuses to go to the pub or drink alcohol? Is she less Australian now? It doesn't make sense, that's not an objective measure to determine whether or not people have integrated into society or not.

The notion of flexible citizenship is not new to the debates of immigrant integration. The term *flexible citizenship* has appeared in debates about the transnational activities of some immigrant groups in Canada and Europe. In the case of Canada, Waters (2010) explains the flexible citizen in the context of Chinese economic immigrants, where at least one parent returns to the country of origin to maximise the families' economic wellbeing while at the same time leaving children behind with their partner so they can obtain a good education. He calls these families "Astronaut families and satellite kids" (Waters, 2010, p. 72).

Productive Citizen

The third of the four schemas that were dominant in the participants' understandings of integration is the notion of the productive citizen. In this schema, topics relating to labour market participation, education and paying taxes took prominence in the discussions of the interviewees and were repeatedly explained as meaning integration. Unlike the other three schemas, the productive citizen schema is noticeably conceptualised consistently, and is explained as having a job, educating oneself and engaging in business and economic activities for the benefit of the individual and the wider society. Sample statements of productive citizen schema include:

Uthman: You can't just be observing people going to their jobs or their work and you staying at home and you just saying that you are integrating.

The schema of the participatory citizen is the most general of all the schemas and encompasses individual immigrants' participation in the national economic, social and political life. Based on personal experiences, attitudes and preference dictated by age, gender and other factors, different people emphasised different participation areas. For instance, the following are comments from some Muslim participants who stated that education was an important factor in participation:

Noah: First of all as I told you I got my bachelor's degree in this country and for me a bachelor's degree from Australia is a big thing. I mean, and then, uh, like, I came from Pakistan, and Pakistan doesn't have that international standard that Australia has got.

Abdullah: What it means to me personally is, integration for me is when I'm, I'm productive within the community, whether I'm going to work or I'm studying and involved with the day to day life in Australia. For me that's integration.

Uthman: Um, second, I'm uh, doing my best to be uh, part of the society in terms of uh, in terms of uh, like, hard work, either by doing my Ph.D. or after that by getting a job on this basis.

Previous research in immigrant community participation in the national life supports education as being an important element in the integration of newly arrived groups. For example, research into Canadian immigrants finds that increased participation in tertiary education is linked to improved career opportunities, thus leading to full integration (Adamuti-Trache & Sweet, 2010). However, in addition to education and training, other examples of the participatory citizen include the economic development of the self and society. As illustrated in the comments below, Muslims' schema of integration is broad and includes having a business, engaging in import and export activities and issues identified as helping Australia's economic progress. Muslim participants' focus on the business side of participatory citizenship came with comments that defend the integration of early Muslim settlers in this country. Specifically referring to early Muslim settlers, the following are the comments made by people who have become successful in business, thus showing their allegiance to Australia.

Noah: Yeah, I think in 1860s Muslims, Afghan Muslims, they came first time in Australia, they started trade in Australia and they changed Australia a little bit, I think, they changed Australia a little bit and now, even now a lot of Muslim countries they are doing business as I'm doing business in Australia. I'm

	importing a lot of stuff from my own country and providing, you know importing and exporting and providing goods to them, as trying to help this country.
Noah:	What I would say, they have a big involvement in developing this country. Especially a very famous family, called the Deen family, which came like uh, 100 or 200 years ago to this country. And they have some big names and they are some people who are in high positions in Australia. And who are doing good for Australia.
Khalid:	Functioning as an employer, functioning with my clients, uh, working in society uh, you know, uh, in my field of work um, you know, inter- uh, what is it? Uh, having to deal with customers, having to deal with clients, who are perhaps 98–99% not Muslim, uh, from all different walks of life.

Despite the above commentary and claims by the Muslim participants that they successfully participated in a number of aspects, issues Muslims identified in their participatory citizen schema of integration above are absent from the current debates about Muslim integration. This absence is not a surprise, as immigrant groups are generally considered to integrate some aspects of the host community faster than other aspects. This is what is termed in the literature as segmented integration. As such, the absence of any debate about these aspects of economic integration could be seen as confirmation of their success in this part of integration.

Respectful Citizen

The fourth schema of integration is that of the respectful citizen. In their conceptualisation of integration, Muslim participants have provided examples of attitudes and behaviours that they considered respectful. At the forefront of interviewees' conceptions of the respectful citizen is respect for the diversity of the Australian population and respect for the rule of law in this country. Again, there are wide-ranging opinions about this schema and the emphasis placed on it varied. For instance,

Noah and Mustapha stress the cultural, religious and racial diversity of Australia which they should respect. Samples of statements referring to the respectful citizen schema include:

Noah: Here because, in my country I mean, like uh, there is only my community. But when I came here I saw, black people, white people, grey, all communities I saw here. So I should rather instead of like uh, talking against them like I should give respect to them, everybody is equal.

Mustapha: I have to give respect to each and every individual in Australia regardless of his background or culture, because if we believe if it is a multicultural society then we should have a rule for accepting others, if we don't have a rule for accepting others then the word integration is wrong.

But on the other hand, Joseph and Abdullah emphasise respect for the norms of the society and following the rule of law. For example, the following statements take the issue of individual Muslims who disregard certain aspects of council laws, specifically the council regulations which assign specific locations for the slaughtering of animals.

Abdullah: As long as you're decent, obeying the laws of this country you do rightful things by your family and the people of this country you're fine.

Joseph: Following the law properly. Whatever form. What I mean is like, you know, could be road rules, could be, for example, people complain about not being able to have *halal* at home, so they want to slaughter in the backyard. There are reasons why it's not allowed in Australia and it's not because the Australian government hates Muslims. It's got nothing to do with it. It's health regulations.

However, in the following statement, Fairuz's schema of the respectful citizen goes further than the other two participants' understandings of integration and appears to be intolerant, as she is against Muslims imposing their culture and values on others.

Fairuz: Respect this country's meanings, we don't as Muslim we don't push so much what we believe, the one the Australian will not understand, and this is what I want, you do it my way, Islam doesn't teach this.

The schema of the respectful citizen appears as if Muslim participants made these comments to fend off the criticism that they lack respect for the law in Australia, and the notion that perhaps they are even trying to change the laws of this country. This is an area in which Muslims are constantly criticised by the media, which feed fears about the Muslim presence in Australia (Black & Abdullah, 2011). Assertions about *Sharia* law in Australia suggesting that Muslims are attempting to impose their religious laws on Australia's majority Christian population are false (Abdalla, 2012). However, despite this, attitudes of the wider non-Muslim society in Australia towards any form of *Sharia* remain negative (Abdalla, 2012). Black and Abdullah (2011, p. 383) classify *Sharia* as the "good *sharia*" and "bad *sharia*" and explain that the Australian government and majority non-Muslim population are more resistant to the family law side of *Sharia* (marriage, divorce, inheritance) than to the banking and finance sector. This contradiction between embracing *Sharia* law in the political and economic arena on one hand, and rejecting it in the personal domain, on the other hand, is referred to as form of neo-liberal multiculturalism (Roose & Possamai, 2015).

Relevant to the Muslim respectful citizen schema is how the Islamic community is viewed by the wider society and its respect and obedience to the laws of the land. An absence of obedience to the law is what is termed in some scholarly literature as delinquent citizenship (Ríos-Rojas, 2011). Some responses and comments made by Muslim participants appear to refute the notion of delinquency, which is a narrative adopted mainly by the media and which has been used in some political rhetoric (Rane & Hersi, 2012). Currently, in Australia, the intelligence assessment is that over sixty Australian Muslim citizens, young men and women, have joined the notorious Islamic State to fight in Iraq and Syria (White, 2014). It is these reports that perhaps create perceptions of delinquency and Muslim immigrants' lack of respect for the law. Internationally, research into the experiences of immigrant youth in Barcelona, Spain, suggests that immigrant youth are confused by contradictory discourses that identify them as terrorists at some times and victims that need to be rescued at other times (Ríos-Rojas, 2011). Although no similar research has been conducted in Australia, it could be argued that Muslim youth in Australia have difficulties navigating their way through similar contradictions.

Loyal Citizen

In their conceptualisations of meanings of integration, the Muslim participants in this study have also invoked notions of the loyal citizen. Terrorism and extremism have been closely linked with Muslim identity in the past decade, and this, together with the constant reference to Muslims as being outside the realm of loyal citizenry, has caused a sense of loyalty to be at the forefront of respondents' concerns, and this was not a surprise. Research shows that there is some suspicion about the loyalty Muslims have to Australia and to parts of Western Europe (Poynting, 2002). For example, Poynting (2002) states that representatives of the tabloid media and personalities on commercial television and talkback radio demand that immigrant leaders of Arabic background declare their allegiance to Australia. Similarly, in his speech to the American Academy of Religion (AAR), Esposito (2014) stated that Muslims in the USA and Europe continued to be visible at every level of society but faced questions regarding their loyalty to their new homeland. Loyalty is another schema that was apparent from the conversations with the interviewees. The schema of the loyal citizen was strongly advanced by a number of informants. Here are a couple of sample statements:

Noah: They really don't like this country. And they say, I mean, uh, I don't know why but they are. I have many experiences I have seen people like, they live here but even then they talk bullshit against Australia.

Fairuz: Like I'm so cranky when in the school when our children singing the national anthem and these parents just refuse it in front of these little kids, that just makes me cranky.

Hamza: Like I said if something should happen to this country, for example, if there's a war, you know. They all have to put their hand together, and if they're all called, ah for war then they have to be accepting it.

As per the above statements, Muslim participants have plainly expressed their patriotism and loyalty towards Australia. For example, saying negative things and not singing the national anthem were identified as being signs of disloyalty. Some participants, however, went even further and explained that loyalty needs to be shown, not only to a visible extent but also in an intangible way, such as being content and satisfied with life. The following are sample statements in this context:

Khalid: Integration to me means that the person not only accepts um, the new country where they're, you know, where their host country where they're settling in, but they're more than happy to be there. They see an obvious benefit in being there.

Uthman: This is a very high sign of integration for them and it's a very high sign of integration for me. Because if this blood is going to mix with anyone's blood in the society, that means you are fully integrated.

Joseph: Now I know of people. Lebanese people for example, but others also, who have had children here, that were born here in Australia and they say I've, I'm fed up with Australia I want to go back and take their kids back to Lebanon, or whatever, and they don't even last a couple of weeks, because their children are completely Australianised.

In the above statements, Muslim participants seem to stress the importance of being loyal to Australia. By employing the schema of loyalty, they appear to understand that being productive, respectful and flexible is not enough to integrate them into the society. However, it is not clear from the analysis whether Muslim participants conveniently provided these responses to counter the documented popular narratives in both the public and political discussions that question Muslim immigrant loyalty to the nation-state. The schema of the loyal citizen informed the author in most of the integration schemas Muslims provided. It appears as though Muslims are aware of the current dominant discourse of integration that emphasises dominant values and norms, and that they define integration through cultural commitment or loyalty (De Leeuw & Van Wichelen, 2012).

However, an inherent problem has been reported in conceptualising integration as being loyal to a particular bounded locality. This is especially problematic at a time of increased ambiguity about where, and to whom, citizens owe loyalty in a globalised society (Canovan, 2000; Johnson, 2013). Interestingly, it is also noted that the Muslim schema of loyalty exists not at an abstract level but is occurring during the experiences of everyday activities and conversations. The emphasis placed on not speaking negatively about Australia and singing the national anthem are examples of participants' focus on everyday activities rather than on a theoretical discussion of integration. Muslim participants appear to be attempting to express loyalty to the dominant majority and want to identify with this majority, and to be included in the society. It is also apparent that they understand the significance the wider society places on the national flag and the national anthem.

Some Western Europe an immigrant-receiving countries, including Britain, Germany, the Netherlands, Denmark, and Austria, have recently introduced formal citizenship tests, loyalty requirements, and ceremonies to increase the value and meaning of citizenship for immigrants who are becoming naturalised (Joppke, 2013). It is specifically these citizenship tests that have become standard in many Western societies since 11 September 2001 that are in direct contradiction to Muslim participants' understandings of integration. For example, in Holland, the tests' emphasis on secular liberalism, and their focus on cultural tropes such as sexual freedom, gender equality, freedom of speech and individuality are seen as indicators of Dutchness (De Leeuw & Van Wichelen, 2012). De Leeuw and Van Wichelen (2012) agree that this definition of integration leaves little room for cultural and religious variations. However, Muslim participants in this study take the opposite view of integration schemas, and while still being loyal to Australia, provide a meaning of integration that provides little room for their cultural and religious variation.

Integration has been conceptualised in a variety of cognitive schematic frames. Broader frames of functional versus cultural schemata of integration were obvious in the Muslims' understandings of integration. Absent from functional integration indicators which Muslim participants identified are housing and health issues. These are notions of integration identified by integration policy documents in Europe and beyond. For example, Ager and Strang (2008) refer to these areas of integration as the markers and means of integration. The apparent absence of these important areas of functional integration could be explained as being related to the privileged position of Australians, including the new migrants, in securing acceptable housing and their accessibility to Australia's universal health care system, Medicare. Migrant integration policies and programs are nation centred and dictated by local circumstances. However, to benchmark itself against other liberal democracies in Europe, Australia has recently joined the Migrant Integration Policy Index (MIPEX), which rates policies of member countries and how they perform against a set of criteria regarding their integration policies. In the conceptual framework of defining core domains of integration, Australia does better than comparable migrant-receiving European countries (MIPEX data in Europe).

Based on information discussed in Chapters 4 and 5, it is the case that Muslims are functionally integrating. However, cultural integration appears to be an area in which Muslims attract criticism from the wider society. Debates about values and culture are included in the general discussions of integration. Emphasising the cultural rather than the functional, talking down and ridiculing Australia is seen to be an indicator of lack of integration. Just as the beach loving, surfing culture is not a measure of integration, Muslim dress such as the *burqa* or Muslim men wearing a beard is not an indicator of lack of integration. Employment is directly referred to as benefitting a migrant's social integration and this is another example of how the cultural and attitudinal markers are not independent of the functional indicators of integration. This study concludes that the demand for conformity to mainstream culture is perceived by some Muslims as being prejudicial. In fact, meanings of integration that suggest conformism tendencies face resistance. Instead, Muslim immigrants who hold participatory realistic notions of integration may have better chances of achieving full integration.

References

Abdalla, M. (2012). Sacred law in secular land: To what extent should Sharia law be followed in Australia? *The Griffith Law Review, 21*(3), 657–679.

Adamuti-Trache, M., & Sweet, R. (2010). Adult immigrants' participation in Canadian education and training. *Canadian Journal for the Study of Adult Education, 22*(2), 1–26.

Ager, A., & Strang, A. (2008). Understanding integration: A conceptual framework. *Journal of Refugee Studies, 21*(2), 166–191.

Australian Bureau of Statistics. (2011). *Australian Standard Classification of Countries (SACC)*. Retrieved from http://www.abs.gov.au/ausstats/abs@.nsf/Lookup/1269.

Beck, U. (2014). We do not live in an age of cosmopolitanism but in an age of cosmopolitization: The 'global other' is in our midst. In U. Beck (Ed.), *Pioneer in Cosmopolitan Sociology and Risk Society* (pp. 169–187). New York: Springer.

Benhabib, S. (2007). Twilight of sovereignty or the emergence of cosmopolitan norms? Rethinking citizenship in volatile times. *Citizenship Studies, 11*(1), 19–36.

Bisin, A., Patacchini, E., Verdier, T., & Zenou, Y. (2011). Ethnic identity and labour market outcomes of immigrants in Europe. *Economic Policy, 26*(65), 57–92.

Black, A., & Abdullah, K. (2011). Good and bad Sharia: Australia's mixed response to Islamic law. *University of New South Wales Law Journal, 34*(1), 383.

Bloemraad, I. (2006). *Becoming a citizen: Incorporating immigrants and refugees in the United States and Canada*. Berkeley: University of California.

Bolzendahl, C., & Coffé, H. (2013). Are 'good' citizens 'good' participants? Testing citizenship norms and political participation across 25 nations. *Political Studies, 61*(S1), 45–65.

Boski, P. (2008). Five meanings of integration in acculturation research. *International Journal of Intercultural Relations, 32*(2), 142–153.

Brubaker, R., Loveman, M., & Stamatov, P. (2004). Ethnicity as cognition. *Theory and Society, 33*(1), 31–64.

Canovan, M. (2000). Patriotism is not enough. *British Journal of Political Science, 30*(3), 413–432.

Carley, K. (1989). The value of cognitive foundations for dynamic social theory. *Journal of Mathematical Sociology, 14*(2–3), 171–208.

Cerulo, K. A. (2002). *Culture in mind: Toward sociology of culture and cognition*. New York: Routledge.

Cerulo, K. A. (2010). Mining the intersections of cognitive sociology and neuroscience. *Poetics, 38*(2), 115–132.

Cicourel, A. V. (1973). *Cognitive sociology*. New York: Free Press.

De Leeuw, M., & Van Wichelen, S. (2012). Civilizing migrants: Integration, culture and citizenship. *European Journal of Cultural Studies, 15*(2), 195–210.

DiMaggio, P., & Markus, H. R. (2010). Culture and social psychology converging perspectives. *Social Psychology Quarterly, 73*(4), 347–352.

Esposito, J. L. (2014). 2013 AAR presidential address: Islam in the public square. *Journal of the American Academy of Religion, 82*(2), 291–306.

Frey, B. S. (2003). Flexible citizenship for a global society. *Politics, Philosophy & Economics, 2*(1), 93–114.

Heckmann, F., & Schnapper, D. (Eds.). (2003). *The integration of immigrants in European societies: National differences and trends of convergence* (Vol. 7). Stuttgart, DE: Lucius & Lucius.

Ignatow, G. (2007). Theories of embodied knowledge: New directions for cultural and cognitive sociology? *Journal for the Theory of Social Behaviour, 37*(2), 115–135.

Johnson, J. M. (2013). National to global citizenship: Reflections on our values, loyalties, and common future. *Cultural Studies ↔ Critical Methodologies, 13*(6), 452–457.

Joppke, C. (2013). Through the European looking glass: Citizenship tests in the USA, Australia, and Canada. *Citizenship Studies, 17*(1), 1–15.

Kashima, Y. (2014). Meaning, grounding, and the construction of social reality. *Asian Journal of Sociol Psychology, 17*, 81–95. https://doi.org/10.1111/ajsp1205.

Kogan, I. (2011). New immigrants-old disadvantage patterns? Labour market integration of recent immigrants into Germany. *International Migration, 49*(1), 91–117.

Krause, K., & Liebig, T. (2011). The labour market integration of immigrants and their children in Austria. *OECD Social, Employment and Migration* (Working Papers No. 127). Paris: OECD Publishing. http://dx.doi.org/10.1787/5kg264fz6p8w-en (see https://www.oecd.org/migration/49205671.pdf).

Kymlicka, W. (2011). Multicultural citizenship within multination states. *Ethnicities, 11*(3), 281–302.

Lawler, P. (2007). Janus-faced solidarity. *Cooperation and Conflict, 42*(1), 101–126.

Mitchell, M. C. (2013). *Religion, identity and politics in Northern Ireland: Boundaries of belonging and belief.* Abingdon: Routledge.

Nyamnjoh, F. B. (2008). From bounded to flexible citizenship. In E. F. Isin, P. Nyers, & B. S. Turner (Eds.), *Citizenship between past and future* (pp. 78–87). London: Routledge.

Nyamnjoh, F. B. (2013). Fiction and reality of mobility in Africa. *Citizenship Studies, 17*(6–7), 653–680.

Petrovic-Lazarevic, S. (2010). Good corporate citizenship in the Australian construction industry. *Corporate Governance, 10*(2), 115–128.

Poynting, S. (2002). Racism and community safety. *Current Issues in Criminal Justice, 13*(3), 328–332.

Pykett, J., Saward, M., & Schaefer, A. (2010). Framing the good citizen. *The British Journal of Politics & International Relations, 12*(4), 523–538.

Rane, H., & Hersi, A. (2012). Meanings of integration in the Australian press coverage of Muslims: Implications for social inclusion and exclusion. *Media International Australia, Incorporating Culture & Policy, 142*(February), 135–147.

Ríos-Rojas, A. (2011). Beyond delinquent citizenships: Immigrant youth's (re)visions of citizenship and belonging in a globalized world. *Harvard Educational Review, 81*(1), 64–95.

Roose, J. M., & Possamai, A. (2015). Between rhetoric and reality: Shari'a and the shift towards neoliberal multiculturalism in Australia. In F. Mansouri (Ed.), *Cultural, religious and political contestations* (pp. 91–105). Cham, Switzerland: Springer.

Russell, C. D., & Kleyn, T. (2013). Impenetrable citizenship. *Refugees, Immigrants, and Education in the Global South: Lives in Motion, 94*, 180.

Schmidt, V. H. (2001). Oversocialised epistemology: A critical appraisal of constructivism. *Sociology, 35*(1), 135–157.

Shapcott, R. (2013). From the good international citizen to the cosmopolitan political community: A constitutional path. *International Politics, 50*(1), 138–157.

Soysal, Y. N. (2012). Post-national citizenship. *The Wiley-Blackwell Companion to Political Sociology, 38*, 383.

Staeheli, L. A. (2011). Political geography: Where's citizenship? *Progress in Human Geography, 35*(3), 393–400.

Thorson, K. (2012). What does it mean to be a good citizen? Citizenship vocabularies as resources for action. *The Annals of the American Academy of Political and Social Science, 644*(1), 70–85.

Van Deth, J. W. (2009). The 'Good European Citizen' congruence and consequences of different points of view. *European Political Science, 8*(2), 175–189.

Waters, J. L. (2010). Becoming a father, missing a wife: Chinese transnational families and the male experience of lone parenting in Canada. *Population, Space and Place, 16*(1), 63–74.

White, A. (2014) Unmasked: Aussie Jihadist heading to the Islamic state terror zones. *Herald Sun.* Retrieved from http://www.heraldsun.com.au/ news/law-order/unmasked-aussie-jihadists-heading-into-islamic-state-terror-zones/story-fni0fee2-1227062790468.

Zerubavel, E. (1997). *Social mindscapes. An invitation to cognitive sociology.* London: Harvard University Press.

7

Clash of Integration Frames

International migration is a topical issue in international affairs. The reasons for this may be because international migration is a phenomenon that crosses national borders and affects two or more nation-states (Castles, 2007). Managing the diversity inherent in international migration is the new, emerging challenge of international migration policies. In most countries of the Western world, those that resettle a significant number of migrants face challenges in incorporating immigrant newcomers. Researchers have noted these challenges in Australia, North America and Europe (see Bloemraad, 2006; Castles, 2007; Li, 2003; Mac Éinrí, 2007; Wets, 2006). As a result, immigrant integration remains an area of significant interest to governments, policymakers, academics and the media. The increase in the global movement of people will be further complicated by the diversity of the people migrating from one country to another.

In the realisation of this ever-increasing diversity, to date, a number of countries in the West are making significant changes to their migration policies. For example, countries like Australia, New Zealand and Canada have started to shift their immigration intake priorities (Akbari & MacDonald, 2014). These countries have become focused on:

© The Author(s) 2018
A. Hersi, *Conceptualisation of Integration*, Palgrave Politics of Identity
and Citizenship Series, https://doi.org/10.1007/978-3-319-91235-6_7

- attracting skilled migration,
- expanding temporary migration visa regimes,
- appealing to international students securing permanent settlement after graduating from universities, as well as
- implementing reforms to their refugee and humanitarian programmes (Akbari & MacDonald, 2014).

Immigration reforms in these countries are not only limited to migrant intake but extend to the successful settlement of new immigrants in their host societies. Australia and some Western European countries have indeed undergone some significant changes in this area (Hollifield, Martin, & Orrenius, 2014). With an increase in the diversity of migrants coming to these countries, the challenges of maintaining a socially cohesive nation have become a reality and have necessitated reform. There has been a shift away from a focus on functional integration to an emphasis on migrants adopting the dominant society's culture and values (McHugh, 2014). It is what is now termed in the contemporary international migration literature "civic integration" (Goodman, 2010). One explanation for this cultural notion of integration is perhaps that some members of host society groups have a perceived fear of immigrants who have an unfamiliar culture and religion (Koopmans, Lancee, & Schaeffer, 2014). Similarly, geopolitical consideration may have led to anxiety about new immigrant groups, especially those which originate in regions where extremist and terrorist groups operate.

Public and political discussions of immigrant integration continue to take a significant space in the scholarly literature of international migration, and this will continue into the future, as constant, large flows of migrants challenge destination countries to find innovative ways to meet their needs and promote their integration (McHugh, 2014). Nation-states often attempt to make the necessary reforms in this significant public policy area. However, the approaches adopted by different nation-states differ and are dictated by local circumstances and the types of groups of immigrants involved (Bertossi & Duyvendak, 2012). They are also influenced by context and country, and by which groups of immigrants are involved (International Organisation for Migration, 2014). For example, the Netherlands is considered to be one Western

European country which is retreating from pluralist forms of integration and is instead adopting an assimilationist form of immigrant integration, due to popular anxiety caused by profound changes in the Dutch society (Entzinger, 2014).

As a country with a long and generally positive history of migration, Australia has introduced a set of citizenship tests for its immigrant communities (Bloemraad, 2012). Civic integration is the latest of Australia's constantly shifting immigrant incorporation policies, which has progressed from segregated assimilative forms to integrationist forms and then to multiculturalism (International Organisation for Migration, 2014). Australia's adoption of civic integration is in line with shifts in the immigrant incorporation policies of many other Western states (Entzinger, 2014). These significant policy shifts are believed to be in response to a perceived lack of migrant integration in general, but Muslim immigrants in particular, who are often seen as a group which poses problematic integration (Bouma, Cahill, Dellal, & Zwartz, 2011; Dunn et al., 2008; Markus, 2011, 2013).

As governments adjust immigrant incorporation policies, they face the difficulties of negotiating the meanings of integration stipulated by the different actors in the integration process. It has previously established in this study that integration is conceived as a loose concept with different interpretations, thus producing multiple meanings (see Chapter 3). However, when it comes to Muslims in Australia, despite the absence of any agreed definition of integration in the scholarly literature, Muslims become the target of those who espouse the view that diversity threatens social cohesion (Fozdar, 2012). This happens without any acknowledgement of the existence of multiple interpretations of integration adopted by different groups, societies and actors. The existence of competing frames of immigrant integration is well-documented in Chapter 3 of this book, in which these discourses were categorised as those adopted by the media, the state and academia. Therefore, the view is taken here that Muslim conceptualisations of integration lie within one of these competing frames of integration. Furthermore, there may not be a problematic integration of Muslims in Australia, but there is certainly a clash of integration frames evident in both the international migration literature and the responses provided by the Muslim participants in this study.

Integration has been defined by many constituent actors, for example, the media, the state and academia, however, none of these actors has provided a consistent and uniform meaning of integration, and in some cases, they have offered competing immigrant integration frames (see Chapter 3). There are also variances in the way in which integration is framed between different countries, cities and regions. For example, in their examination of the integration frames of eight Italian regions, Campomori and Caponio (2013, pp. 169–171) found, "A social welfare frame, an assimilationist frame and a would-be citizen frame". In an examination of the findings of this research, it is apparent that Muslims have made a hefty contribution to this clash of integration frames.

Muslims have accepted and embraced certain frames of integration, mainly those which relate to the functional elements of integration, such as social and economic participation in the host society. For the most part, the meanings of integration Muslims provided were similar to those advanced by immigrant integration literature. In fact, for Muslims in Australia, the prevailing conceptualisation of integration was participation in the social, economic and political life of Australia. However, even within these conceptualisations, there were discrepancies in how much emphasis was placed on one integration factor (employment integration) over another (political integration). For instance, while the participants' responses to questions about employment integration were forthcoming, their responses to questions about political integration were much more reserved.

The question is what are the barriers that impede individual Muslims from participating in the political systems of Australia? It is difficult to answer this question without empirical examination, but in a speech at the Sydney Institute after losing the election of 2004 in the seat of Greenway for the Labor party, the current Muslim Federal Member of Parliament hints that Islam and religion was used against him in the national election campaign of 2004 (Husic, 2006). Husic does not, however, blame this alone as the reason for his loss but cites other factors such as the effective use of fear of interest rate hikes under a Labor government. However, it can be reasonably hypothesised that the current Islamophobia experienced by many Muslim citizens in Australia could be one factor contributing to the lower level of Muslim political participation.

While agreeing with the general understandings of integration in the wider scholarly literature, there were discrepancies between individual participants' responses to these conceptualisations. There were notable differences in their preferences of one form of integration over another. These thematically varied definitions of integration offered by study participants reflect the larger disagreements about the meanings of integration in the literature. It is believed that these variances are not limited to group differences, but are obvious in personal and individual spheres. The study stresses that participants have also subscribed to integration frames that emphasise civic duties and citizenship—in particular, the rights and responsibilities of a citizen.

The integration frames that Muslims question are assimilationist and culturally dense frames of integration. In particular, Muslims appear to be contesting the new and popular discourse of integration which emphasises dominant values and norms, one that defines civic membership through cultural commitment (De Leeuw & Van Wichelen, 2012). At the same time, the study found that while the meanings Muslims generally assign to the term *integration* are by and large similar to those prevalent in the scholarly literature on integration, it is, however, the case that emphasis was placed on how perceptions, belief systems, culture and values play a part in how integration is defined. In analysing the research data, it is apparent that Muslims had mixed reactions and responses to issues around cultural integration. In this study, religion and integration were at the forefront of many of the discussions with participants. This was not a surprise, as these findings are supported by the findings from previous research, which found that beliefs, values and symbols weigh into the policy debates about immigration, specifically in discussions relating to immigrant integration (Lahav, 2004).

The findings of this study are also strengthened by findings of previous research which confirm that religiosity is an important determinant of how new immigrants self-identify by ethnicity or religion (Mitchell, 2013; Zimmermann, Gataullina, Constant, & Zimmermann, 2008). Religiosity is key to how integration is framed by Muslims. It is important to note that in addition to religion, research conducted in Germany found that different characteristics have also played a role in determining immigrants' feelings about being German (Zimmermann et al., 2008). In this particular study, for males, the research found that religion, education in the home country and ethnicities are pre-migration characteristics which influenced how immigrants felt about being German (Zimmermann et al., 2008). For females, the research found that both pre- and post-migration characteristics played a role in how females felt about Germany. It can be concluded from this observation that belief systems, values and cultures influence not only immigrant communities but also their host societies' acceptance of newcomers. As van der Noll (2014, p. 63) explains, "Traditional morality is expected to induce opposition towards the visibility and presence of Islam in the German public sphere because this conflicts with the traditional beliefs and behaviours and provides space for other lifestyles".

The findings of this research also confirm the suggestion by Cesari (2007, p. 56) that "Religion and Islam are powerful elements of identity formation that can weave together people of different nations, cultures and countries". Despite the diversity of the focus group and interview participants in terms of nationalities, cultures and countries of origin, it was found that issues of integration were always defined by what is perceived to be acceptable to a Muslim person. While Muslims condition their integration to what is permissible within their religion, similarly, Jackson (2011) refers to immigrant integration in relation to the biblical and mythological insights. However, it is the phenomenon of Islam as a transnational religion that is perceived as presenting a dilemma to the notion and concept of immigrant integration. This dilemma has only become an issue in the recent past, as Islam as a religion and Muslims as people have a history of migration to non-Muslim societies with no major concerns. According to Eickelman and Piscatori (1990) Muslim societies have a long history of movement to non-Muslim countries for migration, pilgrimage and commerce and other reasons.

Not only does Muslim society's history of migration predate modern migration times, but also the causes and precursors of Muslim migration to places of non-Muslim populations are centuries old. A noteworthy example is the contemporary issue of asylum-seeking, where individuals and groups who face persecution for racial and religious reasons seek protection in other places. In his time, the prophet Mohammad asked a group of his close companions to flee from the persecution they faced from the Meccan Arabs in what is today Saudi

Arabia, and migrate to the Abyssinian land of a just Christian king, Negus (Elmadmad, 2008). Abyssinia today is Ethiopia, and in this country, Muslims and Christians share a history of living together harmoniously.

The notion of more secularised Western society encountering a heightened resurgence of Islam and its alleged transnational Islamic agenda is of particular interest. Globalisation poses challenges in this sphere and whether or not Muslim individuals should identify with the nation or the global Islamic identity (*Ummah*) is contentious (Hassan, 2006). According to Hassan (2006, p. 311) "The concept of *Ummah* embodies the universalism of Islam and provides a framework for religious unity, which accommodates the cultural diversity of believers". However, pledging allegiance to the community of faith (*Ummah*) beyond the national boundaries of the state may create a tension between a more secular host society and the Muslims in its midst. In our analysis of research data, participants did not indicate identification with *Ummah* (community of faith) but were instead seeking acceptance and accommodation of their faith by the wider society.

At the outset, it was noted that there could well be a discrepancy between what Muslim participants say in the group discussions and how they behave individually outside the group discussions. The observations show there are clear indications that Muslim participants who were the children of third or fourth generation Muslims had slightly altered their performative outlook as Muslims. This means that even though the majority of Muslim participants stated the importance of the faith in the integration process, there is a subtle process of mutual adaptation and integration between Muslims and the wider society. Studies show that ties to homeland gradually fade to some extent, but religious ties may not fade as quickly, and individuals who have spent a longer time in their receiving countries certainly accommodate other people of different faith more than do those who have settled more recently (Harles, 1997).

Australia is a nation of people of multiple faiths and Muslims know their constitutional rights to practise their faith. Muslim participants appear to be making substantial claims to conditioning their integration on acceptance of their religion. Their conceptualisation of integration in this way is also a rejection of complete assimilation. As much as Australia is a multicultural society, it is also a multi-faith society due to a large number of religious belief systems practised by diverse citizen groups. Researchers have already noted that Australian citizenship has "religious features" and suggest that multicultural countries like Australia should consider themselves to be multi-faith rather than secular (Hudson, 2003, p. 429). Despite their small number, Muslims in Australia are already attracting significant attention in public and political discussions relating to terrorism, radicalisation and extremism. In this climate of fear, the proposition of turning multicultural Australia into multi-faith Australia is somewhat enthusiastic and is not beneficial to the debate.

In fact, there is an outright rejection of any call for the accommodation of *Sharia* law in Australia (Abdalla, 2012), but what is perhaps missed in the debate is the fact that only small number of Muslims call for the partial application of *Sharia* law, and this is mainly in the areas of marriage and divorce, Islamic banking and female circumcision. While the argument for implementing *Sharia* law for matters relating to marriage and divorce is perceived to have some merit, the idea is unworkable in the present climate of suspicion and fear overshadowing the wider society's consciousness about Muslims and *Sharia* law (Abdalla, 2012, p. 659). Despite this fact, there are advocates for the recognition of *Sharia* law in Australia, especially concerning family issues (Black, 2008; Black & Abdullah, 2011). These scholars stress that Australia as a multi-ethnic and multi-faith society needs to embrace legal pluralism. However, this author asserts that the proposition of Australia partially adopting *Sharia* law is provocative when considering the general debates about Muslims and *Sharia* law.

At a technical detail level, the extent to which *Sharia* law should be followed in Australia is debatable. In his work, *Sacred Law In a Secular Land: To What Extent Should Sharī 'a Law be Followed in Australia?* Abdalla (2012) extensively documents the extent to which Muslims are obliged to follow *Sharia* in a non-Muslim context. Relying on the views of leading classical and contemporary Islamic scholars, Abdalla (2012) argues that in a non-Muslim country, Muslims are only obliged to follow certain aspects of personal status law. What is missing in the debate is the fact some proposals suggest that Muslims are about to change the cultural and religious landscape of Australia by imposing harsh *Sharia* laws. The participants in this study mentioned that they would prefer accommodation for cultural and religious differences, but none provided responses even mildly suggestive of an imposition of their faith on others.

The above discussions of religion and *Sharia* law and their influence on the integration debate are not independent of the much broader debates of culture and values that are consistently becoming part of this debate (Arai, Karlsson, & Lundholm, 2011; Bisin, Patacchini, Verdier, & Zenou, 2011; Tolsma, Lubbers, & Gijsberts, 2012). In addition to religion, the cultural debate undeniably presents another challenge to the definition and meaning of integration. It specifically presents considerable risks where integration is conceptualised as an interaction between an inferior (Muslim) subordinate culture and value into a superior (Western) one. This erroneous conception of imagined superior culture and values has the potential to lead to what Huntington (1993) describes as a cultural and civilizational clash (Huntington, 1993). Regrettably, this culturally dense debate of integration is prevalent in public and policy discussions, and there are indications that it is becoming the immigrant integration policy choice of many liberal and conservative-led governments in Western Europe (Kymlicka, 2011).

It is acknowledged that the particular meanings that actors such as political organisations assign to integration are normally dictated by a set of political philosophies and ideological underpinnings. The clashes of frames of integration are also manifested in the way different political parties approach the concept of integration. In some cases, variations have been made between liberal and conservative ideologies in regard to the propensity to use a more culturally dense definition of integration. For instance, Kundnani (2012) observes the differences between the liberal and the conservative parties in Britain over issues concerning immigrant integration. He argues that while the conservative discourse of integration emphasises Enlightenment and its legacy of secularism, individualism and freedom of expression, the conservatives mark out racial difference and use British values, comparing these with those of others such as Muslim community values (Kundnani, 2012).

Correspondingly, the findings reveal that Muslim meanings of integration are also influenced by cultural, philosophical and ideological underpinnings as well as individual circumstances and experiences. This is absent from current immigrant integration discourse, but presents another argument which is informed by how Muslim participants frame the concept of integration. The link between integration and religion and what is acceptable in the participants' faith is a clear example of the fact that their conceptualisation of the term is informed by religion and culture. The participants in this study appear to downplay possible limitations that their faith might impose on their integration levels, and they reject an apparent contradiction between being a Muslim and being well-integrated into the Australian community. Similarly, a study of 30 prominent Australian Muslim leaders finds that Islamic texts and teachings do not cause problems with social integration (Sohrabi & Farquharson, 2015).

In recognition of the complexity of Australian society following postwar mass immigration, this author supports the view of Mason (2010) who calls for a new policy of inclusion which does not oblige immigrants to surrender their cultural heritage. In fact, he points out that cultural landscapes were central to migrants' ongoing relationships with Australia (Mason, 2010). As with other important actors of the debate such as members of the host society, it is not a surprise that Muslims bring their own culture, beliefs, customs and values to the debates of immigrant integration. Since Huntington's (1993) theory of a clash of civilisations, it appears as if culture and values are noticeable in matters relating to Islam and West relations. It is evident that a clash of integration frames is emerging in this debate.

Certain difficulties may be caused by this emerging clash of integration frames. For example, it might confirm that a clash of integration frames is an unexpressed form of cultural and civilizational clash (Huntington, 1993). The arguments advanced in this book are supported by findings of other researchers who reach the same conclusion. For example, Kuran and Sandholm (2008) argue that policies which aggressively support social integration serve to homogenise preferences amongst communities and may have the effect of undermining multiculturalism. It is also the case that there is an apparent contradiction between cultural integration and the pursuit of policies of multiculturalism, which in essence is to preserve the multiplicity of cultures. The findings of this research show that the concept of civic integration faces challenges from globalisation. While the concept of civic integration is intended to create a harmonious, socially cohesive society, minority ethnic and religious groups may see it as being a tool of exclusion. For these groups, it appears that there are two constituent groups who are talking at cross purposes, that is, the immigrant groups and the members of host communities. It was found that Muslims are willing to be functionally integrated into wider society, and statistics and other available measures indicate that they are fully integrated in this aspect. However, there appears to be some discontent amongst Muslims in aspects of cultural integration. In the contemporary debates about integration and what it might mean, what is now emerging is a new and contested concept of citizenship that is operating both as a force for inclusion and a force for exclusion.

Kuran and Sandholm (2008) conclude that cultural integration will continue both within and across boundaries. Practically, this means that in coming decades today's cultures will undergo major transformations; efforts to protect existing cultures from foreign influences seem doomed to fail. At the same time, cultural integration will induce conflicts within and amongst countries. Indeed, today's political instabilities are rooted partly in tensions fuelled by cultural integration (Kuran & Sandholm, 2008). Overall, this study challenges previous studies which solely considered that the philosophical sense of nationhood and national identity of the host society informs what the concept of integration means (Heckmann & Schnapper, 2003, p. 12). Instead, it was found that any definitional proposition which squarely focuses on the philosophies and expectations of the host society while neglecting the philosophical and expectations of the newcomer is erroneous. This study shows that Muslims' understandings of integration are correspondingly informed by the lived experiences, attitudes, faith and values held by the Muslim immigrant group.

However, this research demonstrates that Muslims conceptualisation of integration is at least far more complex and dynamic than is widely acknowledged by available scholarly literature. For example, there is little mention in the scholarly literature of how religion and faith influence how individual Muslims interpret integration. Quite often, the scholarly literature conflates issues with integration, religion, culture and values without clear demarcations and boundaries of how these frames and schemas interact with each other. Despite the clashes of integration frames apparent in the discussions above, there were conceptualisations of integration which Muslim participants contested. For example, one particular frame of integration that Muslims appear to contest and challenge is the new and developing theme of civic integration. This theme introduces a host of new hard-line policies that condition status on immigrants' cultural integration. These policies may take the form of citizenship tests, language proficiency, learning dominant society history, values and culture (Bocker & Strik, 2011; Goodman, 2010; Joppke, 2013; Wiesbrock, 2011). In fact, Muslim participants challenge defining integration in this narrow cultural tradition and advance the view that the increasingly complex global environment requires integration to be defined in a globally meaningful and less rigid fashion.

Instead, Muslims tend to advocate a cosmopolitan meaning of integration, despite the fact that, to date, no country has accepted cosmopolitanism as a form of immigrant incorporation. As the cosmopolitan nature and realities of the increasingly high levels of diversity in some nation-states demand a change, perhaps it is time to revisit how states and policymakers define integration. The concept of cosmopolitanism, however, is weak in the sense that it generally refers to the individual as opposed to the group (Meer & Modood, 2012). It could be argued that a secular liberal view of integration does not fit in the multicultural and multireligious landscape which is characterised by many Western societies. Drawing on the findings of this study, it is clear that Muslims' definition of integration is one that is attempting to discredit those narratives.

It is clear that there are meanings which Muslims attach to the concept of integration which are in line with the themes, models and frames of integration adopted by Australia and other Western countries. These include participatory citizen frames of integration, where Muslims emphasise the importance of making social and economic contributions to the host society and pledging loyalty to Australia. While that is positive in itself, Muslim participants in this study acknowledge that there are other meanings of integration adopted by some members of the host society which have the potential to fragment social cohesion, to increase distrust between Muslims and members of the host society. This author concurs with interpretations of notable scholars in this field such as Modood (2013) who argues that the symbolic framework of integration (identity, religion, perception of the "other", collective memory, and so on) is no less important than its functional or material framework.

An understanding of how Muslims in Australia conceptualise integration is vital because it is indeed the case that despite these divergent conceptualisations of integration, while seeming conflictual, the debates are at the same time influencing each other. For instance, it is necessary to understand the influential role that the media plays in this important area of public policy discussion. In the Netherlands, one study of how issues of immigration and integration are debated in the parliament and the press reveals that an increase in the use of a frame by the media led to the increase of the same frame by the parliament (Roggeband & Vliegenthart, 2007).

The manifestation of the clash of frames of integration and contestable frames of integration risks the production of a competitive framing process of integration. This competition is between the integration processes' actors, namely, the immigrant, the members of the host society, the state and the media. It is apparent that each constituent actor prefers a frame of integration deemed as serving their particular narrative. The absence of an agreement between all frames of integration is, therefore, the new challenge that is posed by the current increasing levels of international migration.

References

Abdalla, M. (2012). Sacred law in secular land: To what extent should Sharia law be followed in Australia? *The Griffith Law Review, 21*(3), 657–679.
Akbari, A. H., & MacDonald, M. (2014). Immigration policy in Australia, Canada, New Zealand, and the United States: An overview of recent trends. *International Migration Review, 48*(3), 801–822.

Arai, M., Karlsson, J., & Lundholm, M. (2011). On fragile grounds: A replication of "Are Muslim immigrants different in terms of cultural integration?" *Journal of the European Economic Association, 9*(5), 1002–1011.

Bertossi, C., & Duyvendak, J. W. (2012). National models of immigrant integration: The costs for comparative research. *Comparative European Politics, 10*(3), 237–247.

Bisin, A., Patacchini, E., Verdier, T., & Zenou, Y. (2011). Ethnic identity and labour market outcomes of immigrants in Europe. *Economic Policy, 26*(65), 57–92.

Black, A. (2008). Accommodating Shariah law in Australia's legal system. *Alternative Law Journal, 33*(4), 214–219.

Black, A., & Abdullah, K. (2011). Good and bad Sharia: Australia's mixed response to Islamic law. *University of New South Wales Law Journal, 34*(1), 383.

Bloemraad, I. (2006). *Becoming a citizen: Incorporating immigrants and refugees in the United States and Canada.* Berkeley: University of California.

Bloemraad, I. (2012). Understanding "Canadian exceptionalism" in immigration and pluralism policy. In B. Stiftung (Ed.), *Rethinking national identity in the age of migration* (pp. 145–170). Washington, DC: Migration Policy Institute.

Bocker, A., & Strik, T. (2011). Language and knowledge tests for permanent residence rights: Help or hindrance for integration. *European Journal of Migration & Law, 13,* 157.

Bouma, G., Cahill, D., Dellal, H., & Zwartz, A. (2011). *Freedom of religion and belief in 21st century Australia.* Canberra: Australian Human Rights Commission.

Campomori, F., & Caponio, T. (2013). Competing frames of immigrant integration in the EU: Geographies of social inclusion in Italian regions. *Policy Studies, 34*(2), 162–179.

Castles, S. (2007). Twenty-first-century migration as a challenge to sociology. *Journal of Ethnic and Migration Studies, 33*(3), 351–371.

Cesari, J. (2007). Muslim identities in Europe: The snare of exceptionalism. In A. Al-Azmeh & E. Fokas (Eds.), *Islam in Europe: Diversity, identity and influence* (pp. 49–67). Cambridge, UK: Cambridge University Press.

De Leeuw, M., & Van Wichelen, S. (2012). Civilizing migrants: Integration, culture and citizenship. *European Journal of Cultural Studies, 15*(2), 195–210.

Dunn, K., Forrest, J., Ip, D., Babacan, H., Paradise, Y., & Pederson, A. (2008). Challenging racism: The anti-racism research project, state-level comparison. In *Proceedings of 4Rs Conference: Rights, Reconciliation, Respect,*

Responsibility (30 September–3 October). Sydney, NSW: University of Technology. Retrieved from http://www.uws.edu.au/__data/assets/pdf_file/0020/42185/State_level_comparison_for_4Rs_conference.pdf.

Eickelman, D. F., & Piscatori, J. (Eds.). (1990). *Muslim travelers, migration, and the religious imagination* (pp. 3–28). Berkley: University of California Press.

Elmadmad, K. (2008). Asylum in Islam and in modern refugee law. *Refugee Survey Quarterly, 27*(2), 51–63.

Entzinger, H. (2014). The growing gap between facts and discourse on immigrant integration in the Netherlands. *Identities, 21*(6), 693–707.

Fozdar, F. (2012). Social cohesion and skilled Muslim refugees in Australia employment, social capital and discrimination. *Journal of Sociology, 48*(2), 167–186.

Goodman, S. W. (2010). Integration requirements for integration's sake? Identifying, categorising and comparing civic integration. *Journal of Ethnic and Migration Studies, 36*(5), 753–772.

Harles, J. C. (1997). Integration before assimilation: Immigration, multiculturalism and the Canadian polity. *Canadian Journal of Political Science, 30*(4), 711–736.

Hassan, R. (2006). Globalisation's challenge to the Islamic Ummah. *Asian Journal of Social Science, 34*(2), 311–323.

Heckmann, F., & Schnapper, D. (Eds.). (2003). *The integration of immigrants in European societies: National differences and trends of convergence* (Vol. 7). Stuttgart, DE: Lucius & Lucius.

Hollifield, J., Martin, P., & Orrenius, P. (Eds.). (2014). *Controlling immigration: A global perspective*. Redwood City, CA: Stanford University Press.

Hudson, W. (2003). Religious citizenship. *Australian Journal of Politics & History, 49*(3), 425–429.

Huntington, S. P. (1993). The clash of civilizations? *Foreign Affairs, 72*(3), 22–49.

Husic, E. (2006). Islam and Australia: Can a Muslim get elected to parliament in a war on terror? *The Sydney Papers, 18*(1), 88–99.

International Organisation for Migration (2014). *Compendium of migrant integration policies and practices*, Retrieved October 22, 2014, from www.iom.int.

Jackson, D. (2011). Europe and the migrant experience: Transforming integration. *Transformation: An International Journal of Holistic Mission Studies, 28*(1), 14–28.

Joppke, C. (2013). Through the European looking glass: Citizenship tests in the USA, Australia, and Canada. *Citizenship Studies, 17*(1), 1–15.

Koopmans, R., Lancee, B., & Schaeffer, M. (Eds.). (2014). *Social cohesion and immigration in Europe and North America: Mechanisms, conditions, and causality*. London: Routledge.

Kundnani, A. (2012). Multiculturalism and its discontents: Left, right and liberal. *European Journal of Cultural Studies, 15*(2), 155–166.

Kuran, T., & Sandholm, W. H. (2008). Cultural integration and its discontents. *The Review of Economic Studies, 75*(1), 201–228.

Kymlicka, W. (2011). Multicultural citizenship within multination states. *Ethnicities, 11*(3), 281–302.

Lahav, G. (2004). *Immigration and politics in the new Europe: Reinventing borders*. Cambridge, UK: Cambridge University Press.

Li, P. S. (2003). Deconstructing Canada's discourses of immigrant integration. *Journal of International Migration and Integration, 4*(3), 315–333.

Mac Éinrí, P. (2007). The challenge of migrant integration in Ireland. *Evidence from New Countries of Immigration, 9*(1), 75–90.

Markus, A. (2011). Attitudes to multiculturalism and cultural diversity. In M. Clyne & J. Jupp (Eds.), *Multiculturalism and integration: A harmonious relationship*. Canberra: Australian National University Press.

Markus, A. (2013). *Mapping social cohesion 2012: The Scanlon foundation survey*. Retrieved from http://www.arts.monash.edu.au/mapping-population/social-cohesion-report.php.

Mason, R. (2010). Australian multiculturalism: Revisiting Australia's political heritage and the migrant presence. *History Compass, 8*, 817–827.

McHugh, M. (2014). *Immigrant civic integration and service access initiatives. Access initiative: City sized solution for city-sized needs*. Washington, DC: Migration Policy Institute.

Meer, N., & Modood, T. (2012). For "Jewish" read "Muslim"? Islamophobia as a form of racialisation of ethno religious groups in Britain today. *Islamophobia Studies Journal, 1*(1), 36–55.

Mitchell, M. C. (2013). *Religion, identity and politics in Northern Ireland: Boundaries of belonging and belief*. Abingdon, UK: Routledge.

Modood, T. (2013). Post-immigration 'difference' and integration. *Meritum, revista de Direito da Universidade FUMEC, 8*(1), 389–415.

Roggeband, C., & Vliegenthart, R. (2007). Divergent framing: The public debate on migration in the Dutch parliament and media, 1995–2004. *West European Politics, 30*(3), 524–548.

Sohrabi, H., & Farquharson, K. (2015). Social integration of Australian Muslims: A dramaturgical perspective. *Journal of Sociology, 52*(2). doi:1440783314562415.

Tolsma, J., Lubbers, M., & Gijsberts, M. (2012). Education and cultural integration among ethnic minorities and natives in the Netherlands: A test of the integration paradox. *Journal of Ethnic and Migration Studies, 38*(5), 793–813.

Van der Noll, J. (2014). Religious toleration of Muslims in the German public sphere. *International Journal of Intercultural Relations, 38,* 60–74.

Wets, J. (2006). The Turkish community in Austria and Belgium: The challenge of integration. *Turkish Studies, 7*(1), 85–100.

Wiesbrock, A. (2011). The integration of immigrants in Sweden: A model for the European union? *International Migration, 49*(4), 48–66.

Zimmermann, L., Gataullina, L., Constant, A., & Zimmermann, K. F. (2008). Human capital and ethnic self-identification of immigrants. *Economics Letters, 98*(3), 235–239.

8

Conclusion

Australia's migration programme is much more inclusive today than in previous times, and migrants are sourced from different parts of the globe. The ever-present diversity of the population is evidence that Australia has sourced its migrants from many different countries and continents. While not facing the discriminatory migration system of the White Australia era, a challenging state of affairs which contemporary Muslim immigrants encounter is the wider society's perception of their lack of integration. The author set out to explore how Muslims in Australia conceptualise the term *integration* and has identified that Muslims' conceptualisation of integration is part of the various interpretations of integration which exist amongst different actors and stakeholders. These stakeholders include members of the wider society and the media. The wider society's perception of Muslim immigrant integration is characterised as being problematic (Celermajer, 2007; Poynting, 2006; Saeed, 2003; Samani, 2007), but the general literature of immigrant integration fails to provide a universal definition of integration. The study of how Muslims in Australia conceptualise integration is appropriate, as a lack of understanding of the meanings of the concept may potentially lead to a complete breakdown in the ability of migrants to integrate.

© The Author(s) 2018   **149**
A. Hersi, *Conceptualisation of Integration*, Palgrave Politics of Identity
and Citizenship Series, https://doi.org/10.1007/978-3-319-91235-6_8

This research stresses the importance of immigrant integration, specifically in reference to the possibility that disintegration or lack of integration of immigrants may cause disturbances in the societal order (Husted, Heinesen, & Andersen, 2009).

The main empirical findings of the study are chapter specific and are supported by discussions of existing literature about the subject of immigrant integration. The examination of this complex subject requires in-depth analysis of how integration is framed by all of its actors. A thorough review of immigrant integration literature uncovered the existence of clashing, and sometimes conflicting, frames of integration. This necessitated the creative use and application of two methods of inquiry. In the first study, focus group discussions were conducted and participants provided their responses to what the concept of integration meant to them. These initial focus group discussions were then followed with one-on-one in-depth interviews to deepen and enhance the study's thoroughness. The latter were analysed using the cognitive psychology theory of schemata. This second phase of data collection allowed the author to more deeply probe the study participants' ideas to gain greater insight into their understandings of integration.

Muslim conceptualisations of integration and, in particular, what practices and behaviours Muslims attach to the meaning of integration, have been investigated in this study. In this investigation, an understanding of how integration is defined in the broader scholarly literature was crucial. This understanding may indicate the extent to which Muslims subscribe to similar, or different and perhaps contradictory, definitions of integration by other important stakeholders, such as the media, academia and composers of public policy documents. The specific aim of the study was to address the question of what activities, behaviours, characteristics and values Muslim people attach to the meaning of integration. For instance, is it to assimilate into the host society? Is it to participate in the host society's economic, social and political fabric, or is it simply to be naturalised and obtain a certificate of citizenship? The importance of understanding the extent to which Muslims define integration in a singular or pluralist form and/or in a cosmopolitan or universalistic fashion is also recognised. The following is a summary of how Muslim participants responded to the three research questions.

The findings of this study demonstrate that Muslims' conceptualisation of integration is part and parcel of an existing clash of integration frames in the debates about immigrant integration. The study finds that Muslims' conceptualisations of integration are part of the general confusion about meanings of integration, and a number of the different interpretations of the meanings of integration offered by Muslims are revealed. Some of these conceptualisations are consistent with interpretations found in the scholarly literature, but in some cases, participants in the study have developed interpretations of what integration means. It is also clear that on occasions those interpretations were in line with meanings stated in the broader literature about immigrant integration. Australian Muslims generally provide meanings of integration that are in line with general definitions of integration available in the academic literature and public policy documents. Nevertheless, they do so with the addition of a strong perception of their own cultural and religious traditions.

The findings also demonstrate the openness and acceptance of Muslim participants towards certain frames of integration, and their reluctance and resistance to other frames of integration. It is demonstrated that Muslims' conceptualisation of integration includes the proposition that they resist assimilation, especially in the sphere of cultural and religious assimilation. For example, the first study in this book focused on what integration means to the Muslim participants. The central research aim of this study was to identify what determinants and/or detractors of integration Muslim participants provide in their responses. Muslim participants tended to focus on the participatory meanings of integration. They provided meanings, such as participation, belonging and acceptance as being determinants of integration, whereas discrimination, isolation and lack of English language are understood to be detractors.

Muslims' definitions of integration are quite often pluralistic and universalistic, and this is revealed in this study. In some cases, Muslim participants deliberately shifted their conceptualisation of integration from one context to another. For example, they contest media discourse that narrowly defines integration in the context of terrorism, extremism and radicalisation which repurposes the meaning of this concept from one context to another. In other situations, Muslim participants broaden the application of the definition of integration and concur with the academic literature which stretches the concept of integration to a universalistic meaning. This makes the concept of integration a subjective term that eludes consensus. With no clear parameters or objective measures of integration, both the host society that receives immigrants and the immigrant groups themselves will doubtless remain confused.

The following two competing and conflicting paradigms in the debates about the meanings of integration arguably influence the meanings of integration adopted by Muslims. The first is the introduction of a new concept of civic integration, which is formulated to reaffirm and preserve the dominant Western society's culture and values. The second paradigm is the emergence of a resurgent Islam that is suspicious of Western powers, perhaps due to a history of colonisation. It is against these two paradigms that the meanings of integration are redefined. For example, civic integration is an example of how dominant Christian communities in Europe, North America and Australia are redefining integration, but at the same time, Muslim communities in Europe perceive that their religion is constantly under attack, and assert that a rise in Islamophobia is a threat to their freedom of religion. The majority Christian communities also perceive Islam as being an invasion of their values.

The paradigm of enforcing immigrant integration through a notion of cultural supremacy is directly at odds with resurgent Islam, where individual Muslims might identify with a community of faith making the nation-state irrelevant in their lives. Both of the above positions are dangerous and risk undermining social cohesion. The author takes the view that commitment to religious practice and the pursuit of spiritual perfection are not to be interpreted to mean an unwillingness to integrate. On the other hand, the notion that Muslims in Australia must show a willingness to fully participate in the social and economic life of the nation and show their loyalty and allegiance to Australia is strong and uncompromised. However, certain contemporary realities pose challenges to the realisation of this middle ground position.

For instance, the debates about immigrant integration are heavily influenced by international events, creating fear and insecurity between Muslims and members of the wider society. This is evident in the tone of their conversations, including the emergence of conservative discourse that warns against "the Islamisation" of Europe (Pilbeam, 2011). This leads to the belief that the integration debate therefore in part suffers from a perceived clash of civilizations. It is specifically the political aspect of Islam that is perceived to be a threat by some in the wider Australian society (Bergin & Townsend, 2007). In response to this perceived threat, a divisive and sometimes harsh political rhetoric directed at Muslims and Muslim leaders have emerged. The findings support those of Jakubowicz (2007), who argues that ill-advised political decisions that are not practical and engaging, and marginal groups gaining leverage in Muslim society, both risk undermining the potential for immigrant integration in Australia.

Muslims in Australia conceptualised the term *integration* more often in its positive aspects than its negative ones. In general, Muslims' conceptualisations of integration appear to have been constructed against a background of their struggle for inclusion. Their responses to the research questions showed that they used significantly more positive interpretations than negative ones. For example, feelings of participation, belonging, loyalty and embracing diversity were all declared as meaning that they felt they were integrated. It is clear from the study that their cognition of integration is not far from the meanings that the concept is assigned in the available academic discourse (Skrbiš, Baldassar, & Poynting, 2007). With the exception of their faith influencing their interpretations of integration, Muslims have stated their belief that a host of universal standards of acceptance, sense of belonging and loyalty to the host society mean integration.

In conclusion, it is apparent that *integration* is a slippery term and one that can mean different things to different individuals, groups and societies. If it is not understood in its contextual framework, the concept can be misleading. Based on an extensive literature review encompassing analysis of multiple actors' perceptions of integration, and as informed by the empirical findings on Muslims' conceptions of integration, the following definition of integration is proposed: *Integration* is an ideologically loaded term that sits at the interface of the settlement of immigrants in a rapidly changing international order. This interface has behavioural, emotional, functional, cultural and political dimensions. These, then produce particular forms of performance of self: for a believing Muslim, it is about membership in a secular Western nation without fundamental compromise to their faith; for the state it is seeking a contributing and obedient citizen; for the host community, it is accommodating newcomers without significant changes to their cultural and historical environment; and for the media it is a normalised social subject. Muslims' meanings of integration may be better understood in the context of the competing interests between these actors.

The dynamics of immigrant integration are social processes, and the above definition of integration obviously presents another difficulty. In Muslims' conceptualisation of integration, the findings reveal a combination of aspirations (functional integration), resistance (faith limitations) and compromise (a middle way). This compromise is generally to integrate in the public sphere but remain separated in the private sphere. This apparent self-selection is something that perhaps the wider society would disendorse. This may then lead to suspicions about the newcomers and tensions may emerge between the new immigrants and members of the host society. Australian Muslims described prejudicial treatment and discrimination as key barriers to their integration into Australia society.

The findings in this book concur with those of Hamid (2011), who confirms the link between integration and discrimination by referring to many young Muslims in the United Kingdom who became fully integrated when they overcame challenges of structural inequality and high levels of deprivation, disadvantage and discrimination. Hamid (2011) further stresses that these inequalities may inhibit opportunities for young British Muslims, thus leading to social exclusion. In this case, the theories of prejudice and group contact are useful and informative. In explaining the Muslim threat narrative in the literature, previous research findings suggest that majority community members who strongly perceive immigrant minorities as being threatening may have fewer friends who come from minority groups (Van Acker, Phalet, Deleersnyder, & Mesquita, 2014).

Overall, the meanings Muslims use in interpreting the concept of integration and their choice of frames and schemas about integration are important. Muslims' understandings of integration are similar to various other interpretations found in the wider scholarly literature about integration. The findings suggest that Muslims have preformed meanings of integration that are produced by their lived experiences as members of the wider society. The term *integration* is viewed differently and its meaning is seen by some of the participants as being ubiquitous and pejorative.

However, the book argues that the meanings Muslims and other immigrant groups attach to the concept of integration will not be static and may be susceptible to continual modifications and adjustment, mainly dictated by individual, group, local and international circumstances.

Implications

Although this study is of a modest scale and deals only with Muslims' understandings of integration, it exposes some valuable dimensions of the public debates on integration. Specifically, it was found that Muslims tend to understand integration in socio-economic terms rather than cultural ones. That is, their emphasis is on dimensions of everyday life, such as employment, education, contributing to society and learning the English language. The author finds the differences between this understanding of integration and understandings of integration that have been adopted by other important actors in the public debate about integration, in particular the media, to be remarkable.

In conclusion, it is clear that variations of how important social actors of public debate define integration may have implications for the building of an inclusive and cohesive society. In this study, the author has sought to understand how Muslims in Australia conceptualise the concept of integration. The findings reveal what practices Muslims attached to the meanings of integration and the cognitive schemes they use in their interpretations of these meanings. This section focuses on the study's implications and suggests possible directions for future research. The implications of this study may be multifaceted and may include the following:

One practical implication is that integration stakeholders may have a better and more informed understanding of how Muslims conceptualise integration. Stemming from the very fact that meanings of integration vary depending on who is defining the concept, uncovering Muslims' conceptualisation of integration may lead to adjustment on how Muslims and members of the wider society negotiate in defining integration in a manner that is acceptable to all its constituent stakeholders. A meaning of integration negotiated between stakeholders is believed to produce less prejudiced public discussions of the concept. This may, in turn, lead to increased social harmony and cohesion.

Amongst other possible implications that merit consideration is that the study's findings may inform policymakers and other interested parties about the possibility that certain frames, schemas and meaning of integration employed by individuals and groups may have positive or negative effects on social inclusion and exclusion. For instance, meanings which advance a pluralist understanding of integration will arguably have inclusivity effects, whereas assimilationist meanings of integration will have the opposite effect. In other words, this study's findings may similarly inform policy makers about how social cohesion and social inclusion should not be detached from the conceptualisation of what integration means.

Another important implication is the fact that frames of problematic community integration and threat narratives which denigrate Muslims provide little or no chance for integration. At this juncture of the national debate about the Muslim community in Australia, this study becomes critical. In a time of heightened terrorism alert, the Australian community needs to be cohesive and trusting. Governments, in particular, have a greater responsibility to develop policies and programmes which help Muslims to integrate and not feel isolated.

The view is adopted here that there is a great deal of risk in the politicisation of the concept of integration, as this dilutes the true meaning of integration. The author asserts that meanings of integration advanced by certain politicians, and the political rhetoric of Muslim integration or its lack, may be counterproductive. Evidence shows that politicisation of integration risks altering the interplay between policy setting and knowledge production, thus creating further confusion about how integration is conceptualised (Entzinger & Scholten, 2015).

Recommendations

The ubiquitous challenges presented by the current debates about immigrant integration, which hardly agree on a common definition of integration are noted. This book provides a suite of recommendations that may help immigrant groups, members of host societies and governments to have a more realistic expectation of each other's conceptualisation of integration. It is expected that these recommendations may help to overcome the dilemmas created by the multiplicity of integration frames. The following are the key recommendations put forward by this study:

This study stresses the importance of conceptualising integration as a two-way street, meaning new immigrants and their receiving societies must be willing to go through a process of adaptation and adjustment. It also notes that the adaptation skills of immigrants vary as much as the reception immigrants receive, which may be warmer from one community to another. This inter-reliance on the mutual integration of the immigrant and the newcomer is arguably missed in contemporary migrant integration literature. The notion that immigrants must integrate with the host society ignores the adjustments that host society members need to make, and this may increase the confusion and misunderstandings about the meanings of integration.

The adaptation of a more conciliatory tone in the debates about immigrant integration is recommended, and all participants in the debate are called on to acknowledge the fact that there are different conceptualisations of integration dictated by different circumstances and situations (see Dukes & Musterd, 2012). An approach that builds bridges between these competing and sometimes contradictory frames of integration is called for (Scholten & Van Nispen, 2008). For this to occur, it is necessary to understand the multiplicity of integration frames existing in debates about integration. It is the author's assessment that Muslims' conceptualisations of integration that focus on loyalty, flexibility, respect and participation concur with calls for the building of bridges between competing frames of integration. These bridges are now being constructed in certain spheres of the debates about immigrant integration. For example, the International Organisation for Migration (IOM), which is the peak intergovernmental organisation in matters relating to international migration, adopts a compromising meaning of integration as follows: "While the term 'integration' can be understood differently depending on the country and context, it is generally defined as the process of mutual adaptation between host society and immigrant" (International Organisation for Migration, 2014, n.p.).

Also, recommended by this study is the adoption of a more generalised conceptualisation of integration, especially one that considerably accepts and accommodates differences in cultural, religious and language differences and emphasises reciprocated mutual integration between immigrant groups and newcomers. It is what Wilkinson (2013) calls for—the development and testing of a generalisable frame of integration, especially one that reconciles differences of cultural practices, religion and language differences. In essence, the author argues that the concept of integration is ambiguous and is often poorly defined by its stakeholders, and that the concept should be context-based and dependent on levels of reception by members of the host society and other environmental factors, in order to integrate new immigrants. It should also factor in the levels of shared cultural and historical features between the host society members and the new immigrants. This allows policymakers to realistically raise the expectations of integration stakeholders.

Another important recommendation is the abandonment of integration frames that are monocultural rather than multicultural. The departure from these types of integration conceptualisations implies that there is an appreciation that a sense of obligation and respect for a core set of values that bind migrants will go further than insisting that new arrivals integrate into a dominant society's culture. A multicultural frame can also be important in giving both immigrants and members of host communities a common purpose. The particular meanings and frames of integration we adopt may have the potential to strengthen and maintain our social cohesion, but can equally create disharmony between societies (Dukes & Musterd, 2012). Today, in this era of thriving global terrorist networks, integration is essential for all stakeholders, not only as a way of providing economic and cultural benefits but also for ensuring the security and stability of societies as a whole (International Organisation for Migration, 2014).

The author also recommends that a holistic integration approach needs to be employed, rather than using piecemeal and selective integration frames. In particular, as Alexander (2013) suggests, a shift is required from a focus on the functional elements of integration, such as employment, education and wealth, to a cultural sociological approach which emphasises meanings and emotions. In countries like the Netherlands, Dukes and Musterd (2012) assert that social cohesion policy would benefit from framing the integration debate differently. Similarly, Carrera (2006) argues that Europe a Union states need to readjust the conceptualisation of their perceived national identity and values, from one that emphasises a mythical national unity to one that is heterogeneous, diverse and multicultural (Carrera, 2006, p. 9).

Research Limitations

The ever-increasing levels of the global movement of people demand the developments of policies and programmes that encourage social inclusion and social cohesion. This book is especially timely and addresses an important question in the field of international migration, particularly the subject of immigrant integration. Thus far, this study has produced empirical knowledge of how Muslims in the region of South East Queensland conceptualise the concept of integration. However, this research is not conducted without certain limitations or shortcomings. Below are some of the limitations and suggested areas of further study in this important field in international migration.

The first limitation is considerations concerning sample size and selection. This book has focused on only Muslim community groups in the South East Queensland region, in Australia. This means that strictly speaking, the conclusions can only be drawn about Muslims in this region. While the findings may imply that other immigrant groups may conceptualise integration differently to the official definitions, conclusions drawn from this research cannot be transferred to other non-Muslim immigrant groups in Australia. This is one area in which the author readily accepts that the work presented can be advanced and strengthened. For example, examining whether other immigrant groups would conceptualise integration similarly or differently to Muslim immigrant groups may confirm or refute the notion that immigrant groups understand integration in the same way.

Additionally, a review of the wider society's conceptualisation of integration would add to the debate and shed light on what factors cause one group to emphasise aspects of integration over another, and how individuals select those preformed perceptions of integration. The absence of this basic research is a limitation to this study, as comparisons between how different groups conceptualise integration cannot be made. While this limitation is worthy of acknowledgement, this book advances the debates about immigrant integration and adds to it a new and untapped research angle that potentially enhances greater understanding of this subject. It concludes that the concept of integration suffers from definitional vagueness and oversimplification.

Integration processes occur in complex social, political and economic environments and require future researchers of the subject to produce more grounded empirical studies which would enhance theoretical arguments and create a universal understanding of integration. The findings of this study may also inspire important questions that may lead to future research in areas and aspects, which this study deemed to be beyond its scope. Further research could address several issues which have emerged from this study. First, because the sample size of this study was relatively small, a new study could target a much wider population size. Second, it would be important to determine whether respondents from a national study share the same conceptions of integration as those reported in this study. Third, it would be important to conduct further studies that examine how Muslim immigrant groups in comparable countries have similar or different conceptions of integration.

Despite the above-stated research limitations, the findings of this book contribute significantly to the growing body of immigrant incorporation literature. This study complements and sometimes contrasts previous research on the subject of immigrant integration. It confirms how culturally, linguistically and religiously diverse groups of people may conceptualise terms such as integration differently to the understandings previously stated in the scholarly literature.

References

Alexander, J. C. (2013). Struggling over the mode of incorporation: Backlash against multiculturalism in Europe. *Ethnic and Racial Studies, 36*(4), 531–556.

Bergin, A., & Townsend, J. (2007). *Responding to radical Islamist ideology: The case of Hizb ut-Tahrir in Australia*. Barton, ACT, Australia: Australian Strategic Policy Institute.

Carrera, S. (2006, March 1). *A comparison of integration programmes in the EU: Trends and weaknesses*. CEPS Challenge Papers No. 1.

Celermajer, D. (2007). If Islam is our other, who are 'we'? *Australian Journal of Social Issues, 42*(1), 103–122.

Dukes, T., & Musterd, S. (2012). Towards social cohesion: Bridging national integration rhetoric and local practice: The case of the Netherlands. *Urban Studies, 49*(9), 1981–1997.

Entzinger, H., & Scholten, P. (2015). The interplay of knowledge production and policymaking: A comparative analysis of research and policymaking on migrant integration in Germany and the Netherlands. *Journal of Comparative Policy Analysis: Research and Practice, 17*(1), 60–74.

Hamid, S. (2011). British Muslim young people: Facts, features and religious trends. *Religion, State and Society, 39*(2–3), 247–261.

Husted, L., Heinesen, E., & Andersen, S. H. (2009). Labour market integration of immigrants: Estimating local authority effects. *Journal of Population Economics, 22*(4), 909–939.

International Organisation for Migration. (2014). *Compendium of migrant integration policies and practices*. Retrieved October 22, 2014, from www.iom.int.

Jakubowicz, A. (2007). Anglo-multiculturalism: Contradictions in the politics of cultural diversity as risk. *International Journal of Media & Cultural Politics, 2*(3), 249–266.

Pilbeam, B. (2011). Eurabian nightmares: American conservative discourses and the Islamisation of Europe. *Journal of Transatlantic Studies, 9*(2), 151–171.

Poynting, S. (2006). What caused the Cronulla riots? *Race and Class, 48*, 85–91.

Saeed, A. (2003). *Islam in Australia*. Crows Nest, NSW: Allen & Unwin.

Samani, S. (2007). Rhetoric and realities of multiculturalism: The perpetuation of negative constructions of Muslims in Australia. *International Journal of Diversity, 7*(2), 113–119.

Scholten, P. W., & Van Nispen, F. K. (2008). Building bridges across frames? *Journal of Public Policy, 28*(02), 181–205.

Skrbiš, Z., Baldassar, L., & Poynting, S. (2007). Introduction–negotiating belonging: Migration and generations. *Journal of Intercultural Studies, 28*(3), 261–269.

Van Acker, K., Phalet, K., Deleersnyder, J., & Mesquita, B. (2014). Do "they" threaten "us" or do "we" disrespect "them": Majority perceptions of inter-group relations and everyday contacts with immigrant minorities. *Group Processes & Intergroup Relations, 17*(5), 617–628.

Wilkinson, L. (2013). Introduction: Developing and testing a generalizable model of immigrant integration. *Canadian Ethnic Studies, 45*(3), 1–7.

Bibliography

Abbas, T. (2007). Muslim minorities in Britain: Integration, multiculturalism and radicalism in the post 7/7 period. *Journal of International Studies, 28*(3), 287–300.

Abdalla, M. (2012). Sacred law in secular land: To what extent should Sharia law be followed in Australia? *The Griffith Law Review, 21*(3), 657–679.

Abid, L. J. (2006). Muslims in Austria: Integration through participation in Austrian society. *Journal of Muslim Minority Affairs, 26*(2), 263–278.

Adamuti-Trache, M., & Sweet, R. (2010). Adult immigrants' participation in Canadian education and training. *Canadian Journal for the Study of Adult Education, 22*(2), 1–26.

Adida, C. L., Laitin, D. D., & Valfort, M. A. (2010). Identifying barriers to Muslim integration in France. *Proceedings of the National Academy of Sciences, 107*(52), 22384–22390.

Ager, A., & Strang, A. (2004). *Indicators of integration*. London: Home Office, Research, Development and Statistics Directorate.

Ager, A., & Strang, A. (2008). Understanding integration: A conceptual framework. *Journal of Refugee Studies, 21*(2), 166–191.

Ajrouch, K. J. (2007). Global contexts and the veil: Muslim integration in the United States and France. *Sociology of Religion, 68*(3), 321–325.

© The Editor(s) (if applicable) and The Author(s) 2018
A. Hersi, *Conceptualisation of Integration*, Palgrave Politics of Identity and Citizenship Series, https://doi.org/10.1007/978-3-319-91235-6

Akbari, A. H., & MacDonald, M. (2014). Immigration policy in Australia, Canada, New Zealand, and the United States: An overview of recent trends. *International Migration Review, 48*(3), 801–822.

Akbarzadeh, S., & Saeed, A. (Eds.). (2001). *Muslim communities in Australia.* Sydney: UNSW Press.

Akresh, I. R., Massey, D. S., & Frank, R. (2014). Beyond English proficiency: Rethinking immigrant integration. *Social Science Research, 45,* 200–210.

Alba, R., Logan, J., Lutz, A., & Stults, B. (2002). Only English by the third generation? Loss and preservation of the mother tongue among the grandchildren of contemporary immigrants. *Demography, 39*(3), 467–484.

Alexander, J. C. (2013). Struggling over the mode of incorporation: Backlash against multiculturalism in Europe. *Ethnic and Racial Studies, 36*(4), 531–556.

Ali, J. A. (2012). *Islamic revivalism: Encounter the modern world (a study of the Tabligh Jama 'at).* New Dehli: Sterling Publishers.

Aly, A. (2007). Australian Muslim responses to the discourse on terrorism in the Australian popular media. *Australian Journal of Social Issues, 42*(1), 27–40.

Andersson, P., & Uthman, A. (2008). Recognition of prior learning as a practice for differential inclusion and exclusion of immigrants in Sweden. *Adult Education Quarterly, 59*(1), 42–60.

Andersson, M. (2012). The debate about multicultural Norway before and after 22 July 2011. *Identities, 19*(4), 418–427.

Arai, M., Karlsson, J., & Lundholm, M. (2011). On fragile grounds: A replication of "are Muslim immigrants different in terms of cultural integration?". *Journal of the European Economic Association, 9*(5), 1002–1011.

Australian Bureau of Statistics. (2011). *Australian Standard Classification of Countries* (SACC). Retrieved from http://www.abs.gov.au/ausstats/abs@.nsf/Lookup/1269.

Australian Housing and Urban Research Institute. (2015). *Addressing recurring or protracted episodes in housing affordability stress 2001–11.* Melbourne: AHURI.

Banting, K., & Kymlicka, W. (2013). Is there really a retreat from multiculturalism policies & quest: New evidence from the multiculturalism policy index. *Comparative European Politics, 11*(5), 577–598.

Beach, C. M., & Worswick, C. (1993). Is there a double-negative effect on the earnings of immigrant women? *Canadian Public Policy/Analyse de Politiques, 6,* 36–53.

Beck, U. (2014). We Do Not Live in an Age of Cosmopolitanism but in an Age of Cosmopolitization: The 'Global Other' is in Our Midst. In U. Beck (Ed.), *Pioneer in Cosmopolitan Sociology and Risk Society* (pp. 169–187). New York: Springer.

Beckford, J., Gale, R., Owen, D., Peach, C., & Weller, P. (2006). *Review of the evidence base on faith communities.* London, UK: Office of the Deputy Prime Minister.

Benhabib, S. (2007). Twilight of sovereignty or the emergence of cosmopolitan norms? Rethinking citizenship in volatile times. *Citizenship Studies, 11*(1), 19–36.

Bergin, A., & Townsend, J. (2007). *Responding to radical Islamist ideology: The case of Hizb ut-Tahrir in Australia.* Barton, ACT, Australia: Australian Strategic Policy Institute.

Bertossi, C., & Duyvendak, J. W. (2012). National models of immigrant integration: The costs for comparative research. *Comparative European Politics, 10*(3), 237–247.

Bevelander, P. (1999). The employment integration of immigrants in Sweden. *Journal of Ethnic and Migration Studies, 25*(3), 445–468.

Bevelander, P. (2000). *Immigrant employment integration and structural change in Sweden, 1970–1995.* Doctoral dissertation, Lund University.

Biddle, N., Khoo, S. E., & Taylor, J. (2015). Indigenous Australia, White Australia, multicultural Australia: The demography of race and ethnicity in Australia. In R. Sáenz, N. Rodriguez, & D. Embrick (Eds.), *The international handbook of the demography of race and ethnicity* (Vol. 4, pp. 599–622). Rotterdam, The Netherlands: Springer.

Bieber, F. (2008). *Minority participation and political parties.* Skopje: Friedrich Ebert Stiftung.

Bisin, A., Verdier, T. H., Pattachini, E., & Zenou, Y. (2008). Are Muslim immigrants different in terms of cultural integration? *Journal of European Economic Association, 6*(2), 445–456.

Bisin, A., Patacchini, E., Verdier, T., & Zenou, Y. (2011). Ethnic identity and labour market outcomes of immigrants in Europe. *Economic Policy, 26*(65), 57–92.

Blanchard, C. M. (2005). *Islam: Sunnis and Shiites.* Washington, DC: Congressional Research Service (Library of Congress).

Black, A. (2008). Accommodating Shariah law in Australia's legal system. *Alternative Law Journal, 33*(4), 214–219.

Black, A., & Abdullah, K. (2011). Good and bad Sharia: Australia's mixed response to Islamic law. *University of New South Wales Law Journal, 34*(1), 383.

Blau, P. M. (1977). *Inequality and heterogeneity: A primitive theory of social structure* (Vol. 7). New York, NY: Free Press.

Bleakley, H., & Chin, A. (2010). Age at arrival, English proficiency, and social assimilation among US immigrants. *American Economic Journal: Applied Economics, 2*(1), 165.

Bloemraad, I. (2006). *Becoming a citizen: Incorporating immigrants and refugees in the United States and Canada.* Berkeley: University of California.

Bloemraad, I. (2012). Understanding "Canadian exceptionalism" in immigration and pluralism policy. In B. Stiftung (Ed.), *Rethinking national identity in the age of migration* (pp. 145–170). Washington, DC: Migration Policy Institute.

Bloemraad, I., Korteweg, A., & Yurdakal, G. (2008). Citizenship and immigration: Multiculturalism, assimilation, and challenges to the nation-state. *Annual Review of Sociology, 34*(1), 153–179.

Bocker, A., & Strik, T. (2011). Language and knowledge tests for permanent residence rights: Help or hindrance for integration. *European Journal of Migration & Law, 13,* 157.

Bodey, M. (2011, September 28). Andrew bolt loses racial vilification court case. *The Australian.* Retrieved April 20, 2016, from http://www.theaustralian.com.au/business/media/andrew-bolt-x-racial-vilification-court-case/story-e6frg996-1226148919092.

Bolt, G., Özüekren, A. S., & Phillips, D. (2010). Linking integration and residential segregation. *Journal of Ethnic and Migration Studies, 36*(2), 169–186.

Bolzendahl, C., & Coffé, H. (2013). Are 'good' citizens 'good' participants? Testing citizenship norms and political participation across 25 nations. *Political Studies, 61*(S1), 45–65.

Boomgaarden, H. G., & Vliegenthart, R. (2007). Explaining the rise of anti-immigrant parties: The role of news media content. *Electoral Studies, 26*(2), 404–417.

Boski, P. (2008). Five meanings of integration in acculturation research. *International Journal of Intercultural Relations, 32*(2), 142–153.

Bouma, G. D. (1994). *Mosques and Muslim settlement in Australia.* Canberra: Australian Government.

Bouma, G., Cahill, D., Dellal, H., & Zwartz, A. (2011). *Freedom of religion and belief in 21st century Australia.* Canberra: Australian Human Rights Commission.

Bowskill, M., Lyons, E., & Coyle, A. (2007). The rhetoric of acculturation: When integration means assimilation. *British Journal of Social Psychology, 46*(4), 793–813.

Bovenkerk, F., Miles, R., & Verbunt, G. (1990). Racism, migration and the state in Western Europe: A case for comparative analysis. *International Sociology, 5*(4), 475–490.

Brasted, H. V., & Khan, A. (2012). Islam and the 'clash of civilizations'? An historical perspective. In S. Akbarzadeh (Ed.), *Routledge handbook of political Islam* (pp. 273–301). Abingdon: Routledge.

Brennan, F. (2015). High court fails high seas detainees. *Eureka Street, 25*(2), 46.

Brubaker, R., Loveman, M., & Stamatov, P. (2004). Ethnicity as cognition. *Theory and Society, 33*(1), 31–64.

Campese, G. (2012). The irruption of migrants: Theology of migration in the 21st century. *Theological Studies, 73*(1), 3–32.

Campomori, F., & Caponio, T. (2013). Competing frames of immigrant integration in the EU: Geographies of social inclusion in Italian regions. *Policy Studies, 34*(2), 162–179.

Canovan, M. (2000). Patriotism is not enough. *British Journal of Political Science, 30*(03), 413–432.

Carley, K. (1989). The value of cognitive foundations for dynamic social theory. *Journal of Mathematical Sociology, 14*(2–3), 171–208.

Carrera, S. (2006, March 1). *A comparison of integration programmes in the EU: Trends and weaknesses.* CEPS Challenge Papers No. 1.

Casanova, J. (2006). Religion, European secular identities, and European integration. In T. Byrnes & P. Katzenstein (Eds.), *Religion in an expanding Europe* (pp. 65–92). Cambridge, UK: Cambridge University Press.

Castles, S. (1992). The Australian model of immigration and multiculturalism: Is it applicable to Europe? *International Migration Review, 26*(2), 549–567.

Castles, S. (1999). *Challenges to national identity and citizenship: A comparative study of immigration and society in Germany, France and Australia.* Wollongong, NSW: University of Wollongong.

Castles, S. (2007). Twenty-first-century migration as a challenge to sociology. *Journal of Ethnic and Migration Studies, 33*(3), 351–371.

Celermajer, D. (2007). If Islam is our other, who are 'we'? *Australian Journal of Social Issues, 42*(1), 103–122.

Celermajer, D., Yasmeen, S., & Saeed, A. (2007). Introduction special edition: Australian Muslims and secularism. *Australian Journal of Social Issues, 42*(1), 1–5.

Cerulo, K. A. (2002). *Culture in mind: Toward sociology of culture and cognition.* New York, NY: Routledge.

Cerulo, K. A. (2010). Mining the intersections of cognitive sociology and neuroscience. *Poetics, 38*(2), 115–132.

Cesari, J. (2007). Muslim identities in Europe: The snare of exceptionalism. In A. Al-Azmeh & E. Fokas (Eds.), *Islam in Europe: Diversity, identity and influence* (pp. 49–67). Cambridge, UK: Cambridge University Press.

Chiswick, B. R., Lee, Y. L., & Miller, P. W. (2004). Immigrants' language skills: The Australian experience in a longitudinal survey. *International Migration Review, 38*(2), 611–654.

Cicourel, A. V. (1973). *Cognitive sociology.* New York, NY: Free Press.

Cleland, B. (2002). *Muslims in Australia: A brief history.* Melbourne: Islamic Council of Victoria.

Colic-Peisker, V. (2011). A new era in Australian multiculturalism? From working-class "ethnics" to a "multicultural middle-class". *International Migration Review, 45*(3), 562–587.

Colic-Peisker, V., & Farquharson, K. (2011). A new era in Australian multiculturalism? The need for critical interrogation. *Journal of Intercultural Studies, 32*(6), 579–586.

Collins, J. (2013). Multiculturalism and immigrant integration in Australia. *Canadian Ethnic Studies, 45*(3), 133–149.

Commission on Multi-Ethnic Britain (CMEB). (2000). *The future of multi-ethnic Britain: Report of the commission the future of multi-ethnic Britain.* London, UK: Runnymede Trust.

Constant, A. F., Roberts, R., & Zimmermann, K. F. (2009). Ethnic identity and immigrant homeownership. *Urban Studies, 46*(9), 1879–1898.

Convy, P., & Monsour, A. (2008). *Lebanese settlement in New South Wales.* Retrieved from http://www.migrationheritage.nsw.gov.au/mhc-reports/ThematicHistoryOfLebaneseNSW.pdf.

Cox, D. R. (1983). Religion and the welfare of immigrants. *Australian Social Work, 36*(1), 3–10.

Crock, M., & Ghezelbash, D. (2010). Do loose lips bring ships—The role of policy, politics and human rights in managing unauthorised boat arrivals. *Griffith Law Review, 19,* 238.

Crul, M., & Schneider, J. (2010). Comparative integration context theory: Participation and belonging in new diverse European cities. *Ethnic and Racial Studies, 33*(7), 1249–1268.

Cruz, G. T. (2008). Between identity and security: Theological implications of migration in the context of globalization. *Theological studies, 69*(2), 357–375.

Das, E., Bushman, B. J., Bezemer, M. D., Kerkhof, P., & Vermeulen, I. E. (2009). How terrorism news reports increase prejudice against outgroups: A terror management account. *Journal of Experimental Social Psychology, 45*(3), 453–459.

Deen, H. (2011). *Ali Abdul v. the king: Muslim stories from the dark days of White Australia*. Crawley, WA: UWA Publishing.

Department of Home Affairs (DHA). (2018). *Welcome to the department of home affairs*. Retrieved from https://www.homeaffairs.gov.au/.

Department of Immigration and Citizenship (DIAC). (2013). *Key facts about immigration*. Retrieved from http://www.immi.gov.au/media/factsheets/02key.htm.

Department of Immigration and Border Protection. (2014). *Operation sovereign borders*. Retrieved from https://www.border.gov.au/about/operation-sovereign-borders.

Department of Immigration and Citizenship. (2009). *The Australian journey: Muslim communities*. Report Retrieved from https://www.dss.gov.au/sites/default/files/documents/01_2014/australian-journey-muslim-communities.pdf.

Department of Industry. (2014). *Adult migrant English program*. Retrieved from http://www.industry.gov.au/skills/AssistanceForIndividuals/AdultMigrantEnglishProgram/Pages/default.aspx.

De Leeuw, M., & Van Wichelen, S. (2012). Civilizing migrants: Integration, culture and citizenship. *European Journal of Cultural Studies, 15*(2), 195–210.

Diehl, C., Koenig, M., & Ruckdeschel, K. (2009). Religiosity and gender equality: Comparing natives and Muslim migrants in Germany. *Ethnic and Racial Studies, 32*(2), 278–301.

DiMaggio, P. (1997). Culture and cognition. *Annual Review of Sociology, 23*(1), 263–287.

DiMaggio, P., & Markus, H. R. (2010). Culture and social psychology converging perspectives. *Social Psychology Quarterly, 73*(4), 347–352.

Doomernik, J. M. J., & Knippenberg, H. (2003). *Migration and immigrants: Between policy and reality: A volume in honor of Hans van Amersfoort*. Amsterdam: Aksant.

Dukes, T., & Musterd, S. (2012). Towards social cohesion: Bridging national integration rhetoric and local practice: The case of the Netherlands. *Urban Studies, 49*(9), 1981–1997.

Dunn, K. M. (2005). Repetitive and troubling discourses of nationalism in the local politics of mosque development in Sydney, Australia. *Environment and Planning D: Society and Space, 23*(1), 29–50.

Dunn, K. M. (2009). Public attitudes towards hijab-wearing in Australia. In T. Dreher & C. Ho (Eds.), *Beyond the hijab debates: New conversations on gender, race and religion* (pp. 31–51). Cambridge, UK: Cambridge Scholars Publishing.

Dunn, K. M., Forrest, J., Burnley, I., & McDonald, A. (2004). Constructing racism in Australia. *Australian Journal of Social Issues, 39*(4), 409–430.

Dunn, K., Forrest, J., Ip, D., Babacan, H., Paradise, Y., & Pederson, A. (2008). Challenging racism: The anti-racism research project, state-level comparison. In *Proceedings of 4Rs Conference: Rights, Reconciliation, Respect, Responsibility* 30 September–3 October. Sydney, NSW: University of Technology. Retrieved fromhttp://www.uws.edu.au/__data/assets/pdf_file/0020/42185/State_level_comparison_for_4Rs_conference.pdf.

Dunn, K. M., Klocker, N., & Salabay, T. (2007). Contemporary racism and Islamophobia in Australia racializing religion. *Ethnicities, 7*(4), 564–589.

Durey, A., Thompson, S. C., & Wood, M. (2012). Time to bring down the twin towers in poor aboriginal hospital care: Addressing institutional racism and misunderstandings in communication. *Internal Medicine Journal, 42*(1), 17–22.

Eickelman, D. F., & Piscatori, J. (Eds.). (1990). *Muslim travelers, migration, and the religious imagination* (pp. 3–28). Berkley: University of California Press.

Elmadmad, K. (2008). Asylum in Islam and in modern refugee law. *Refugee Survey Quarterly, 27*(2), 51–63.

Entzinger, H. (2006). Changing the rules while the game is on: From multiculturalism to assimilation in the Netherlands. In Y. M. Bodemann & G. Yurdakul (Eds.), *Migration, citizenship, ethnos: Incorporation regimes in Germany, Western Europe and North America* (pp. 121–144). New York, NY: Palgrave Macmillan.

Entzinger, H. (2014). The growing gap between facts and discourse on immigrant integration in the Netherlands. *Identities, 21*(6), 693–707.

Entzinger, H. B., & Biezeveld, R. L. (2003). *Benchmarking in immigrant integration. A report by the European Research Centre on Migration and Ethnic Relations* (ERCOMER, pp. 1–50). Rotterdam, The Netherlands: Erasmus University Rotterdam.

Entzinger, H., & Scholten, P. (2015). The interplay of knowledge production and policymaking: A comparative analysis of research and policymaking on migrant integration in Germany and the Netherlands. *Journal of Comparative Policy Analysis: Research and Practice, 17*(1), 60–74.

Ercan, S. A. (2015). Creating and sustaining evidence for "failed multiculturalism" the case of "honor killing" in Germany. *American Behavioral Scientist, 59*(6), 658–678.

Esposito, J. L. (2014). 2013 AAR presidential address: Islam in the public square. *Journal of the American Academy of Religion, 82*(2), 291–306.

Farouque, F., Petrie, A., & Miletic, D. (2007). Minister cuts African refugee intake. *The Age*. Retrieved from http://www.theage.com.au/articles/2007/10/01/1191091031242.html.

Foner, N., & Alba, R. (2008). Immigrant religion in the US and Western Europe: Bridge or barrier to inclusion? *International Migration Review, 42*(2), 360–392.

Forrest, J., Johnston, R., & Poulsen, M. (2014). Ethnic capital and assimilation to the great Australian (homeownership) dream: The early housing experience of Australia's skilled immigrants. *Australian Geographer, 45*(2), 109–129.

Fozdar, F. (2012). Social cohesion and skilled Muslim refugees in Australia employment, social capital and discrimination. *Journal of Sociology, 48*(2), 167–186.

Freedman, J. (2004). Secularism as a barrier to integration? The French Dilemma. *International Migration, 42*(3), 5–27.

Frey, B. S. (2003). Flexible citizenship for a global society. *Politics, Philosophy & Economics, 2*(1), 93–114.

Furtado, D., & Theodoropoulos, N. (2009). *Intermarriage and immigrant employment: The role of networks*. (Discussion Paper Series 06/09). London, UK: Centre for Research and Analysis of Migration.

Ganter, R. (2012). Remembering Muslim histories of Australia. *The La Trobe Journal, 89*, 48–62.

Garbutt, R. (2009). Social inclusion and local practices of belonging. *Cosmopolitan Civil Societies: An Interdisciplinary Journal, 1*(3), 84–108.

Gardner, R., Karakaşoğlus, Y., & Luchtenberg, S. (2008). Islamophobia in the media: A response from multicultural education 1. *Intercultural Education, 19*(2), 119–136.

Goodman, S. W. (2010). Integration requirements for integration's sake? Identifying, categorising and comparing civic integration. *Journal of Ethnic and Migration Studies, 36*(5), 753–772.

Guo, S. (2009). Difference, deficiency, and devaluation: Tracing the roots of non-recognition of foreign credentials for immigrant professionals in Canada. *Canadian Journal for the Study of Adult Education, 22*(1), 37–52.

Hagan, J. (2006). Negotiating social membership in the contemporary world. *Social Forces, 85*(2), 631–642.

Hamel, C. E. (2002). Muslim diaspora in Western Europe: The Islamic headscarf (hijab), the media and Muslim's integration in France. *Citizenship Studies, 6*(3), 293–308.

Hamid, S. (2011). British Muslim young people: Facts, features and religious trends. *Religion, State and Society, 39*(2–3), 247–261.

Harles, J. C. (1997). Integration before assimilation: Immigration, multiculturalism and the Canadian polity. *Canadian Journal of Political Science, 30*(4), 711–736.

Harrison, D. S. (1984). The impact of immigration on a depressed labour market: The South Australian experience. *Economic Record, 60*(1), 57–67.

Hassan, R. (2006). Globalisation's challenge to the Islamic Ummah. *Asian Journal of Social Science, 34*(2), 311–323.

Hassan, R. (2009). Social and economic conditions of Australian Muslims: Implications for social inclusion. *National Centre of Excellence for Islamic Studies, 2*(4), 1–13. Retrieved from http://www.nceis.unimelb.edu.au/sites/nceis.unimelb.edu.au/files/NCEIS_Research_Paper_Vol2,No4_Hassan.pdf.

Hassan, R. (2010). Socio-economic marginalization of Muslims in contemporary Australia: Implications for social inclusion. *Journal of Muslim Minority Affairs, 30*(4), 575–584.

Hassan, R. (2015). *Australian Muslims—A demographic, social and economic profile of Muslims in Australia 2015*. International Centre for Muslim and Non-Muslim Understanding, University of South Australia. Retrieved from http://www.unisa.edu.au/Global/EASS/MnM/Publications/Australian_Muslims_Report_2015.pdf.

Heckmann, F., & Schnapper, D. (Eds.). (2003). *The integration of immigrants in European societies: National differences and trends of convergence* (Vol. 7). Stuttgart, DE: Lucius & Lucius.

Heilbrunn, S., Kushnirovich, N., & Zeltzer-Zubida, A. (2010). Barriers to immigrants' integration into the labour market: Modes and coping. *International Journal of Intercultural Relations, 34*(3), 244–252.

Ho, C. (2007). Muslim women's new defenders: Women's rights, nationalism and Islamophobia in contemporary Australia. *Women's Studies International Forum, 30*(4), 290–298.

Hollifield, J., Martin, P., & Orrenius, P. (Eds.). (2014). *Controlling immigration: A global perspective.* Redwood City, CA: Stanford University Press.

Huddleston, T., Niessen, J., Ni Chaoimh, E., & White, E. (2011). *Migrant Integration Policy Index III.* Brussels, Belgium: British Council and Migration Policy Group. Retrieved from: http://www.mipex.eu/.

Hudson, W. (2003). Religious citizenship. *Australian Journal of Politics & History, 49*(3), 425–429.

Hugo, G. (2005). *Migrants in society: Diversity and cohesion.* Geneva: Global Commission on International Migration.

Humphrey, M. (2001). Muslim Lebanese. In J. Jupp (Ed.), *The Australian people* (pp. 564–567). Cambridge, UK: Cambridge University Press.

Huntington, S. P. (1993). The clash of civilizations? *Foreign Affairs, 72*(3), 22–49.

Husic, E. (2006). Islam and Australia: Can a Muslim get elected to parliament in a war on terror? [online]. *The Sydney Papers, 18*(1), 88–99.

Husted, L., Heinesen, E., & Andersen, S. H. (2009). Labour market integration of immigrants: Estimating local authority effects. *Journal of Population Economics, 22*(4), 909–939.

Hwang, S. S., Xi, J., & Cao, Y. (2010). The conditional relationship between english language proficiency and earnings among US immigrants. *Ethnic and Racial Studies, 33*(9), 1620–1647.

Ignatow, G. (2007). Theories of embodied knowledge: New directions for cultural and cognitive sociology? *Journal for the Theory of Social Behaviour, 37*(2), 115–135.

International Organisation for Migration. (2014). *Compendium of migrant integration policies and practices.* Retrieved October 22, 2014, from http://www.iom.int.

Jackson, D. (2011). Europe and the migrant experience: Transforming integration. *Transformation: An International Journal of Holistic Mission Studies, 28*(1), 14–28.

Jacobson, J. (2006). *Islam in transition: Religion and identity among British Pakistani youth.* London: Routledge.

Jakubowicz, A. (2007). Anglo-multiculturalism: Contradictions in the politics of cultural diversity as risk. *International Journal of Media & Cultural Politics, 2*(3), 249–266.

Jakubowicz, A. (2011). Chinese walls: Australian multiculturalism and the necessity for human rights. *Journal of Intercultural Studies, 32*(6), 691–706.

Jayasuria, L. (1990). Rethinking Australian multiculturalism: Towards a new paradigm. *The Australian Quarterly, 62*(1), 50–63.

Johnson, C. (2000). *Governing change: Keating to Howard.* Brisbane: University of Queensland Press.

Johnson, J. M. (2013). National to global citizenship: Reflections on our values, loyalties, and common future. *Cultural Studies ↔ Critical Methodologies, 13*(6), 452–457.

Johnston, R., Forrest, J., Jones, K., Manley, D., & Owen, D. (2015). The melting-pot and the economic integration of immigrant families: Ancestral and generational variations in Australia. *Environment and Planning A, 47*(12), 2663–2682.

Jones, G. W. (1993). Is demographic uniformity inevitable? *Journal of the Australian Population Association, 10*(1), 1–16.

Jones, P. G., & Kenny, A. (2007). *Australia's Muslim cameleers: Pioneers of the inland, 1860s–1930s.* Mile End, SA: Wakefield Press.

Jongkid, F. (1992). Ethnic identity, societal integration and migrant's alienation: State policy and academic research in the Netherlands. *Ethnic and Racial Studies, 15*(3), 365–380.

Joppke, C. (2004). The retreat of multiculturalism in the liberal state: Theory and policy. *The British Journal of Sociology, 55*(2), 237–257.

Joppke, C. (2007). Transformation of immigrant integration: Civic integration and antidiscrimination in the Netherlands, France, and Germany. *World Politics, 59*(2), 243–273.

Joppke, C. (2013). Through the European looking glass: Citizenship tests in the USA, Australia, and Canada. *Citizenship Studies, 17*(1), 1–15.

Jupp, J. (1997). Tacking into the wind: Immigration and multicultural policy in the 1990s. *Journal of Australian Studies, 21*(53), 29–39.

Jupp, J. (2002). *From white Australia to Woomera: The story of Australian immigration.* Cambridge, UK: Cambridge University Press.

Jupp, J. (2011). Politics, public policy and multiculturalism. In M. Clyne & J. Jupp (Eds.), *Multiculturalism & integration: A harmonious relationship* (pp. 41–52). Canberra, ACT: ANU Press.

Kabir, N. A. (2004). *Muslims in Australia: Immigration, race relations and cultural history.* London, UK: Routledge.

Kaida, L. (2013). Do host country education and language training help recent immigrants exit poverty? *Social Science Research, 42*(3), 726–741.

Kalantzis, M., & Cope, B. (1988). Why we need multicultural education: A review of the 'ethnic disadvantage' debate 1. *Journal of Intercultural Studies, 9*(1), 39–57.

Kalantzis, M., & Cope, B. (1999). Multicultural education: Transforming the mainstream. In S. May (Ed.), *Critical multiculturalism: Rethinking multicultural and antiracist education* (pp. 245–276). London, UK: Falmer Press.

Kalmijn, M., & Van Tubergen, F. (2006). Ethnic intermarriage in the Netherlands: Confirmations and refutations of accepted insights. *European Journal of Population/Revue Européenne de Démographie, 22*(4), 371–397.

Kashima, Y. (2014). Meaning, grounding, and the construction of social reality. *Asian Journal of Sociology. Psychol, 17*, 81–95. https://doi.org/10.1111/ajsp.12051.

Kastoryano, R. (2004). Religion and incorporation: Islam in France and Germany. *International Migration Review, 38*(3), 1234–1255.

Klocker, N., & Dunn, K. M. (2003). Who's driving the asylum debate: Newspaper and government representations of asylum seekers. *Media International Australia Incorporating Culture and Policy, 109*, 71–92.

Koenig, M. (2007). Europeanising the governance of religious diversity: An institutionalist account of Muslim struggles for public recognition. *Journal of Ethnic and Migration Studies, 33*(6), 911–932.

Kogan, I. (2011). New immigrants-old disadvantage patterns? Labour market integration of recent immigrants into Germany. *International Migration, 49*(1), 91–117.

Kolig, E., & Kabir, N. (2008). Not friend, not foe: The rocky road of enfranchisement of Muslims into multicultural nationhood in Australia and new Zealand. *Immigrants & Minorities, 26*(3), 266–300.

Koopmans, R. (2013). Multiculturalism and immigration: A contested field in cross-national comparison. *Annual Review of Sociology, 39*, 147–169.

Koopmans, R., Lancee, B., & Schaeffer, M. (Eds.). (2014). *Social cohesion and immigration in Europe and North America: Mechanisms, conditions, and causality.* London: Routledge.

Koser, K. (2010). *Responding to boat arrivals in Australia: Time for a reality check—Analysis.* http://m.lowyinstitute.org/files/pubfiles/Koser,_Responding_web.pdf.accessed17/03/2014.

Kostakopoulou, D. (2010). The anatomy of civic integration. *The Modern Law Review, 73*(6), 933–958.

Krause, K., & Liebig, T. (2011). The labour market integration of immigrants and their children in Austria. *OECD social, employment and migration* (Working Papers, No. 127). OECD Publishing. http://dx.doi.org/10.1787/5kg-264fz6p8w-en (seehttps://www.oecd.org/migration/49205671.pdf).

Kuenssberg, L. (2011, February). State multiculturalism has failed, says David Cameron. *BBC News.*

Kundnani, A. (2012). Multiculturalism and its discontents: Left, right and liberal. *European Journal of Cultural Studies, 15*(2), 155–166.

Kuran, T., & Sandholm, W. H. (2008). Cultural integration and its discontents. *The Review of Economic Studies, 75*(1), 201–228.

Kymlicka, W. (2010). The rise and fall of multiculturalism? New debates on inclusion and accommodation in diverse societies. *International Social Science Journal, 61*(199), 97–112.

Kymlicka, W. (2011). Multicultural citizenship within multination states. *Ethnicities, 11*(3), 281–302.

Kymlicka, W. (2012). Comment on Meer and Modood. *Journal of Intercultural Studies, 33*(2), 211–216.

Lacroix, C. (2010). *Immigrants, literature and national integration*. Retrieved from http://www.palgraveconnect.com/pc/doifinder/10.1057/9780230281219.

Lahav, G. (2004). *Immigration and politics in the new Europe: Reinventing borders*. Cambridge, UK: Cambridge University Press.

Lawler, P. (2007). Janus-faced solidarity. *Cooperation and Conflict, 42*(1), 101–126.

Lenard, P. (2012). The report of multiculturalism's death are greatly exaggerated. *Politics, 32*(3), 186–196.

Lentin, A., & Titley, G. (2012). The crisis of 'multiculturalism' in Europe: Mediated minarets, intolerable subjects. *European Journal of Cultural Studies, 15,* 123–138.

Li, P. S. (2003). Deconstructing Canada's discourses of immigrant integration. *Journal of International Migration and Integration, 4*(3), 315–333.

Löwenheim, O., & Gazit, O. (2009). Power and examination: A critique of citizenship tests. *Security Dialogue, 40*(20), 145–167.

Lowy Institute. (2014). *Poll*. Retrieved April 16, 2014. http://www.lowyinstitute.org/publications/lowy-institute-poll-2014.

Mac Éinrí, P. (2007). The challenge of migrant integration in Ireland. *Evidence from New Countries of Immigration, 9*(1), 75–90.

Mahar, A. L., Cobigo, V., & Stuart, H. (2013). Conceptualizing belonging. *Disability and Rehabilitation, 35*(11), 1026–1032.

Mahtani, M. (2001). Representing minorities: Canadian media and minority identities. *Canadian Ethnic Studies, 33*(3), 99–133.

Markus, A. (2011). Attitudes to multiculturalism and cultural diversity. In M. Clyne & J. Jupp (Eds.), *Multiculturalism and integration: A harmonious relationship*. Canberra: Australian National University Press.

Markus, A. (2013). *Mapping social cohesion 2012: The Scanlon foundation survey*. Retrieved from http://www.arts.monash.edu.au/mapping-population/social-cohesion-report.php.

Marranci, G. (2004). Multiculturalism, Islam and the clash of civilisations theory: Rethinking Islamophobia. *Culture and Religion, 5*(1), 105–117.

Mason, R. (2010). Australian multiculturalism: Revisiting Australia's political heritage and the migrant presence. *History Compass, 8,* 817–827.

Matejskova, T. (2013). "But one needs to work!": Neoliberal citizenship, work-based immigrant integration, and post-socialist subjectivities in Berlin-Marzahn. *Antipode, 45*(4), 984–1004.

Maxwell, R. (2010). Evaluating migrant integration: Political attitudes across generations in Europe. *International Migration Review, 44*(1), 25–52.

Mayne, A. J. C. (2009). *Delineating multicultural Australia.* Doctoral dissertation, Wakefield Press.

McAllister, I. (2003). Border protection, the 2001 Australian election and the coalition victory. *Australian Journal of Political Science, 38*(3), 445–463.

McHugh, M. (2014). *Immigrant civic integration and service access initiatives. Access initiative: City sized solution for city-sized needs.* Washington, DC: Migration Policy Institute.

Meer, N., Dwyer, C., & Modood, T. (2010). Embodying nationhood? Conceptions of British national identity, citizenship, and gender in the 'veil affair'. *The Sociological Review, 58*(1), 85–111.

Meer, N., & Modood, T. (2009). The multicultural state we're in: Muslims, 'multiculture' and the 'civic re-balancing 'of British multiculturalism. *Political Studies, 57,* 473–497.

Meer, N., & Modood, T. (2012). For "Jewish" read "Muslim"? Islamophobia as a form of racialisation of ethno religious groups in Britain today. *Islamophobia Studies Journal, 1*(1), 36–55.

Meer, N., & Modood, T. (2013). *Interculturalism, multiculturalism, or both?* European University Institute Robert Schuman Centre for Advanced Studies, RSCAS Policy Paper 2013/18.

Meer, N., & Nayak, A. (2013). Race ends where? Race, racism and contemporary sociology. *Sociology E-special, 2,* 1–18.

Minkenberg, M. (2008). Religious legacies, churches, and the shaping of immigration policies in the age of religious diversity. *Politics and Religion, 1*(03), 349–383.

Mitchell, M. C. (2013). *Religion, identity and politics in Northern Ireland: Boundaries of belonging and belief.* Abingdon, UK: Routledge.

Modood, T. (2013). Post-immigration 'difference' and integration. *Meritum, revista de Direito da Universidade FUMEC, 8*(1), 389–415.

Modood, T., Hansen, R., Bleich, E., O'Leary, B., & Carens, J. H. (2006). The Danish cartoon affair: Free speech, racism, Islamism, and integration. *International Migration, 44*(5), 3–62.

Mogahed, D., & Nyiri, Z. (2007). Re-inventing integration: Muslims in the West. *Courting Africa, 29*(2), 2–20.

Murdie, R. A. (2002). The housing careers of Polish and Somali newcomers in Toronto's rental market. *Housing Studies, 17*(3), 423–443.

Muste, C. P. (2013). The dynamics of immigration opinion in the United States, 1992–2012. *Public Opinion Quarterly, 77*(1), 398–416.

National Multicultural Advisory Council. (1999). *Australian multiculturalism for a new century: Towards inclusiveness.* Retrieved September 19, 2013, from http://www.immi.gov.au/media/publications/multicultural/nmac/chapt_2a.htm.

Newman, L. (2013). Seeking asylum, trauma, mental health, and human rights: An Australian perspective. *Journal of Trauma & Dissociation, 14*(2), 213–223.

Northcote, J., & Casimiro, S. (2010). Muslim citizens and belonging in Australia: Negotiating the inclusive/exclusive divide in a multicultural context. In S. Yasmeen (Ed.), *Muslims in Australia: The dynamics of exclusion and inclusion* (pp. 141–161). Carlton, VIC: Melbourne University Press.

Norris, P., & Inglehart, R. F. (2012). Muslim integration into Western cultures: Between origins and destinations. *Political Studies, 60*(2), 228–251.

Novotný, V. (2011). Opening the door: Immigration and integration in the European Union. *European View, 10*(2), 269–271.

Nyamnjoh, F. B. (2008). From bounded to flexible citizenship. In E. F. Isin, P. Nyers, & B. S. Turner (Eds.), *Citizenship between past and future* (pp. 78–87). London, UK: Routledge.

Nyamnjoh, F. B. (2013). Fiction and reality of mobility in Africa. *Citizenship Studies, 17*(6–7), 653–680.

O'Doherty, K., & Le Couter, A. (2007). "Asylum seekers", "boat people" and "illegal immigrants": Social categorisation in the media. *Australian Journal of Psychology, 59*(1), 1–12.

Owusu, T. Y. (1998). To buy or not to buy: Determinants of home ownership among Ghanaian immigrants in Toronto. *The Canadian Geographer/Le Géographe Canadien, 42*(1), 40–52.

Peschke, D. (2009). The role of religion for the integration of migrants and institutional responses in Europe: Some reflections. *The Ecumenical Review, 61*(4), 367–380.

Petrovic-Lazarevic, S. (2010). Good corporate citizenship in the Australian construction industry. *Corporate Governance, 10*(2), 115–128.

Petrusevska, T. (Ed.). (2009). *A guide to minorities and political participation in South-East Europe.* Brussels: King Baudouin Foundation.

Pettus, K. I. (2013). *Felony disenfranchisement in America: Historical origins, institutional racism, and modern consequences.* Albany: SUNY Press.

Peucker, M., & Akbarzadeh, S. (2014). *Muslim active citizenship in the West.* Abingdon-on-Thames, UK: Routledge.

Peucker, M., Roose, J. M., & Akbarzadeh, S. (2014). Muslim active citizenship in Australia: Socioeconomic challenges and the emergence of a Muslim elite. *Australian Journal of Political Science, 49*(2), 282–299.

Pew Forum. (2009). *Mapping the global Muslim population.* http://www.pewforum.org/2009/10/07/mapping-the-global-muslim-population/ accessed12/05/2014.

Phillimore, J., & Goodson, L. (2008). Making a place in the global city: The relevance of indicators of integration. *Journal of Refugee Studies, 21*(3), 305–325.

Phillips, C. (2011). Institutional racism and ethnic inequalities: An expanded multilevel framework. *Journal of Social Policy, 40*(01), 173–192.

Phillips, D. (2006). Moving towards integration: The housing of asylum seekers and refugees in Britain. *Housing Studies, 21*(4), 539–553.

Pickering, S. (2001). Common sense and original deviancy: News discourses and asylum seekers in Australia. *Journal of Refugee Studies, 14*(2), 169–186.

Pilbeam, B. (2011). Eurabian nightmares: American conservative discourses and the Islamisation of Europe. *Journal of Transatlantic Studies, 9*(2), 151–171.

Pilkington, A. (2011). *Institutional racism in the academy: A case study.* Stoke On Trent, UK: Trentham Books.

Poppelaars, C., & Scholten, P. (2008). Two worlds apart: The divergence of national and local immigrant integration policies in the Netherlands. *Administration & Society, 40*(4), 335–357.

Portes, A., Rumbaut, R. G., Fernandez-Kelly, P., & Haller, W. (2006). *Religion: The enduring presence.* Unpublished manuscript.

Poynting, S. (2002). Racism and community safety. *Current Issues in Criminal Justice, 13*(3), 328–332.

Poynting, S. (2006). What caused the Cronulla riots? *Race and Class, 48,* 85–91.

Poynting, S., & Mason, V. (2007). The resistible rise of Islamophobia anti-Muslim racism in the UK and Australia before 11 September 2001. *Journal of Sociology, 43*(1), 61–86.

Poynting, S., & Mason, V. (2008). The new integrationism, the state and Islamophobia: Retreat from multiculturalism in Australia. *International Journal of Law, Crime and Justice, 36,* 230–246.

Pykett, J., Saward, M., & Schaefer, A. (2010). Framing the good citizen. *The British Journal of Politics & International Relations, 12*(4), 523–538.

Ramadan, T. (2003). *Western Muslims and the future of Islam.* Oxford: Oxford University Press.

Ramli, M. A. (2013). Postmodernism approach in Islamic jurisprudence (fiqh). *Middle-East Journal of Scientific Research, 13*(1), 33–40.

Rane, H., & Hersi, A. (2012). Meanings of integration in the Australian press coverage of Muslims: Implications for social inclusion and exclusion. *Media International Australia, Incorporating Culture & Policy, 142*(February), 135–147.

Rane, H., Nathie, M., Isakhan, B., & Abdalla, M. (2011). Towards understanding what Australia's Muslims really think. *Journal of Sociology, 47*(2), 1–21. http://doi.org/10.1177/1440783310386829.

Ray, B. K., & Moore, E. (1991). Access to homeownership among immigrant groups in Canada. *Canadian Review of Sociology/Revue canadienne de sociologie, 28*(1), 1–29.

Ríos-Rojas, A. (2011). Beyond delinquent citizenships: Immigrant youth's (re) visions of citizenship and belonging in a globalized world. *Harvard Educational Review, 81*(1), 64–95.

Roberts, J. (2006, October 27). Media blamed for Islam bias. *The Australian.* p. 5.

Roggeband, C., & Vliegenthart, R. (2007). Divergent framing: The public debate on migration in the Dutch parliament and media, 1995–2004. *West European Politics, 30*(3), 524–548.

Roose, J. M., & Possamai, A. (2015). Between rhetoric and reality: Shari'a and the shift towards neoliberal multiculturalism in Australia. In F. Mansouri (Ed.). *Cultural, religious and political contestations* (pp. 91–105). Cham, Switzerland: Springer.

Russell, C. D., & Kleyn, T. (2013). 11 Impenetrable citizenship. *Refugees, Immigrants, and Education in the Global South: Lives in Motion, 94,* 180.

Saeed, A. (2003). *Islam in Australia.* Crows Nest, NSW: Allen & Unwin.

Saeed, A. (2004). *Muslim Australians: Their beliefs, practices and institutions.* Melbourne: Department of Immigration and Multicultural and Indigenous Affairs and Australian Multicultural Foundation.

Saeed, A. (2006). *Islamic thought: An introduction.* London: Routledge.

Saeed, A. (2007a). Trends in contemporary Islam: A preliminary attempt at a classification. *The Muslim World, 97*(3), 395–404.

Saeed, A. (2007b). Media, racism and Islamophobia: The representation of Islam and Muslims in the media. *Sociology Compass, 1*(2), 443–462.

Samani, S. (2007). Rhetoric and realities of multiculturalism: The perpetuation of negative constructions of Muslims in Australia. *International Journal of Diversity, 7*(2), 113–119.

Samers, M. (2002). Immigration and the global city hypothesis: Towards an alternative research agenda. *International Journal of Urban and Regional Research, 26*(2), 389–3402.

Schaeffer, M. (2013). Inter-ethnic neighbourhood acquaintances of migrants and natives in Germany: On the brokering roles of inter-ethnic partners and children. *Journal of Ethnic and Migration Studies, 39*(8), 1219–1240.

Schmidt, V. H. (2001). Oversocialised epistemology: A critical appraisal of constructivism. *Sociology, 35*(1), 135–157.

Scholten, P. W., & Van Nispen, F. K. (2008). Building bridges across frames? *Journal of Public Policy, 28*(2), 181–205.

Segovia, F., & Defever, R. (2010). The polls—Trends American public opinion on immigrants and immigration policy. *Public Opinion Quarterly, 74*(2), 375–394.

Shadid, W. A. (1991). The integration of Muslim minorities in the Netherlands. *International Migration Review, 25*(2), 355–374.

Shapcott, R. (2013). From the good international citizen to the cosmopolitan political community: A constitutional path. *International Politics, 50*(1), 138–157.

Sinning, M. (2010). Homeownership and economic performance of immigrants in Germany. *Urban Studies, 47*(2), 387–409.

Skrbiš, Z., Baldassar, L., & Poynting, S. (2007). Introduction–Negotiating belonging: Migration and generations. *Journal of Intercultural Studies, 28*(3), 261–269.

Sohrabi, H., & Farquharson, K. (2015). Social integration of Australian Muslims: A dramaturgical perspective. *Journal of Sociology, 52*(2). https://doi.org/10.1177/1440783314562415.

Soysal, Y. N. (1994). *Limits of citizenship: Migrants and postnational membership in Europe.* Chicago: University of Chicago.

Soysal, Y. N. (2012). Post-national Citizenship. *The Wiley-Blackwell Companion to Political Sociology, 38,* 383.

Spoonley, P., Peace, R., Butcher, A., & O'Neill, D. (2005). Social cohesion: A policy and indicator framework for assessing immigrant and host outcomes. *Social Policy Journal of New Zealand, 24,* 85–110.

Staeheli, L. A. (2011). Political geography: Where's citizenship? *Progress in Human Geography, 35*(3), 393–400.

Tastsoglou, E., & Preston, V. (2012). Gender, immigration and labour market integration: Where we are and what we still need to know. *Critical Studies in Gender, Culture & Social Justice, 30*(1), 46–59.

Tate, J. W. (2009). John Howard's "nation": Multiculturalism, citizenship, and identity. *Australian Journal of Politics & History, 55*(1), 97–120.

Tavan, G. (2012). No going back? Australian multiculturalism as a path-dependent process. *Australian Journal of Political Science, 47*(4), 547–561.

Thorson, K. (2012). What does it mean to be a good citizen? Citizenship vocabularies as resources for action. *The Annals of the American Academy of Political and Social Science, 644*(1), 70–85.

Tilbury, F. (2007, November). The retreat from multiculturalism: The Australian experience. Paper presented at *Pluralism, Inclusion and Citizenship, 3rd Global Conference*, Interdisciplinary.net, Salzburg. Available at http://www.inter-disciplinary.net/ati/diversity/pluralism/pl3/Tilbury%20paper.pdf.

Tip, L. K., Zagefka, H., Gonzalez, R., Brown, R., Cinnirella, M., & Na, X. (2012). Is support for multiculturalism threatened by … threat itself? *International Journal of Intercultural Relations, 36,* 22–30.

Tolsma, J., Lubbers, M., & Gijsberts, M. (2012). Education and cultural integration among ethnic minorities and natives in the Netherlands: A test of the integration paradox. *Journal of Ethnic and Migration Studies, 38*(5), 793–813.

Tran-Nam, B., & Neville, J. W. (1988). The effects of birthplace on male earnings in Australia. *Australian Economic Papers, 27*(50), 83–101.

Treas, J., & Mazumdar, S. (2002). Older people in America's immigrant families: Dilemmas of dependence, integration, and isolation. *Journal of Aging Studies, 16*(3), 243–258.

Trepagnier, B. (2010). *Silent racism: How well-meaning white people perpetuate the racial divide*. Boulder, CO: Paradigm.

Van Tubergen, F., & Sindradottir, J. I. (2011). The religiosity of immigrants in Europe: A cross-national study. *Journal for the Scientific Study of Religion, 50*(2), 272–288.

Tufail, W., & Poynting, S. (2013). A common 'outlawness': Criminalisation of Muslim minorities in the UK and Australia. *International Journal for Crime, Justice and Social Democracy, 2*(3), 43–54.

Van Acker, K., Phalet, K., Deleersnyder, J., & Mesquita, B. (2014). Do "they" threaten "us" or do "we" disrespect "them": Majority perceptions of intergroup relations and everyday contacts with immigrant minorities. *Group Processes & Intergroup Relations, 17*(5), 617–628.

Van der Noll, J. (2014). Religious toleration of Muslims in the German public sphere. *International Journal of Intercultural Relations, 38*, 60–74.

Van Deth, J. W. (2009). The 'good European citizen' congruence and consequences of different points of view. *European Political Science, 8*(2), 175–189.

Van Dijk, T. A. (2000). On the analysis of parliamentary debates on immigration. In M. Reisigl & R. Wodak (Eds.), *The semiotics of racism. Approaches in critical discourse analysis* (pp. 85–104). Vienna: Passagen Verlag.

Van Heerden, S., de Lange, S. L., van der Brug, W., & Fennema, M. (2014). The immigration and integration debate in the Netherlands: Discursive and programmatic reactions to the rise of anti-immigration parties. *Journal of Ethnic and Migration Studies, 40*(1), 119–136.

Van Onselen, P., & Errington, W. (2007). From vitriolic criticism to ungainly praise: Locating John Howard's political success. *Australian Quarterly, 79*(2), 4–39.

Verkaaik, O. (2012). Designing the 'anti-mosque': Identity, religion and affect in contemporary European mosque design. *Social Anthropology, 20*(2), 161–176.

Vertovec, S., & Wassendorf, S. (2009) *The multiculturalism backlash: European discourses, policies and practices, (e-book).* London: Routledge.

Wagner, R., & Childs, M. (2006). Exclusionary narratives as barriers to the recognition of qualifications, skills and experience—A case of skilled migrants in Australia. *Studies in Continuing Education, 28*(1), 49–62.

Waldrauch, H., & Hofinger, C. (1997). An index to measure the legal obstacles to the integration of migrants. *Journal of Ethnic and Migration Studies, 23*(2), 271–285.

Waters, J. L. (2010). Becoming a father, missing a wife: Chinese transnational families and the male experience of lone parenting in Canada. *Population, Space and Place, 16*(1), 63–74.

Waters, M. C., & Jiménez, T. R. (2005). Assessing immigrant assimilation: New empirical and theoretical challenges. *Annual Review of Sociology, 31*(1), 105–125.

Weaver, M. (2010, October 17). Angela Merkel: German multiculturalism has utterly failed. *The Guardian Newspaper*. Retrieved April 22, 2016, from http://www.theguardian.com/world/2010/oct/17/angela-merkel-german-multiculturalism-failed.

Weiner, M. (1996). Determinants of immigrant integration: An international comparative analysis. In S. Vertovec (Ed.), *Migration and social cohesion*. Northampton, MA: Edward Elgar.

Wets, J. (2006). The Turkish community in Austria and Belgium: The challenge of integration. *Turkish Studies, 7*(1), 85–100.

White, A. (2014) Unmasked: Aussie Jihadist heading to the Islamic state terror zones. *Herald Sun*. Retrieved from http://www.heraldsun.com.au/news/law-order/unmasked-aussie-jihadists-heading-into-islamic-state-terror-zones/story-fni0fee2-1227062790468.

Wiesbrock, A. (2011). The integration of immigrants in Sweden: A model for the European Union? *International Migration, 49*(4), 48–66.

Wilkinson, L. (2013). Introduction: Developing and testing a generalizable model of immigrant integration. *Canadian Ethnic Studies, 45*(3), 1–7.

Woodward, I., Skrbiš, Z., & Bean, C. (2008). Attitudes towards globalisation and cosmopolitanism: Cultural diversity, personal consumption and the national economy. *The British Journal of Sociology, 59*(2), 207–226.

Wright, M., & Bloemraad, I. (2012). Is there a trade-off between multiculturalism and socio-political integration? Policy regimes and immigrant incorporation in comparative perspective. *Perspectives on Politics, 10*(1), 77–95.

Wyss, D., Beste, S., & Bächtiger, A. (2015). A decline in the quality of debate? The evolution of splexity in Swiss parliamentary debates on immigration (1968–2014). *Swiss Political Science Review, 21*(4), 636–653.

Xi, J. (2013). English fluency of the US immigrants: Assimilation effects, cohort variations, and periodical changes. *Social Science Research, 42,* 1109–1121.

Yasmeen, S. (2008). *Understanding Muslim identities: From perceived relative exclusion to inclusion*. Canberra: Department of Immigration and Citizenship.

Zagefka, H., & Brown, R. (2002). The relationship between acculturation strategies, relative fit and intergroup relations: Immigrant-majority relations in Germany. *European Journal of Social Psychology, 32*(2), 171–188.

Zerubavel, E. (1997). *Social mindscapes. An invitation to cognitive sociology*. London, UK: Harvard University Press.

Zimmermann, L., Gataullina, L., Constant, A., & Zimmermann, K. F. (2008). Human capital and ethnic self-identification of immigrants. *Economics Letters, 98*(3), 235–239.

Index

A

Abbott, Tony 13
Adult Migrant English Language
    Program 98
Afghan 21
Afghan cameleers 19, 20
Afghanistan 23, 36, 37
Afghan Muslims 119
Africa 8, 36, 54
    South Africa 36
    Zambia 36
    Zimbabwe 36
Albania 23
allegiance 46, 51, 56, 119, 123, 152
anti-discrimination 87
anti-immigrant 6, 93, 98
anti-Islamic 43, 55
anti-terrorism 89
Asia 23, 44, 54
assimilation 7, 12, 34, 57, 72, 101
    cultural and religious 151

effect 98
language 50, 98
rejection 138
assimilationist 10, 46, 47, 133, 135,
    156
    frame 134
asylum seekers 6, 8, 9
Australia 2, 4, 5, 7, 8, 10, 131
Australian Labor Party 8
Australian Muslims 14, 23, 25, 27,
    65, 93, 106, 113, 151, 154
    background 19
    context 19
    diversity of 23
    first settlement 20
    higher education 28
    post-September 11 43
    social and economic position of
        25
    successful integration 51
    unemployment 30, 87

youth unemployment 30, 32
Australian population 25
  diversity 120
  non-Muslim 34
Australians 6, 9–11, 23, 26, 33, 71, 126
  first 19
Austria 7, 51, 93, 125

B

belonging 2, 46, 100, 109, 116, 151, 153
  a sense of 77
boat people 7, 9
Bolt, Andrew 89
border protection 13
Britain 44, 87, 125, 139
British 10, 23, 48, 139
British India 20
British Muslims 154
burqa 51, 53, 126

C

Cameron, David 6, 48
Canada 36, 46, 76, 98, 118, 131
Census 25
Chinese 21, 98
  economic immigrant 118
Christian Democratic Union party 6
Christians 71, 116, 137
Church of England 23
citizenship 13
citizenship test 12, 49, 99, 125, 133, 142
civic integration 46, 49, 132, 141, 142, 152
  Australia 133

cognitive complexity 7
cognitive psychology 105, 106, 150
cognitive psychology theory 4
cognitive schematic frames 126
compromise 154
conformism 127
cosmopolitan citizenship 116
cosmopolitanism 142
Cronulla riots 43
cultural capital 11, 36
cultural integration 46, 108, 126, 141, 142
cultural unity 13
Cyprus 22

D

Denmark 125
Department of Home Affairs 13
Department of Immigration and Border Protection 9, 10, 13
Department of Immigration and Citizenship 13
Department of Immigration and Multicultural Affairs 13
detention 9
determinants of integration 50
  acceptance 151
  belonging 151
  participation 151
detractors of integration
  faith 68
  influence 89
  self-isolation 94
discrimination 21, 50, 70, 151, 154
  anti-discrimination 49
  barriers to integration 84, 88
  clothing 86
  employment 86

religious 21, 32
    systematic 99
discriminatory 10, 20, 86, 149
diversity
    Australia 149
    Australian muslim 23
    Australian Muslim community 37
    Australian population 120
    cultural 11, 23, 69, 121
    Dutch 46
    ethnic 23
    mosque congregants 23
    Muslilm legal and ideological
        domains 24
    religious 23, 69, 116, 121
Dunston, Don 11
Dutch. *See* Netherlands

E

economic immigrant 118
educational attainment 26, 27, 50
education
    postgraduate 26, 29
employment access 50
employment integration 134
English
    Adult Migrant English Language
        Program 98
    colonial system 59
    determinant of integration 96
    detractors of integration 151
    lack of 83, 96
    language 72
    language skills 51, 91
    names 56
    non English-speaking 53
Ethiopian 75

Europe 5, 6, 12, 13, 19, 20, 22, 30,
    36, 44, 46, 47, 49–51, 54, 65,
    69, 70, 74, 93, 98, 100, 114,
    118, 123, 125, 126, 131, 139,
    152, 159
European 21
extremism 123, 138, 151

F

failure of integration 84–86, 98
failure to integration 55, 74, 83, 93,
    94
faith limitations 154
Federal Member of Parliament
    Muslim 76
first Australians 19
flexible citizen 114
frames of integration 107
    bridging approach 157
    competing 133
    dominant values 135
    participatory citizen 142
    resistance to 151
France 32, 44, 69, 70, 98
Fraser, Malcolm 11
freedom
    of choice 109
    of religion 152
    of speech 46, 125
    sexual 46, 125
French 32, 59
functional indicators of integration
    126, 134, 158
    socio-economic status 50
functional integration 154
fundamentalism 92

G

Germany 6, 7, 44, 48, 69, 74, 125, 135, 136
globalisation 137, 141
good citizen 111
government 3
Greeks 98

H

halal 21, 66, 95, 109, 115, 121
Hanafi 24
Hanbali 24
haram 74
Hawke, Bob 11
hijab 22, 70, 85, 86, 88, 93. *See also* Muslim dress
Hindus 23, 26
Holt, Harold 11
home ownership 26, 34, 36, 51
honour killings 7
housing 126
housing affordability stress 35
Howard, John 7, 11, 13
human capital 28, 36, 50

I

identificational integration 108
identity 46, 66, 95
    cultural 12, 46, 116
    ethnic 12, 46
    formation 136
    framework of integration 143
    group 88
    ideological 25
    Islamic 137
    Muslim 22, 25, 123
    narratives of 94

national 70, 79, 141, 159
    religious 52, 68, 69, 116
    social 77
illiberalism 48
imams 22
immigrant 3
immigration
    illegal 7
Immigration Restriction Act 10, 21
incorporation 1, 7, 10, 12, 44, 45, 69, 99, 116, 133, 142, 160
    assimilationist 48
India 36
indicator of integration 26, 49
    average weekly household income 26
    earnings 32
    education 26
    functional 50
    home ownership 26
    labour market participation 26, 29
    media definition 91
    occupational attainment 32
indigenous. *See* first Australians
individualism 139
Indonesia 9, 19, 20
Indonesian Muslim 19
inequality 69
    income 69
    social 88
    structural 154
integratability 44, 56
integration
    definition 46
    Muslim definition 52
    problematic 2
    processes 7
integrationism 12, 55
integrationist 133

interactive integration 108
interculturalism 48
inter-marriage
    rate of 50
Iraq 22, 36, 37, 92, 122
Islamic State 92
Islamophobia 55, 87, 88, 134, 152
Israel 22, 74
Italian(s) 98, 134

K

Keating, Paul 11

L

labor 8, 12, 13, 76, 134
labour market participation 26, 29,
    32, 52, 118
language proficiency 46, 96–99, 142
law enforcement 13
Lebanese 21
Lebanon 21, 23
11 September 2001 2, 6, 8, 43, 79,
    87, 88, 92, 100, 125
Liberal 13
Liberal-National 8, 11–13, 89
loyal citizen 123

M

Macassan fishermen 19
Malays 20
Malaysia 9
Maliki 24
mandatory detention 9
Manus Island 9
measures of integration 49
media 3, 68, 110

barrier to integration 92
bias 84, 100
criticism 122
definition of integration 91
distorted reporting 89
influence 89, 143
negative representation of Islam
    44
negative representations 55, 93
stereotypes 43
stigmatising minority groups 93
tabloid 123
Melanesians 21
Merkel, Angela 6, 48
Middle East 22, 25, 54
migration program 28, 149
business and skills 36
consequences 23
monocultural 11, 23, 158
moral conservatism 70
mosque 20, 22, 23, 56, 66, 67, 88,
    95, 109
multiculturalism 6, 10, 11, 46, 87,
    100, 133
neo-liberal 122
multi-faith 138
Muslim Australians. *See* Australian
    Muslims
Muslim dress
    burqa 51, 126
    covered hair 53
    women 22, 56, 59, 70, 71, 92,
    117
Muslim migration 4, 20, 22, 136
history of 19
Muslims
    classifications 24
    extremist 24
    moderate 24

N

Nationality and Citizenship Act 1948 11
national security 8, 13
Naturalisation Act 21
Nauru 9
Netherlands 44, 46, 87, 98, 125, 132, 143, 159
New Zealand 131
Nigeria 23
niqab 92
non-Christians 23
non-Muslim
  attitudes toward Sharia 122
  Australian 24
  average weekly income 34
  drinking 66
  education 27
  faith groups 21
  home ownership 35
  immigrant groups 74, 98, 159
  labour force 33
  religion 27
  UK integration 69
  unemployment rates 30
  volunteer work 113
no religion 26, 27
North America 5

O

Operation Sovereign Borders 9
other 43, 143
out-groups 8, 79, 88, 101
outsider 44, 58
overseas
  born 10, 23, 53

P

Pakistan 23, 36, 119
Papua New Guinea 9
patriotism 113, 124
pluralism 70, 138
pluralist 46, 100, 133, 151, 156
Poland
  refugees 36
polarised debates 5, 48
policies 1, 3, 6, 9, 133, 142, 143
  assimilation 11, 13
  failed 48
  humanitarian 11
  immigrant integration 11, 139
  inclusion 140
  integration 11, 45, 49, 126
  integration through participation 51
  migrant 131
  migrant integration policy index rankings 49
  migration 10
  multicultural 47, 87
  multiculturalism 11, 47, 87, 141
  settlement 98
  social cohesion 156, 159
  social inclusion 32, 156, 159
  social integration 49, 140
  White Australia Policy 10
political integration 134
political literalist *Salafism* 24
post-multiculturalism 10, 55
productive citizen 118

R

racial
  labelling 6

Racial Discrimination Act 89
racial diversity 121
racialise 88
racism 85, 88
    definition 88
radicalisation 70, 90, 91, 110, 138, 151
rationalist reformism 24
refugee and humanitarian program 36
refugee and humanitarian programme 53
refugee and humanitarian visas 37
refugees 8, 10, 12, 13, 36
religion
    framework of integration 143
religious affiliation 24, 25, 75, 113
    Australian Muslims 26
    educational attainment 27
research limitations 159
respectful citizen 120
riba 36
right-wing political parties 6

S
Salafi literalism 24
Salafi reformism 24
Sarkozy, Nicolas 6
scholastic traditionalism 24
sectoral integration 77
secular 24, 46, 69–71, 138, 142, 153
secularism 139
secular liberalism 125
segregation 10, 133
settlement in Australia 19
Shafi'i 24
Sharia law 122, 138, 139

Shiites 24
skilled migrants 28
social cohesion 87, 133, 156, 158, 159
social harmony 2, 156
social inclusion 2, 44, 79, 93, 156
social integration 12, 46, 49, 50, 126, 140
social welfare frame 134
society 3
socio-economic 50, 70, 73, 87, 100
    marginalisation of migrants 88
socio-economic integration 46, 50
socio-economic status 36, 50
Somalia 36, 37
Somali
    refugees 36
structural integration 108
Sudan 8
Sufism 24
Sunnis 24
Switzerland 7

T
Tampa 8
terrorism 90–92, 110, 123, 138, 151
Turkish 21, 22
Turnbull, Malcolm 13

U
Ummah 137
underemployment 30, 32
unemployment 30, 69
United Kingdom (UK) 6, 48, 50, 51, 154

United Nations' Refugee Convention
    10
unity 12, 46
    cultural 13
    in diversity 116
    national 159
    religious 137
USA 8, 12, 69, 98, 100, 123

V

volunteerism 110

W

White Australia era 149
Whitlam, Gough 11
would-be citizen frame 134

Y

Yugoslavia 22, 51

Printed by Printforce, the Netherlands